THE PENGUIN SHAKESPEARE
EDITED FROM THE ORIGINAL TEXT
BY G. B. HARRISON
B 36
HENRY THE SIXTH

D0773806

WILLIAM SHAKESPEARE

The Three Parts of Henry the Sixth

PENGUIN BOOKS

Penguin Books Ltd, Harmondsworth, Middlesex
AUSTRALIA: Penguin Books Pty Ltd, 762 Whitehorse Road,
Mitcham, Victoria

—

This edition first published 1959

The Editor gratefully acknowledges
the kindness of Dr J. C. Adams in
allowing the Penguin Shakespeare to
reproduce an engraving of his
model of the stage of the
Globe Playhouse

The portraits on the cover and on the title page
were engraved by Reynolds Stone

—

Made and printed in Great Britain
by Wyman & Sons Ltd, London, Fakenham and Reading

CONTENTS

THE WORKS OF SHAKESPEARE

PLAYS

WILLIAM SHAKESPEARE

William Shakespeare was born at Stratford upon Avon in April, 1564. He was the third child, and eldest son, of John Shakespeare and Mary Arden. His father was one of the most prosperous men of Stratford, who held in turn the chief offices in the town. His mother was of gentle birth, the daughter of Robert Arden of Wilmcote. In December, 1582, Shakespeare married Ann Hathaway, daughter of a farmer of Shottery, near Stratford; their first child Susanna was baptized on May 6, 1583, and twins, Hamnet and Judith, on February 22, 1585. Little is known of Shakespeare's early life; but it is unlikely that a writer who dramatized such an incomparable range and variety of human kinds and experiences should have spent his early manhood entirely in placid pursuits in a country town. There is one tradition, not universally accepted, that he fled from Stratford because he was in trouble for deer stealing, and had fallen foul of Sir Thomas Lucy, the local magnate; another that he was for some time a schoolmaster.

From 1592 onwards the records are much fuller. In March, 1592, the Lord Strange's players produced a new play at the Rose Theatre called *Harry the Sixth*, which was very successful, and was probably the *First Part of Henry VI*. In the autumn of 1592 Robert Greene, the best known of the professional writers, as he was dying wrote a letter to three fellow writers in which he warned them against the ingratitude of players in general, and in particular against an 'upstart crow' who 'supposes he is as much able to bombast out a blank verse as the best of you: and being an absolute Johannes Factotum is in his own conceit the only Shake-scene in a country.' This is the first reference to

Shakespeare, and the whole passage suggests that Shakespeare had become suddenly famous as a playwright. At this time Shakespeare was brought into touch with Edward Alleyne the great tragedian, and Christopher Marlowe, whose thundering parts of Tamburlaine, the Jew of Malta, and Dr Faustus Alleyne was acting, as well as Hieronimo, the hero of Kyd's *Spanish Tragedy*, the most famous of all Elizabethan plays.

In April, 1593, Shakespeare published his poem *Venus and Adonis*, which was dedicated to the young Earl of Southampton: it was a great and lasting success, and was reprinted nine times in the next few years. In May, 1594, his second poem, *The Rape of Lucrece*, was also dedicated to Southampton.

There was little playing in 1593, for the theatres were shut during a severe outbreak of the plague; but in the autumn of 1594, when the plague ceased, the playing companies were reorganized, and Shakespeare became a sharer in the Lord Chamberlain's company who went to play in the Theatre in Shoreditch. During these months Marlowe and Kyd had died. Shakespeare was thus for a time without a rival. He had already written the three parts of *Henry VI*, *Richard III*, *Titus Andronicus*, *The Two Gentlemen of Verona*, *Love's Labour's Lost*, *The Comedy of Errors*, and *The Taming of the Shrew*. Soon afterwards he wrote the first of his greater plays – *Romeo and Juliet* – and he followed this success in the next three years with *A Midsummer Night's Dream*, *Richard II*, and *The Merchant of Venice*. The two parts of *Henry IV*, introducing Falstaff, the most popular of all his comic characters, were written in 1597–8.

The company left the Theatre in 1597 owing to disputes over a renewal of the ground lease, and went to play at the Curtain in the same neighbourhood. The disputes continued throughout 1598, and at Christmas the players settled the matter by demolishing the old Theatre and re-erecting a new playhouse on the South bank of the Thames, near Southwark Cathedral. This playhouse was named the Globe. The expenses of the new building were shared by the chief members of the Company, including Shakespeare, who was now a man of some means. In 1596 he had bought New Place, a large house in the centre of Stratford, for £60 and through his father purchased a coat-of-arms from the Heralds, which was the official recognition that he and his family were gentlefolk.

By the summer of 1598 Shakespeare was recognized as the greatest of English dramatists. Booksellers were printing his more popular plays, at times even in pirated or stolen versions, and he received a remarkable tribute from a young writer named Francis Meres, in his book *Palladis Tamia*. In a long catalogue of English authors Meres gave Shakespeare more prominence than any other writer, and mentioned by name twelve of his plays.

Shortly before the Globe was opened, Shakespeare had completed the cycle of plays dealing with the whole story of the Wars of the Roses with *Henry V*. It was followed by *As You Like It*, and *Julius Caesar*, the first of the maturer tragedies. In the next three years he wrote *Troylus and Cressida*, *The Merry Wives of Windsor*, *Hamlet*, and *Twelfth Night*.

On March 24, 1603, Queen Elizabeth I died. The company had often performed before her, but they found her successor a far more enthusiastic patron. One of the first acts of King James was to take over the company and to promote them to be his own servants, so that henceforward they were known as the King's Men. They acted now very frequently at Court, and prospered accordingly. In the early years of the reign Shakespeare wrote the more sombre comedies, *All's Well that Ends Well*, and *Measure for Measure*, which were followed by *Othello*, *Macbeth*, and *King Lear*. Then he returned to Roman themes with *Antony and Cleopatra* and *Coriolanus*.

Since 1601 Shakespeare had been writing less, and there were now a number of rival dramatists who were introducing new styles of drama, particularly Ben Jonson (whose first successful comedy, *Every Man in his Humour*, was acted by Shakespeare's company in 1598), Chapman, Dekker, Marston, and Beaumont and Fletcher who began to write in 1607. In 1608 the King's Men acquired a second playhouse, an indoor private theatre in the fashionable quarter of the Blackfriars. At private theatres, plays were performed indoors; the prices charged were higher than in the public playhouse, and the audience consequently was more select. Shakespeare seems to have retired from the stage about this time: his name does not occur in the various lists of players after 1607. Henceforward he lived for the most part at Stratford, where he was regarded as one of the most important citizens. He still wrote a few plays, and he tried his hand at the new form of tragi-comedy – a play with tragic incidents but a happy ending – which Beaumont and Fletcher had popularized. He wrote four of these – *Pericles*, *Cymbeline*, *The Winter's Tale*, and *The Tempest*, which was acted at Court in 1611. For the last four years of his life he lived in retirement. His son Hamnet had died in 1596: his two daughters were now married. Shakespeare died at Stratford upon Avon on April 23, 1616, and was buried in the chancel of the church, before the high altar. Shortly afterwards a memorial which still exists, with a portrait bust, was set up on the North wall. His wife survived him.

When Shakespeare died fourteen of his plays had been separately published in Quarto booklets. In 1623 his surviving fellow actors, John Heming and Henry Condell, with the co-operation of a number of printers, published a collected edition of thirty-six plays in one Folio volume, with an engraved portrait, memorial verses by Ben Jonson and others, and an Epistle to the Reader in which Heming and Condell make the interesting note that Shakespeare's 'hand and mind went together, and what he thought, he uttered with that easiness that we have scarce received from him a blot in his papers'.

The plays as printed in the Quartos or the Folio differ considerably from the usual modern text. They are often not divided into scenes, and sometimes not even into acts. Nor are there place-headings at the beginning of each scene, because in the Elizabethan theatre there was no scenery. They are carelessly printed and the spelling is erratic.

THE ELIZABETHAN THEATRE

Although plays of one sort and another had been acted for many generations, no permanent playhouse was erected in England until 1576. In the 1570s the Lord Mayor and Aldermen of the City of London and the players were constantly at variance. As a result James Burbage, then the leader of the great Earl of Leicester's players, decided that he would erect a playhouse outside the jurisdiction of the Lord Mayor, where the players would no longer be hindered by the authorities. Accordingly in 1576 he built the Theatre in Shoreditch, at that time a suburb of London. The experiment was successful, and by 1592 there were two more playhouses in London, the Curtain (also in Shoreditch), and the Rose on the south bank of the river, near Southwark Cathedral.

Elizabethan players were accustomed to act on a variety of stages; in the great hall of a nobleman's house, or one of the Queen's palaces, in town halls and in yards, as well as their own theatre.

The public playhouse for which most of Shakespeare's plays were written was a small and intimate affair. The outside measurement of the Fortune Theatre, which was built in 1600 to rival the new Globe, was but eighty feet square. Playhouses were usually circular or octagonal, with three tiers of galleries looking down upon the yard or pit, which was open to the sky. The stage jutted out into the yard so that the actors came forward into the midst of their audience.

Over the stage there was a roof, and on either side doors by which the characters entered or disappeared. Over the back of the stage ran a gallery or upper stage, with windows on either side, which was used whenever an upper scene was needed, as when Romeo climbs up to Juliet's bedroom, or the citizens of Angiers address King John from the walls. The space beneath this upper stage was known as the tiring house; it was concealed from the audience by a curtain which would be drawn back to reveal an inner stage, for such scenes as the witches' cave in *Macbeth*, Prospero's cell, or Juliet's tomb.

There was no general curtain concealing the whole stage, so that all scenes on the main stage began with an entrance and ended with an exit. Thus in tragedies the dead must be carried away. There was no scenery, and therefore no limit to the number of scenes, for a scene came to an end when the characters left the stage. When it was necessary for the exact locality of a scene to be known, then Shakespeare indicated it in the dialogue; otherwise a simple property or a garment was sufficient; a chair or stool showed an indoor scene, a man wearing riding boots was a messenger, a king wearing armour was on the battlefield, or the like. Such simplicity was on the whole an advantage; the spec-

THE GLOBE THEATRE
Wood-engraving by R. J. Beedham after a reconstruction by J. C. Adams

tator was not distracted by the setting and Shakespeare was able to use as many scenes as he wished. The action passed by very quickly: a play of 2500 lines of verse could be acted in two hours. Moreover, since the actor was so close to his audience, the slightest subtlety of voice and gesture was easily appreciated.

The company was a 'Fellowship of Players', who were all partners and sharers. There were usually ten to fifteen full members, with three or four boys, and some paid servants. Shakespeare had therefore to write for his team. The chief actor in the company was Richard Burbage, who first distinguished himself as Richard III; for him Shakespeare wrote his great tragic parts. An important member of the company was the clown or low comedian. From 1594 to 1600 the company's clown was Will Kemp; he was succeeded by Robert Armin. No women were allowed to appear on the stage, and all women's parts were taken by boys.

HENRY THE SIXTH

On 3 March 1592, Philip Henslowe noted in his famous *Diary* the performance of a new play called 'harey the vi', for which his share of the takings was £3. 16s. 8d. This was the largest sum recorded for any of the 105 performances by the Lord Strange's players at the Rose playhouse between 19 February and 22 June when playing ceased in London for six months. *Harry the Sixth* was performed fifteen times during that period, and the takings were well above the average. The popularity of the play is further confirmed by the enthusiastic praise of Thomas Nashe in *Piers Penniless*, which was sent to the press in August. Although Shakespeare's name does not appear in the *Diary*, it is likely that 'harey the vi' is *I Henry VI* – unless some other writer at the same time wrote a rival play on the reign of Henry VI. Shakespeare's play thus seems to date from the end of 1591 or the beginning of 1592.

The Third Part (and presumably also the Second Part) was in existence by the summer of 1592. When Robert Greene in his last days made his bitter attack on the players in *The Groatsworth of Wit* (see p. 7), he sneered at 'an upstart Crow, beautified with our feathers, that with his Tygers hart wrapt in a Players hyde', thereby parodying a line in *III Henry VI* – 'O tiger's heart wrapped in a woman's hide' (P. 259 L. 17). Greene died on 3 September 1592. Yet there is no trace of *II* or *III Henry VI* in Henslowe's *Diary*, and various conjectures have been made to explain the origin and ownership of the Second and Third Parts. It has indeed been suggested that the Second and Third Parts may have been written before the First, which was – as the *Diary* shows – the property of the company acting at the Rose Theatre.

The First Part was not printed during Shakespeare's life-
time and did not appear in printed form until the First
Folio of 1623. The complete texts of the Second and Third
Parts also first appeared in the First Folio, but versions of
both had been printed in 1594 and 1595 respectively. These
were entitled: *The First part of the Contention betwixt the two
famous Houses of Yorke and Lancaster, with the death of the
good Duke Humphrey: And the banishment and death of the
Duke of Suffolke, and the Tragicall end of the proud Cardinall
of Winchester, with the notable Rebellion of Iacke Cade: And
the Duke of Yorkes first claime vnto the Crowne. London.
Printed by Thomas Creed, for Thomas Millington, and are to be
sold at his shop vnder Saint Peters Church in Cornwall. 1594.*
And:
*The true Tragedie of Richard Duke of Yorke, and the death of
good King Henrie the Sixt, with the whole contention betweene
the two Houses Lancaster and Yorke, as it was sundrie times acted
by the Right Honourable the Earle of Pembrooke his seruants.
Printed at London by P. S. for Thomas Millington, and are to
be sold at his shoppe vnder Saint Peters Church in Cornwal. 1595.*

Both Quartos were reprinted in 1600, and again in 1619
when they were reissued as one play with the title – *The
Whole Contention betweene the two Famous Houses, Lancaster
and Yorke. With the Tragicall ends of the good Duke Humfrey,
Richard Duke of Yorke, and King Henrie the sixt. Diuided into
two Parts: And newly corrected and enlarged. Written by
William Shakespeare, Gent. Printed at London, for T. P.* It
will be noted that Shakespeare's name is added to the title
page in this edition.

The Quartos are considerably shorter than the Folio
texts, and in the main they tell the story in similar episodes.
Occasionally speeches or lines are identical in Quarto and
Folio; at other times the passage in the Quarto is a para-
phrase of the Folio; more usually there is only general

resemblance. Thus, for example, King Henry's pathetic lamentation (*III Hen VI*, P. 276 L. 2) appears in *The True Tragedy* as follows:

> Oh gratious God of heauen looke downe on vs,
> And set some endes to these incessant griefes,
> How like a mastlesse ship vpon the Seas,
> This wofull battaile doth continue still:
> Now leaning this way, now to that side driue,
> And none doth know to whome the day will fall.
> O would my death might stay these cruell iarres;
> Would I had neuer raignde, nor nere bin king.
> *Margret* and *Clifford*, chide me from the field,
> Swearing they had best successe when I was thence:
> Would God that I were dead, so all were well,
> Or would my crowne suffice, I were content,
> To yeeld it them and liue a priuate life.

On the other hand, the last speech of King Henry (P. 338 L. 31 – P. 339 L. 18) is mostly the same, and Gloucester's speech (P. 339 L. 26 – P. 340 L. 25) is almost identical in both versions.

Until modern scholars began to re-examine the original quartos it was generally assumed that the Folio versions of *II* and *III Henry VI* were revisions by Shakespeare of *The Contention* and *The True Tragedy*, which were the work of other dramatists. This theory, first proposed by Edmund Malone in 1787, was based on Greene's words in *The Groatsworth of Wit* which were interpreted as Greene's accusation that his own work had been rewritten by Shakespeare. The argument was partially confirmed by some prefatory verses by 'R.B.' in a pamphlet called *Greene's Funerals*, which came out in 1594:

> Greene gave the ground to all that wrote upon him.
> Nay more the men that so eclipsed his flame
> Purloined his plumes; can they deny the same?

Malone's theory thus involved two different proposals:
(*a*) The Folio version of *II* and *III Henry VI* is a rewriting
of *The Contention* and *The True Tragedy;* and (*b*) *Henry VI*
is not Shakespeare's work, but his revision of the work of
others.

The first proposal (*a*) has been questioned by modern
scholars who claim that *The Contention* and *The True
Tragedy* were not original plays but pirated versions of *II*
and *III Henry VI*, put together in the same way as other
pirated Quartos. This view was argued at length by Peter
Alexander in *Shakespeare's 'Henry VI' and 'Richard III'* in
1926. Alexander's view has been disputed by C. T.
Prouty, in '*The Contention*' *and Shakespeare's '2 Henry VI'*.
A Comparative Study, 1954. The matter may thus still be
said to be 'hot in question'. It may be noted, however, that
The Contention and *The True Tragedy* are reasonably good
texts and would not have been questioned had there not
been the differing Folio version of these two plays.

The second proposal (*b*) is not so easily confuted, for the
answer depends solely on the judgement of style. There are
manifest differences of style between various episodes and
speeches in the *Henry VI* plays, and especially in the First
Part. It is hard, for instance, to believe that all the speeches
of the heroic Talbot are the work of one man. Thus, at P.
56 L. 24 – P. 59 L. 15 his eloquence runs smooth and even,
and in the same tone he laments over Salisbury (P. 65 L. 11):

Bring forth the body of old Salisbury,
And here advance it in the Market-Place,
The middle centre of this cursed Town.
Now have I paid my vow unto his soul:
For every drop of blood was drawn from him,
There hath at least five Frenchmen died tonight.
And that hereafter Ages may behold

What ruin happen'd in revenge of him,
Within their chiefest Temple I'll erect
A Tomb, wherein his corpse shall be interr'd:
Upon the which, that every one may read,
Shall be engrav'd the sack of Orleans,
The treacherous manner of his mournful death,
And what a terror he had been to France.
But Lords, in all our bloody massacre,
I muse we met not with the Dolphin's Grace,
His new-come Champion, virtuous Joan of Arc,
Nor any of his false confederates.

But the style of his speech to the King at the beginning of
III. iv is a far less able piece of writing:

My gracious Prince, and honourable Peers,
Hearing of your arrival in this Realm,
I have a while given truce unto my wars,
To do my duty to my Sovereign:
In sign whereof, this arm, that hath reclaim'd
To your obedience, fifty fortresses,
Twelve Cities, and seven walled Towns of strength,
Beside five hundred prisoners of esteem;
Lets fall his sword before your Highness' feet:
And with submissive loyalty of heart
Ascribes the glory of his conquest got,
First to my God and next unto your Grace.

Here the author laboriously builds up the speech line by
line and stress by stress. Just before his death, Talbot for no
very obvious reason drops into a ranting and strained
rhyme as he addresses his gallant son (P. 109 L. 8):

When from the Dolphin's crest thy sword struck fire,
It warm'd thy Father's heart with proud desire
Of bold-faced Victory. Then leaden age,
Quicken'd with youthful spleen, and warlike rage,

Beat down Alanson, Orleans, Burgundy,
And from the pride of Gallia rescued thee. . . .
If I today die not with Frenchmen's rage,
Tomorrow I shall die with mickle age.
By me they nothing gain, and if I stay,
'Tis but the short'ning of my life one day.
In thee thy Mother dies, our Household's Name,
My death's revenge, thy youth, and England's Fame:
All these, and more, we hazard by thy stay;
All these are sav'd, if thou wilt fly away.

It may be that in these, his first plays, Shakespeare's touch
was so unsure that he could vary in this manner, but it is
more likely that *Henry VI* was the work of more than one
author. Various names have been suggested – Greene, Marlowe, Peele, Nashe – but there is not sufficient evidence to
identify the style of any one of them and the case cannot be
proved either way. An inexperienced writer who has not
yet developed his own style and technique is often power-
fully influenced by the work of more established contemporaries, and Heminge and Condell would hardly
have included the three parts of *Henry VI* in the folio unless
they had known that these plays were mainly Shakespeare's
work.

THE FIRST PART OF
HENRY THE SIXTH

Shakespeare's plays dealing with English history were
based on the English Chronicles, particularly the volumes
compiled by Raphael Holinshed in 1577, and reissued in
1587. Early chroniclers were not restricted by the laws of
copyright or plagiarism, and they borrowed freely from
their predecessors. Holinshed, for the period covered by

the reign of Henry VI, copied or paraphrased Edward
Halle's *Chronicle* so closely that it is uncertain at times
whether Shakespeare was using Holinshed or Halle; probably he used both, for occasionally he adapted incidents
which appear in Halle but not in Holinshed. In his later
Chronicle plays – the two parts of *Henry IV* and *Henry V* –
Shakespeare kept closely to history, but in *Henry VI* he was
very free with historical facts. *The First Part of Henry VI*,
for instance, opens with the funeral of Henry V, which
occurred on 7 November 1422. As the procession pauses,
Bedford and Gloucester pronounce their eulogies over the
dead hero, but at once quarrels break out between Henry
Beaufort, Bishop of Winchester, and Humphrey Duke of
Gloucester. Gloucester taunts Winchester with his fondness
for

> an effeminate Prince,
> Whom like a schoolboy you may over-awe –

forgetting that the little King Henry VI was at this time
less than a year old. Bedford stops the quarrel to utter a
somewhat pagan invocation to Henry V's ghost, but he is
himself interrupted by the arrival of three messengers.
From the first messenger the English nobles learn of the
loss of Guienne, Champagne, Rheims, Orleans, Paris,
Guysors, Poictiers, and Rouen. Actually Rheims was sur-
rendered in 1429, Paris in 1436, Guysors and Rouen in
1449. Moreover, Orleans and Poictiers were not in English
hands at the death of Henry V. A second messenger enters
to declare that Charles the Dauphin has been crowned in
Rheims (an event that occurred in 1429); and a third messenger tells of the capture of Talbot, which happened on
18 June 1429 – some weeks after the siege of Orleans which
is *later* shown in Act II.

I Henry VI is thus quite unreliable as sober history. In
effect the play covers a period of twenty years, from the

funeral of Henry V to the negotiations for the marriage of Henry VI to Margaret of Anjou (V. 2 and 5) in 1444; but the death of Sir John Talbot (IV.5 and 6) – the most effective scene in the play – occurred in 1453, twenty-two years after the burning of Joan of Arc (V.4).

Apart from this wild chronology, some of the episodes in the play are quite unhistorical. These include the famous incident of the plucking of the roses (II.4) and the Countess of Auvergne's attempt to capture Talbot (II.2).

Modern readers, however, are not greatly disturbed by such romantic inaccuracies; but they are acutely distressed by the unpleasant portrait of Joan of Arc, which is even further from actual history than George Bernard Shaw's *St Joan*. In *I Henry VI* Joan is shown as mistress to Charles the Dauphin and a dabbler in the occult arts, who owes her abilities and successes to the infernal powers; and she is finally led to the stake as a witch and a strumpet. It is perhaps a slight excuse for her persecutors in the play that the seasoned warriors whom she defeated could find no natural or divine explanation for the prowess and generalship of a girl of eighteen. Moreover, Shakespeare found most of the calumnies in Holinshed.

Some examples from Holinshed will show the use made of the *Chronicles* in the play.

I. THE COMING OF JOAN LA PUCELLE
(I.2, P. 48 L. 26 – P. 52 L. 5)

In the time of this siege at Orleans (French stories say) the first week of March 1429, unto Charles the Dolphin at Chinon, as he was in very great care and study how to wrestle against the English nation, by one Robert Badricourt, captain of Vacoleurs (made after Marshal of France by the Dolphin's creation), was carried a young wench of an eighteen years old, called Joan Arc, by name of her father (a sorry shepherd) James of Arc, and Isabel her mother; brought up poorly in their trade of keeping cattle; born at Domprin (therefore reported by Bale, Joan Domprin) upon Meuse in Loraine, within the diocese of Thoule. Of favour was she counted likesome, of person strongly made and manly, of courage great, hardy and stout withal; an understander of counsels though she were not at them; great semblance of chastity both of body and behaviour; the name of Jesus in her mouth about all her businesses; humble, obedient; and fasting divers days in the week. A person (as their books make her) raised up by power divine, only for succour to the French estate then deeply in distress; in whom, for planting a credit the rather, first the company that toward the Dolphin did conduct her, through places all dangerous, was holden by the English (where she never was afore) all the way and by nightertale safely did she lead: then at the Dolphin's sending by her assignment, from St Katherine's church of Fierbois in Touraine (where she never had been and knew not) in a secret place there among old iron, appointed she her sword to be sought out and brought her (that with five flower-de-luces was graven on both sides), wherewith she fought and did many slaughters by her own hands. On warfare rode she in armour cap-a-pie and mustered as a man; before her an ensign all white, wherein was Jesus Christ painted with a flower de luce in his hand.

Unto the Dolphin into his gallery when first she was brought, and he, shadowing himself behind, setting other gay Lords before him to try her cunning, from all the company with a salutation (that indeed mars all the matter) she picked him out alone; who thereupon had her to the end of the gallery, where she held him an hour in secret and private talk, that of his privy chamber was thought very long, and therefore would have broken it off; but he made them a sign to let her say on. In which (among other), as likely it was, she set out unto him the singular feats (for sooth) given her by revelation divine, that in virtue of that sword she should achieve; which were, how with honour and victory she would raise the siege at Orleans, set him in state of the crown of France, and drive the English out of the country, thereby he to enjoy the kingdom alone. Hereupon he heartened at full, appointed her a sufficient army with absolute power to lead them, and they obediently to do as she bade them. Then fell she to work, and first defeated, indeed, the siege at Orleans; by and by encouraged him to crown himself King of France at Reims, that a little before from the English she had won. Thus after pursued she many bold enterprises to our great displeasure a two year together; for the time she kept in state until she were taken and for heresy and witchery burned.

2. THE DEATH OF SALISBURY

(I. 4, P. 55 L. 22 – P. 59 L. 16)

In the tower that was taken at the bridge end (as before you have heard) there was an high chamber, having a grate full of bars of iron, by the which a man might look all the length of the bridge into the city; at which grate many of the chief captains stood many times, viewing the city, and devising in what place it was best to give the assault. They within the city well perceived this tooting hole and laid a piece of ordnance directly against the window.

It so chanced that the nine and fiftieth day after the siege was laid, the Earl of Salisbury, Sir Thomas Gargrave and William Glasdale, with divers other went into the said tower, and so into the high chamber, and looked out at the grate; and, within a short space, the son of the master gunner, perceiving men looking out at the window, took his match (as his father had taught him; who was gone to dinner) and fired the gun; the shot whereof brake and shivered the iron bars of the grate, so that one of the same bars strake the Earl so violently on the head that it stroke away one of his eyes and the side of his cheek. Sir Thomas Gargrave was likewise stricken and died within two days.

3. THE CAPTURE OF ORLEANS
(II.1, P. 62 L. 7 – P. 63 L. 24)

[Orleans was not captured in the manner shown in II.1 of the play. This scene was based on the capture of Mans. The English withdrew from the town and reported to Talbot who sent out Matthew Gough to spy on the state of the French garrison.]

Matthew Gough so well sped his business that privily in the night he came into the castle, where he learned that the Frenchmen very negligently used themselves, without taking heed in their watch, as though they had been out of all danger; which well understood, he returned again, and within a mile of the city met the Lord Talbot and the Lord Scales, and opened unto them all things according to his credence. The Lords then to make haste in the matter (because the day approached) with all speed possible came to the postern gate, and alighting from their horses, about six of the clock in the morning, they issued out of the castle crying, 'Saint George! Talbot!'

The Frenchmen, being thus suddenly taken, were sore amazed; in so much that some of them, being not out of their beds, got up in their shirts and leaped over the walls. Others ran naked out of the gates to save their lives, leaving all their apparel, horses, armour, and riches behind them: none was hurt but such as resisted.

4. THE END OF JOAN LA PUCELLE
(V.4, P. 123 L. 24 – P. 124 L. 28)

[Joan was tried before Peter Cauchon, Bishop of Beauvais, who] caused her life and belief, after order of law, to be inquired upon and examined. Wherein found though a virgin, yet first, shamefully rejecting her sex abominably in acts and apparel, to have counterfeit mankind, and then, all damnably faithless, to be a pernicious instrument to hostility and bloodshed in devilish witchcraft and sorcery, sentence accordingly was pronounced against her. Howbeit, upon humble confession of her iniquities with a counterfeit contrition pretending a careful sorrow for the same, execution spared and all mollified into this, that thenceforth she should cast off her unnatural wearing of man's habiliments and keep her to garments of her own kind, abjure her pernicious practices of sorcery and witchery, and have life and leisure in perpetual prison to bewail her misdeeds. Which to perform (according to the manner of abjuration) a solemn oath very gladly she took.

But herein (God help us!) she fully afore possessed of the fiend, not able to hold her own in any towardness of grace, falling straight into her former abominations (and yet seeking to eke out life as long as she might) stake not (though the shift were shameful) to confess herself a strumpet, and (unmarried as she was) to be with child.[1] For trial, the Lord Regent's lenity gave her nine months' stay, at the end whereof she (found herein as false as

[1] There is no truth in this calumny.

wicked in the rest, an eight days after, upon a further definitive sentence declared against her to be relapse and a renouncer of her oath and repentance) was thereupon delivered over to secular power, and so executed by consumption of fire in the old market place at Rouen, in the selfsame stead where now St Michael's Church stands: her ashes afterward without the town walls shaken into the wind.

The story of *I Henry VI* is thus mainly concerned with the wars in France, and it ends where the Second Part begins – with the marriage of the King, now grown up, with the French Princess Margaret.

THE SECOND PART OF
HENRY THE SIXTH

The Second Part of Henry VI continues the story from the marriage of the young King Henry VI and the Lady Margaret of Anjou to the victory of Richard Duke of York at the battle of St Albans.

A general atmosphere of jealousy and hatred pervades the whole play. The young Queen Margaret is shown as a ruthless and domineering woman; she despises her meek husband and takes Suffolk as her lover; she resents and insults the Duchess of Gloucester and exults in her disgrace and in the downfall and death of Humphrey, the 'good Duke of Gloucester'. She hates York and his supporters and all his family – which is understandable – and she is the inspiration of the party of the Red Rose, the Lancastrians.

Opposed to the Queen and her followers are Richard Duke of York and his sons and supporters, especially the Earl of Warwick, known in English history as 'the Kingmaker', the most powerful of all the English nobles. Richard of York is a good specimen of the ambitious villain – a type popular on the English stage in the early 1590s; but he is mild compared with his youngest son Richard, afterward Duke of Gloucester and King Richard III. York's motives, as he explains in the first soliloquy (P. 141 L. 33 – P. 143 L. 11) are mixed – a desire to claim his rights as legal heir of Edward III, disgust at the bookish King's misrule, and a personal hatred of the House of Lancaster. At the beginning of the play he is overshadowed by Humphrey Duke of Gloucester, but he bides his time until Humphrey's fall. When he is sent off to deal with the rebellion in Ireland, he realizes that his opportunity has come (P. 185 L. 19 – P. 187 L. 5). He resolves that he will stir up troubles in England and then at the head of his army return to reap his harvest and win the crown.

The fourth act of the play is wholly concerned with the rebellion of Jack Cade.

The play ends with York's return to claim the crown. The civil wars begin; at first the White Rose is victorious, and York and Warwick go forth in triumph to receive the submission of London.

In *II Henry VI* Shakespeare was not quite so reckless with the facts of history and chronology as he had been in Part I; but it may be noted that the quarrel between Queen Margaret and the Duchess of Gloucester could not have occurred, as the Duchess was disgraced three and a half years before Margaret came to England. Nor was Suffolk actually the Queen's lover. Moreover, certain episodes in the rebellion of Jack Cade were taken over from incidents in the Wat Tyler rebellion of seventy years earlier.

The sources for *II Henry VI*, as for *I Henry VI*, were for the most part the *Chronicles* of Halle and Holinshed. Some examples will show how Shakespeare used these sources.

I. THE CHARACTER OF HENRY VI

[Halle gives the following character sketch of Henry VI:]

King Henry was of stature goodly, of body slender, to which proportion all other members were correspondent; his face beautiful, in the which continually was resident the bounty of mind with which he was inwardly endowed. He did abhor of his own nature all the vices, as well of the body as of the soul; and from his very infancy he was of honest conversation and pure integrity; no knower of evil, and a keeper of all goodness; a despiser of all things which were wont to cause the minds of mortal men to slide or appair. Besides this, patience was so radicate in his heart that of all the injuries to him committed (which were no small number) he never asked vengeance nor punishment, but for that rendered to Almighty God, his Creator, hearty thanks, thinking that by this trouble and adversity his sins were to him forgotten and forgiven.

2. THE DEATH OF SUFFOLK

(IV.i, P. 201 L. 24 – P. 206 L. 16)

But God's justice would not that so ungracious a person should so escape; for, when he shipped in Suffolk, intending to transport himself over into France, he was encountered with a ship of war, appertaining to the Duke of Exeter, Constable of the Tower of London, called *The Nicholas of the Tower*. The captain of that bark with small fight entered into the Duke's ship, and perceiving his person present, brought him to Dover Road and there on the one side of a cockboat caused his head to be stricken off, and left his body with the head lying there on the sands.

3. THE DEATH OF CADE

(IV.10, P. 224 L. 18 – P. 227 L. 5)

[Halle relates that when Cade saw his men suddenly disperse, he fled into Sussex in disguise.]

But all his metamorphosis or transfiguration little prevailed. For, after a proclamation made that whosoever could apprehend the said Jack Cade should have for his pain a thousand marks, many sought for him but few espied him, till one Alexander Iden, esquire of Kent, found him in a garden and there in his defence manfully slew the caitiff Cade and brought his dead body to London, whose head was set on London Bridge.

4. THE 'MIRACLE' AT ST ALBANS

(II.1, P. 159 L. 22 – P. 163 L. 7)

[This episode was taken from Sir Thomas More's *Dialogue*, concerning the veneration and worship of images, etc.]

When the King was comen and the town full, suddenly this blind man at Saint Alban's Shrine had his sight again; and a miracle solemnly rongen and *Te Deum* songen, so that nothing was talked of in all the town but this miracle. So happened it that Duke Humphrey of Gloucester, a great wise man and very well learned, having great joy to see such a miracle, called the poor man unto him. And first showing himself joyous of God's glory, so showed in the getting of his sight; and exhorting him to meekness, and to none ascribing of any part the worship to himself, nor to be proud of the people's praise, which would call him a good and godly man thereby. At last he looked well into his eyen, and asked whether he could never see nothing at all in all his life before. And when as well his wife as himself affirmed fastly no, then he looked advisedly upon his eyen again and said, 'I believe you very well, for me thinketh that ye cannot see so well yet.' 'Yes, sir,' quoth he, 'I thank God and his holy martyr, I can now see as well as any man.' 'Ye can?' quoth the Duke; 'what colour is my gown?' Then anon the beggar told him. 'What colour is this man's gown?' He told him also; and so forth, without any sticking, he told him the names of all the colours that could be showed him. And when my Lord saw that, he had him 'walk, faitor!' and made him be set openly in the stocks; for though he could have seen suddenly by miracle the difference between divers colours, yet he could not by the sight so suddenly tell the names of all these colours but if he had known them before, no more than the names of all the men that he should suddenly see.

II Henry VI as it stands is an incomplete play and needs its sequel to finish the story.

THE THIRD PART OF HENRY THE SIXTH

The Third Part of Henry the Sixth begins with a scene in Parliament – more symbolic than realistic – in which Richard sets himself on the throne and treats King Henry VI with deliberate contempt. York, however, agrees to the compromise that Henry shall remain nominally King for life but that Richard shall succeed on his death. Queen Margaret and her friends, especially Clifford, will have none of this weakness and withdraw to renew the war. York, on the advice of his youngest son Richard (afterward Duke of Gloucester and King Richard III), breaks his oath to Henry. But at the battle of Wakefield Fortune turns against him; his young son Rutland is cruelly murdered and he himself is captured by the ruthless Margaret, who

mocks and taunts him vilely before she herself aids Clifford
to stab him.

The claims of York thus fall to his eldest son Edward
Earl of March, who still has the all-powerful support of
Warwick. For a while, however, the Red Rose of Lancaster is in the ascendant. The two parties defy each other
and battle is joined; Edward and his party are defeated and
flee for their lives. During the turmoil the poor King wan-
ders in alone and sits down to lament his hard fate – called
to be a King yet despised by Queen, friends, and foes. Then
Fortune once more changes sides. Clifford, the most fero-
cious of Queen Margaret's party, is killed, and Edward
marches off to London to be crowned King, his first act
being to promote his two brothers – Richard to be Duke of
Gloucester and George to be Duke of Clarence – while
Warwick remains the acknowledged chief prop of the new
reign.

In the third Act Edward commits the fatal error which
ultimately brings about the downfall of his house. While
Warwick is in France negotiating a marriage with the
French King's sister-in-law, Lady Bona, Edward makes
love to Lady Grey, a widow who has come to beg for restitution of her husband's lands; but she resists his sugges-
tions until he asks her to marry him and become his Queen.

Richard Duke of Gloucester now reveals himself in a
tremendous soliloquy (P. 292 L. 10 – P. 294 L. 14); and from
this point until his death in *Richard III* (V.5) he is the domi-
nant figure, a colossal monster of unmitigated evil. Edward's ill-advised marriage alienates Warwick (and even
turns him into the ally of the exiled Queen Margaret). It
also annoys the King's brothers, Clarence and Gloucester,
so that when Warwick returns he justifies his name of 'the
Kingmaker' by unkinging Edward and restoring Henry
VI. However, Edward escapes from his captivity, with the

aid of Richard, and rallies his friends. In the battle of Barnet, Warwick is killed (V.2) and in the final battle at Tewkesbury (V.3 and 4) the last hopes of the Lancastrians are destroyed. Margaret and her son, the young Edward Prince of Wales, are captured, and the boy is mercilessly slain before the eyes of his mother by King Edward and his brothers; Richard rides off to London to murder the saintly King Henry in the Tower. The play thus ends with the triumph of the White Rose of York. From this point *Richard the Third*, the last of the four plays on the Hour of the Curse on the House of Lancaster, is the natural sequel.

As with *I* and *II Henry VI* the source of the Third Part was mainly the *Chronicles* of Halle and Holinshed, of which the following passages are representative:

I. THE CRUELTY OF CLIFFORD

(I.3, P. 253 L. 7 – P. 255 L. 2)

[Halle tells that during the battle of Wakefield:]

A priest called Sir Robert Aspall, chaplain and schoolmaster to the young Earl of Rutland (second son to the above named Duke of York, scarce of the age of twelve years, a fair gentleman and a maiden-like person), perceiving that flight was more safeguard than tarrying both for him and his master, secretly conveyed the Earl out of the field, by the Lord Clifford's band, toward the town; but, or he could enter into a house, he was by the said Lord Clifford espied, followed, and taken, and by reason of his apparel demanded what he was. The young gentleman, dismayed, had not a word to speak, but kneeled on his knees, imploring mercy and desiring grace, both with holding up his hands and making dolorous countenance, for his speech was gone for fear. 'Save him,' said his chaplain, 'for he is a Prince's son, and peradventure may do you good hereafter.' With that word,

B

the Lord Clifford marked him and said, 'By God's blood! Thy father slew mine, and so will I do thee and all thy kin!' And with that word, stack the Earl to the heart with his dagger, and bade his chaplain bear the Earl's mother and brother word what he had done and said. In this act the Lord Clifford was accounted a tyrant and no gentleman, for the property of the lion (which is a furious and unreasonable beast) is to be cruel to them that withstand him, and gentle to such as prostrate or humiliate themselves before him.

2. THE WOOING OF THE LADY GREY

(III.2, P. 287 L. 17 – P. 292 L. 8)

[Both Halle and Holinshed record that the King first met the Lady Elizabeth Grey while he was out hunting.]

When the King beheld and heard her speak, as she was both fair and of a goodly favour, moderate of stature, well made and very wise, he not only pitied her but also waxed enamoured of her. And, taking her afterward secretly aside, began to enter in talking more familiarly. Whose appetite when she perceived, she virtuously denied him.

But that she did so wisely, and with so good manner, and words so well set, that she rather kindled his desire than quenched it. And finally after many a meeting, much wooing, and many great promises, she well espied the King's affection toward her so greatly increased that she durst the more boldly say her mind as to him whose heart she perceived more fervently set than to fall off for a word. And in conclusion she showed him plain that, as she wist herself too simple to be his wife, so she thought herself too good to be his concubine. The King, much marvelling at her constancy (as he that had not been wont elsewhere to be so stiffly said nay) so much esteemed her continency and chastity that he set her virtue in the stead of possession and riches; and thus taking counsel of his desire, determined in all possible haste to marry her.

3. THE ANGER OF WARWICK
(III.3, P. 299 L. 33 – P. 302 L. 11)

The French King was not well pleased to be thus dallied with; but he shortly (to appease the grief of his wife and her sister, the Lady Bona) married the said Lady Bona to the Duke of Milan.

Now when the Earl of Warwick had knowledge by letters sent to him out of England from his trusty friends that King Edward had gotten him a new wife, he was not a little troubled in his mind; for that he took it his credence thereby was greatly minished, and his honour much stained, namely, in the Court of France, for that it might be judged he came rather like an espial, to move a thing never minded, and to treat a marriage determined before not to take effect. Surely he thought himself evil used, that when he brought the matter to his purposed intent and wished conclusion, then to have it quail on his part; so as all men might think at the least wise that his Prince made small account of him to send him on such a sleeveless errand.

All men for the most part agree that this marriage was the only cause why the Earl of Warwick conceived an hatred against King Edward whom he so much before favoured.

4. THE CHARACTER OF RICHARD, DUKE OF GLOUCESTER

Richard, the third son, of whom we now intreat, was in wit and courage equal with either of them [Edward

IV and Clarence], in body and prowess far under them both; little of stature, ill-featured of limbs, crookbacked, his left shoulder much higher than his right, hard-favoured of visage, and such as is in states called warly, in other men otherwise; he was malicious, wrathful, envious, and from afore his birth ever froward. It is for truth reported that the Duchess his mother had so much ado in her travail that she could not be delivered of him uncut; and that he came into the world with the feet forward, as men be borne outward, and (as the fame runneth also) not untoothed . . .

None evil captain was he in the war, as to which his disposition was more meetly than for peace. Sundry victories had he, and sometimes overthrows, but never on default, as for his own person, either of hardiness or politic order. Free was he called of dispense, and somewhat above his power liberal; with large gifts he gat him unsteadfast friendship, for which he was fain to pill and spoil in other places, and got him steadfast hatred. He was close and secret, a deep dissembler, lowly of countenance, arrogant of heart, outwardly companionable where he inwardly hated, not letting to kiss whom he thought to kill; despitious and cruel, not for evil will alway, but ofter of ambition and either for the surety or increase of his estate.

Friend and foe was much what indifferent, where his advantage grew; he spared no man's death whose life withstood his purpose . . .

As he was small and little of stature, so was he of body greatly deformed, the one shoulder higher than the other. His face was small, but his countenance cruel, and such that at the first aspect a man would judge it to savour and smell of malice, fraud, and deceit. When he stood musing, he would bite and chaw busily his nether lip, as who said that his fierce nature in his cruel body always chafed, stirred, and was ever unquiet. Beside that, the dagger which he ware, he would, when he studied with his hand pluck up and down in the sheath to the midst, never drawing it fully out. He was of a ready, pregnant, and quick wit, wily to feign, and apt to dissemble. He had a proud mind, and an arrogant stomach, the which accompanied him even to his death; rather choosing to suffer the same by dint of sword than, being forsaken and left helpless of his unfaithful companions, to preserve by cowardly flight such a frail and uncertain life, which by malice, sickness, or condign punishment was like shortly to come to confusion.

The text of this edition follows the Folio closely, in accordance with the principles adopted for the Penguin Shakespeares. Spelling has been modernized, but the punctuation (which shows how the speeches should be delivered) and the original arrangement have been kept, except in a few places where they seemed clearly wrong and likely to cause confusion. The excessive use of capital letters has been somewhat modified. Some of the more striking stage directions in *The Contention* and *The True Tragedie* are recorded in the Notes. For reference purposes, the accepted Act and Scene division have been noted. In the Folio there is an incomplete attempt to divide the First Part into Acts and Scenes, but the texts of the Second and Third Parts have no divisions throughout. The reader who is used to the 'accepted text' will find some unfamiliarities, but the text is nearer to that used in Shakespeare's own playhouse.

The First Part of
Henry the Sixth

THE ACTORS' NAMES

KING HENRY THE SIXTH

DUKE OF GLOUCESTER, uncle to the King, and Protector

DUKE OF BEDFORD, uncle to the King, and Regent of France

THOMAS BEAUFORT, Duke of Exeter, great-uncle to the King

HENRY BEAUFORT, great-uncle to the King, Bishop of Winchester, and afterwards Cardinal

JOHN BEAUFORT, Earl, afterwards Duke, of Somerset

RICHARD PLANTAGENET, son of Richard (late Earl of Cambridge) afterwards Duke of York

EARL OF WARWICK, EARL OF SALISBURY, EARL OF SUFFOLK

LORD TALBOT, afterwards Earl of Shrewsbury

JOHN TALBOT, his son

EDMUND MORTIMER, Earl of March

SIR JOHN FALSTAFFE   SIR WILLIAM GLANSDALE

SIR WILLIAM LUCY   SIR THOMAS GARGRAVE

Mayor of London

WOODVILE, Lieutenant of the Tower

VERNON, of the White-Rose or York faction

BASSETT, of the Red-Rose or Lancaster faction

A Lawyer   Mortimer's Keepers

CHARLES, the Dolphin (afterwards King of France)

REIGNIER, Duke of Anjou, and titular King of Naples

DUKE OF BURGUNDY   BASTARD OF ORLEANS

DUKE OF ALANSON   Governor of Paris

Master-Gunner of Orleans and his Son

General of the French forces in Bourdeaux

A French Sergeant   A Porter

An old Shepherd, father to Joan

MARGARET, daughter to Reignier, afterwards married to King Henry

COUNTESS OF AUVERGNE

JOAN DE PUZELL, commonly called Joan of Arc

Lords, Warders, Heralds, Officers, Soldiers, Messengers, Attendants, etc., Sundry Fiends.

I. 1

Dead March.

Enter the Funeral of King Henry the Fifth, attended on by the Duke of Bedford, Regent of France; the Duke of Gloucester, Protector; the Duke of Exeter, Warwick, the Bishop of Winchester, and the Duke of Somerset.

BEDFORD: Hung be the heavens with black, yield day to
    night;
Comets importing change of Times and States,
Brandish your crystal tresses in the sky,
And with them scourge the bad revolting stars,
That have consented unto Henry's death:
King Henry the Fifth, too famous to live long,
England ne'er lost a King of so much worth.

GLOUCESTER: England ne'er had a King until his time:
Virtue he had, deserving to command,
His brandish'd sword did blind men with his beams,
His arms spread wider than a Dragon's wings:
His sparkling eyes, replete with wrathful fire,
More dazzled and drove back his enemies,
Than mid-day Sun, fierce bent against their faces.
What should I say? his deeds exceed all speech:
He ne'er lift up his hand, but conquered.

EXETER: We mourn in black, why mourn we not in
    blood?
Henry is dead, and never shall revive:
Upon a wooden coffin we attend;
And Death's dishonourable victory,
We with our stately presence glorify,
Like captives bound to a triumphant car.
What? shall we curse the planets of mishap,

That plotted thus our Glory's overthrow?
Or shall we think the subtle-witted French,
Conjurers and sorcerers, that afraid of him,
By magic verses have contriv'd his end?

WINCHESTER: He was a King, bless'd of the King of
Kings.
Unto the French, the dreadful Judgement-Day
So dreadful will not be, as was his sight.
The battles of the Lord of Hosts he fought:
The Church's prayers made him so prosperous.

GLOUCESTER: The Church? where is it?
Had not Church-men pray'd,
His thread of life had not so soon decay'd.
None do you like, but an effeminate Prince,
Whom like a school-boy you may over-awe.

WINCHESTER: Gloucester, whate'er we like, thou art
Protector,
And lookest to command the Prince and Realm.
Thy Wife is proud, she holdeth thee in awe,
More than God or religious Churchmen may.

GLOUCESTER: Name not Religion, for thou lov'st the
flesh,
And ne'er throughout the year to church thou go'st,
Except it be to pray against thy foes.

BEDFORD: Cease, cease these jars, and rest your minds in
peace:
Let's to the Altar: Heralds wait on us;
Instead of gold, we'll offer up our arms,
Since arms avail not, now that Henry's dead,
Posterity await for wretched years,
When at their mothers' moist'ned eyes, babes shall suck,
Our Isle be made a nourish of salt tears,
And none but women left to wail the dead.
Henry the Fifth, thy ghost I invocate:

Prosper this Realm, keep it from civil broils,
Combat with adverse Planets in the Heavens;
A far more glorious Star thy soul will make,
Than Julius Caesar, or bright –

Enter a Messenger.

MESSENGER: My honourable Lords, health to you all:
Sad tidings bring I to you out of France,
Of loss, of slaughter, and discomfiture:
Guienne, Champagne, Rheims, Orleans,
Paris, Guysors, Poictiers, are all quite lost.

BEDFORD: What say'st thou man, before dead Henry's
corse?
Speak softly, or the loss of those great Towns
Will make him burst his lead, and rise from death.

GLOUCESTER: Is Paris lost? is Roan yielded up?
If Henry were recall'd to life again,
These news would cause him once more yield the ghost.

EXETER: How were they lost? what treachery was us'd?

MESSENGER: No treachery, but want of men and money.
Amongst the soldiers this is muttered,
That here you maintain several factions;
And whilst a field should be dispatch'd and fought,
You are disputing of your Generals.
One would have lingering wars, with little cost;
Another would fly swift, but wanteth wings:
A third thinks, without expense at all,
By guileful fair words, Peace may be obtain'd.
Awake, awake, English Nobility,
Let not sloth dim your honours, new begot;
Cropp'd are the flower-de-luces in your arms
Of England's coat, one half is cut away.

EXETER: Were our tears wanting to this funeral,
These tidings would call forth their flowing tides.

BEDFORD: Me they concern, Regent I am of France:

Give me my steeled coat, I'll fight for France.
Away with these disgraceful wailing robes;
Wounds will I lend the French, instead of eyes,
To weep their intermissive miseries.

Enter to them another Messenger.

MESSENGER: Lords view these letters, full of bad mischance.

France is revolted from the English quite,
Except some petty towns, of no import.
The Dolphin Charles is crowned King in Rheims:
The Bastard of Orleans with him is join'd;
Reignier, Duke of Anjou, doth take his part;
The Duke of Alanson flieth to his side.

Exit.

EXETER: The Dolphin crown'd King? all fly to him?
O whither shall we fly from this reproach?

GLOUCESTER: We will not fly, but to our enemies' throats.

Bedford, if thou be slack, I'll fight it out.

BEDFORD: Gloucester, why doubt'st thou of my forwardness?

An army have I muster'd in my thoughts,
Wherewith already France is overrun.

Enter another Messenger.

MESSENGER: My gracious Lords, to add to your laments,
Wherewith you now bedew King Henry's hearse,
I must inform you of a dismal fight,
Betwixt the stout Lord Talbot, and the French.

WINCHESTER: What? wherein Talbot overcame, is't so?

3 MESSENGER: O no: wherein Lord Talbot was o'erthrown:

The circumstance I'll tell you more at large.
The tenth of August last, this dreadful Lord,
Retiring from the siege of Orleans,

Having full scarce six thousand in his troop,
By three and twenty thousand of the French
Was round encompassed, and set upon:
No leisure had he to enrank his men.
He wanted pikes to set before his archers:
Instead whereof, sharp stakes pluck'd out of hedges
They pitched in the ground confusedly,
To keep the horsemen off, from breaking in.
More than three hours the fight continued:
Where valiant Talbot, above human thought,
Enacted wonders with his sword and lance.
Hundreds he sent to Hell, and none durst stand him:
Here, there, and every where enrag'd, he slew:
The French exclaim'd, the Devil was in arms,
All the whole Army stood agaz'd on him.
His soldiers spying his undaunted spirit,
A Talbot, a Talbot, cried out amain,
And rush'd into the bowels of the battle.
Here had the conquest fully been seal'd up,
If Sir John Falstaffe had not play'd the coward.
He being in the vaward, plac'd behind,
With purpose to relieve and follow them,
Cowardly fled, not having struck one stroke.
Hence grew the general wrack and massacre:
Enclosed were they with their enemies.
A base Walloon, to win the Dolphin's grace,
Thrust Talbot with a spear into the back,
Whom all France, with their chief assembled strength,
Durst not presume to look once in the face.

BEDFORD: Is Talbot slain then? I will slay myself,
  For living idly here, in pomp and ease,
  Whilst such a worthy Leader, wanting aid,
  Unto his dastard foemen is betray'd.

3 MESSENGER: O no, he lives, but is took prisoner,

And Lord Scales with him, and Lord Hungerford:
Most of the rest slaughter'd, or took likewise.
BEDFORD: His ransom there is none but I shall pay.
I'll hale the Dolphin headlong from his Throne,
His Crown shall be the ransom of my friend:
Four of their Lords I'll change for one of ours.
Farewell my Masters, to my task will I,
Bonfires in France forthwith I am to make
To keep our great Saint George's Feast withal.
Ten thousand soldiers with me I will take,
Whose bloody deeds shall make all Europe quake.
3 MESSENGER: So you had need, for Orleans is besieg'd,
The English Army is grown weak and faint:
The Earl of Salisbury craveth supply,
And hardly keeps his men from mutiny,
Since they so few, watch such a multitude.
EXETER: Remember Lords your oaths to Henry sworn:
Either to quell the Dolphin utterly,
Or bring him in obedience to your yoke.
BEDFORD: I do remember it, and here take my leave,
To go about my preparation.
                    Exit Bedford.
GLOUCESTER: I'll to the Tower with all the haste I can,
To view th' artillery and munition,
And then I will proclaim young Henry King.
                    Exit Gloucester.
EXETER: To Eltham will I, where the young King is,
Being ordain'd his special Governor,
And for his safety there I'll best devise.
                    Exit.
WINCHESTER: Each hath his place and function to attend:
I am left out; for me nothing remains:
But long I will not be Jack out of office.
The King from Eltham I intend to steal

And sit at chiefest stern of public Weal.
Exeunt.

I. 2

Sound a Flourish.
Enter Charles, Alanson, and Reignier, marching
with Drum and Soldiers.

CHARLES: Mars his true moving, even as in the Heavens,
So in the Earth, to this day is not known.
Late did he shine upon the English side:
Now we are victors, upon us he smiles.
What Towns of any moment, but we have?
At pleasure here we lie, near Orleans:
Otherwhiles, the famish'd English, like pale ghosts,
Faintly besiege us one hour in a month.

ALANSON: They want their porridge, and their fat bull
beeves:
Either they must be dieted like mules,
And have their provender tied to their mouths,
Or piteous they will look, like drowned mice.

REIGNIER: Let's raise the siege: why live we idly here?
Talbot is taken, whom we wont to fear:
Remaineth none but mad-brain'd Salisbury,
And he may well in fretting spend his gall,
Nor men nor money hath he to make war.

CHARLES: Sound, sound alarum, we will rush on them.
Now for the honour of the forlorn French:
Him I forgive my death, that killeth me,
When he sees me go back one foot, or fly.
Exeunt.
Here Alarum, they are beaten back by the English,
with great loss.
Enter Charles, Alanson, and Reignier.

CHARLES: Who ever saw the like? what men have I?
  Dogs, cowards, dastards: I would ne'er have fled,
  But that they left me 'midst my enemies.
REIGNIER: Salisbury is a desperate homicide,
  He fighteth as one weary of his life:
  The other Lords, like lions wanting food,
  Do rush upon us as their hungry prey.
ALANSON: Froissart, a countryman of ours, records,
  England all Olivers and Rowlands bred,
  During the time Edward the Third did reign:
  More truly now may this be verified;
  For none but Samsons and Goliases
  It sendeth forth to skirmish: one to ten?
  Lean raw-bon'd rascals, who would e'er suppose,
  They had such courage and audacity?
CHARLES: Let's leave this Town,
  For they are hare-brain'd slaves,
  And hunger will enforce them to be more eager:
  Of old I know them; rather with their teeth
  The walls they'll tear down, than forsake the siege.
REIGNIER: I think by some odd gimmors or device
  Their arms are set, like clocks, still to strike on;
  Else ne'er could they hold out so as they do:
  By my consent, we'll even let them alone.
ALANSON: Be it so.

Enter the Bastard of Orleans.

BASTARD: Where's the Prince Dolphin? I have news for
  him.
CHARLES: Bastard of Orleans, thrice welcome to us.
BASTARD: Methinks your looks are sad, your cheer
  appal'd.
  Hath the late overthrow wrought this offence?
  Be not dismay'd, for succour is at hand:
  A holy Maid hither with me I bring,

Which by a Vision sent to her from Heaven,
Ordained is to raise this tedious siege,
And drive the English forth the bounds of France:
The spirit of deep prophecy she hath,
Exceeding the nine Sibyls of old Rome:
What's past, and what's to come, she can descry.
Speak, shall I call her in? believe my words,
For they are certain, and unfallible.

CHARLES: Go, call her in: [*Exit Bastard.*] But first, to try
 her skill,
Reignier stand thou as Dolphin in my place;
Question her proudly, let thy looks be stern,
By this means shall we sound what skill she hath.

Enter Joan Puzell.

REIGNIER: Fair Maid, is 't thou wilt do these wondrous
 feats?

JOAN: Reignier, is 't thou that thinkest to beguile me?
Where is the Dolphin? Come, come from behind,
I know thee well, though never seen before.
Be not amaz'd, there's nothing hid from me;
In private will I talk with thee apart:
Stand back you Lords, and give us leave awhile.

REIGNIER: She takes upon her bravely at first dash.

JOAN: Dolphin, I am by birth a Shepherd's Daughter,
My wit untrain'd in any kind of Art:
Heaven and our Lady gracious hath it pleas'd
To shine on my contemptible estate.
Lo, whilst I waited on my tender lambs,
And to Sun's parching heat display'd my cheeks,
God's Mother deigned to appear to me,
And in a Vision full of majesty,
Will'd me to leave my base vocation,
And free my Country from calamity:
Her aid she promis'd, and assur'd success.

In complete glory she reveal'd herself:
And whereas I was black and swart before,
With those clear rays, which she infus'd on me,
That beauty am I bless'd with, which you see.
Ask me what question thou canst possible,
And I will answer unpremeditated:
My courage try by combat, if thou dar'st,
And thou shalt find that I exceed my sex.
Resolve on this, thou shalt be fortunate,
If thou receive me for thy warlike Mate.

CHARLES: Thou hast astonish'd me with thy high terms:
Only this proof I'll of thy valour make,
In single combat thou shalt buckle with me;
And if thou vanquishest, thy words are true,
Otherwise I renounce all confidence.

JOAN: I am prepar'd: here is my keen-edg'd sword,
Deck'd with five flower-de-luces on each side,
The which at Touraine, in S. Katherine's Churchyard,
Out of a great deal of old iron, I chose forth.

CHARLES: Then come a' God's name, I fear no woman.

JOAN: And while I live, I'll ne'er fly from a man.

Here they fight, and Joan de Puzel overcomes.

CHARLES: Stay, stay thy hands, thou art an Amazon,
And fightest with the sword of Debora.

JOAN: Christ's Mother helps me, else I were too weak.

CHARLES: Whoe'er helps thee, 'tis thou that must help
me:
Impatiently I burn with thy desire,
My heart and hands thou hast at once subdu'd.
Excellent Puzel, if thy name be so,
Let me thy servant, and not Sovereign be,
'Tis the French Dolphin sueth to thee thus.

JOAN: I must not yield to any rites of Love,
For my profession's sacred from above:

When I have chased all thy foes from hence,
Then will I think upon a recompence.

CHARLES: Meantime look gracious on thy prostrate thrall.

REIGNIER: My Lord methinks is very long in talk.

ALANSON: Doubtless he shrives this woman to her
smock,
Else ne'er could he so long protract his speech.

REIGNIER: Shall we disturb him, since he keeps no mean?

ALANSON: He may mean more than we poor men do
know,
These women are shrewd tempters with their tongues.

REIGNIER: My Lord, where are you? what devise you on?
Shall we give o'er Orleans, or no?

JOAN: Why no, I say: distrustful recreants,
Fight till the last gasp: I'll be your guard.

CHARLES: What she says, I'll confirm: we'll fight it out.

JOAN: Assign'd am I to be the English Scourge.
This night the siege assuredly I'll raise:
Expect Saint Martin's Summer, halcyons' days,
Since I have enter'd into these wars.
Glory is like a circle in the water,
Which never ceaseth to enlarge itself,
Till by broad spreading, it disperse to nought.
With Henry's death, the English circle ends,
Dispersed are the glories it included:
Now am I like that proud insulting ship,
Which Caesar and his fortune bare at once.

CHARLES: Was Mahomet inspired with a dove?
Thou with an eagle art inspired then.
Helen, the Mother of great Constantine,
Nor yet S. Philip's daughters were like thee.
Bright Star of Venus, fall'n down on the Earth,
How may I reverently worship thee enough?

ALANSON: Leave off delays, and let us raise the siege.

REIGNIER: Woman, do what thou canst to save our
honours,

Drive them from Orleans, and be immortaliz'd.

CHARLES: Presently we'll try: come, let's away about it,

No Prophet will I trust, if she prove false.

Exeunt.

I.3

Enter Gloucester, with his Serving-men.

GLOUCESTER: I am come to survey the Tower this day;

Since Henry's death, I fear there is conveyance:

Where be these warders, that they wait not here?

Open the gates, 'tis Gloucester that calls.

1 WARDER: Who's there, that knocks so imperiously?

1 SERVING-MAN: It is the noble Duke of Gloucester.

2 WARDER: Whoe'er he be, you may not be let in.

1 SERVING-MAN: Villains, answer you so the Lord Protector?

1 WARDER: The Lord protect him, so we answer him,

We do no otherwise than we are will'd.

GLOUCESTER: Who willed you? or whose will stands but
mine?

There's none Protector of the Realm, but I:

Break up the gates, I'll be your warrantize;

Shall I be flouted thus by dunghill grooms?

*Gloucester's men rush at the Tower Gates, and Wood-
vile the Lieutenant speaks within.*

WOODVILE: What noise is this? what traitors have we
here?

GLOUCESTER: Lieutenant, is it you whose voice I hear?

Open the gates, here's Gloucester that would enter.

WOODVILE: Have patience noble Duke, I may not open,

The Cardinal of Winchester forbids:

From him I have express commandment,
That thou nor none of thine shall be let in.

GLOUCESTER: Faint-hearted Woodvile, prizest him 'fore
me?
Arrogant Winchester, that haughty Prelate,
Whom Henry our late Sovereign ne'er could brook?
Thou art no friend to God, or to the King:
Open the gates, or I'll shut thee out shortly.

SERVING-MEN: Open the gates unto the Lord Protector,
Or we'll burst them open, if that you come not quickly.
*Enter to the Protector at the Tower Gates, Winchester
and his men in tawny coats.*

WINCHESTER: How now ambitious Humphrey, what
means this?

GLOUCESTER: Peel'd Priest, dost thou command me to be
shut out?

WINCHESTER: I do, thou most usurping Proditor,
And not Protector of the King or Realm.

GLOUCESTER: Stand back thou manifest conspirator,
Thou that contrived'st to murther our dead Lord,
Thou that givest whores Indulgences to sin,
I'll canvass thee in thy broad Cardinal's hat,
If thou proceed in this thy insolence.

WINCHESTER: Nay, stand thou back, I will not budge a
foot:
This be Damascus, be thou cursed Cain,
To slay thy brother Abel, if thou wilt.

GLOUCESTER: I will not slay thee, but I'll drive thee back:
Thy scarlet robes, as a child's bearing-cloth,
I'll use, to carry thee out of this place.

WINCHESTER: Do what thou dar'st, I beard thee to thy
face.

GLOUCESTER: What? am I dar'd, and bearded to my
face?

Draw men, for all this privileged place,
Blue Coats to Tawny Coats. Priest, beware your beard,
I mean to tug it, and to cuff you soundly.
Under my feet I stamp thy Cardinal's hat:
In spite of Pope, or dignities of Church,
Here by the cheeks I'll drag thee up and down.

WINCHESTER: Gloucester, thou wilt answer this before
   the Pope.

GLOUCESTER: Winchester Goose, I cry, a rope, a rope.
Now beat them hence, why do you let them stay?
Thee I'll chase hence, thou Wolf in Sheep's array.
Out, Tawny Coats, out Scarlet Hypocrite.

   Here Gloucester's men beat out the Cardinal's men,
   and enter in the hurly-burly the Mayor of London,
   and his Officers.

MAYOR: Fie Lords, that you being supreme Magistrates,
Thus contumeliously should break the peace.

GLOUCESTER: Peace Mayor, thou know'st little of my
   wrongs:
Here's Beaufort, that regards nor God nor King,
Hath here distrain'd the Tower to his use.

WINCHESTER: Here's Gloucester, a foe to Citizens,
One that still motions war, and never peace,
O'ercharging your free purses with large fines;
That seeks to overthrow Religion,
Because he is Protector of the Realm;
And would have armour here out of the Tower,
To crown himself King, and suppress the Prince.

GLOUCESTER: I will not answer thee with words, but
   blows.

   Here they skirmish again.

MAYOR: Nought rests for me, in this tumultuous strife,
But to make open Proclamation.
Come Officer, as loud as e'er thou canst, cry:

*All manner of men, assembled here in arms this day, against
God's Peace and the King's, we charge and command you, in
his Highness' Name, to repair to your several dwelling-places,
and not to wear, handle, or use any sword, weapon, or
dagger henceforward, upon pain of death.*

GLOUCESTER: Cardinal, I'll be no breaker of the Law:
    But we shall meet, and break our minds at large.

WINCHESTER: Gloucester, we'll meet to thy cost, be sure:
    Thy heart-blood I will have for this day's work.

MAYOR: I'll call for Clubs, if you will not away:
    This Cardinal's more haughty than the Devil.

GLOUCESTER: Mayor farewell: thou dost but what thou
    may'st.

WINCHESTER: Abominable Gloucester, guard thy head,
    For I intend to have it ere long.

> *Exeunt, Gloucester and Winchester*
> *with their Serving-men.*

MAYOR: See the coast clear'd, and then we will depart.
    Good God, these Nobles should such stomachs bear,
    I myself fight not once in forty year.

> *Exeunt.*

I.4

Enter the Master Gunner of Orleans, and his Boy.

MASTER GUNNER: Sirrah, thou know'st how Orleans is
    besieg'd,
    And how the English have the suburbs won.

BOY: Father I know, and oft have shot at them,
    Howe'er unfortunate, I miss'd my aim.

MASTER GUNNER: But now thou shalt not. Be thou rul'd
    by me:
    Chief Master Gunner am I of this Town,
    Something I must do to procure me grace:

The Prince's espials have informed me,
How the English, in the suburbs close entrench'd,
Wont through a secret grate of iron bars,
In yonder tower, to overpeer the City,
And thence discover, how with most advantage
They may vex us with shot or with assault.
To intercept this inconvenience,
A piece of ordnance 'gainst it I have plac'd,
And even these three days have I watch'd,
If I could see them. Now do thou watch,
For I can stay no longer.
If thou spy'st any, run and bring me word,
And thou shalt find me at the Governor's.

Exit.

BOY: Father, I warrant you, take you no care,
I'll never trouble you, if I may spy them.

Exit.

*Enter Salisbury and Talbot on the turrets, with
Gargrave and Glansdale.*

SALISBURY: Talbot, my life, my joy, again return'd?
How wert thou handled, being prisoner?
Or by what means got'st thou to be releas'd?
Discourse I prithee on this turret's top.

TALBOT: The Duke of Bedford had a prisoner,
Call'd the brave Lord Ponton de Santrayle,
For him was I exchang'd and ransom'd.
But with a baser man of arms by far,
Once in contempt they would have barter'd me:
Which I disdaining, scorn'd, and craved death,
Rather than I would be so pill'd esteem'd:
In fine, redeem'd I was as I desir'd.
But O, the treacherous Falstaffe wounds my heart,
Whom with my bare fists I would execute,
If I now had him brought into my power.

SALISBURY: Yet tell'st thou not, how thou wert entertain'd.

TALBOT: With scoffs and scorns, and contumelious taunts,
In open Market-place produc'd they me,
To be a public spectacle to all:
Here, said they, is the Terror of the French,
The scar-crow that affrights our children so.
Then broke I from the Officers that led me,
And with my nails digg'd stones out of the ground,
To hurl at the beholders of my shame.
My grisly countenance made others fly,
None durst come near, for fear of sudden death.
In iron walls they deem'd me not secure:
So great fear of my name 'mongst them was spread,
That they suppos'd I could rend bars of steel,
And spurn in pieces posts of adamant.
Wherefore a guard of chosen shot I had,
That walk'd about me every minute while:
And if I did but stir out of my bed,
Ready they were to shoot me to the heart.

Enter the Boy with a linstock.

SALISBURY: I grieve to hear what torments you endur'd,
But we will be reveng'd sufficiently.
Now it is supper time in Orleans:
Here, through this grate, I count each one,
And view the Frenchmen how they fortify:
Let us look in, the sight will much delight thee:
Sir Thomas Gargrave, and Sir William Glansdale,
Let me have your express opinions,
Where is best place to make our batt'ry next?

GARGRAVE: I think at the North Gate, for there stands Lords.

GLANSDALE: And I here, at the bulwark of the Bridge.

TALBOT: For aught I see, this City must be famish'd,

Or with light skirmishes enfeebled.
> *Here they shoot, and Salisbury falls down.*

SALISBURY: O Lord have mercy on us, wretched sinners.

GARGRAVE: O Lord have mercy on me, woeful man.

TALBOT: What chance is this, that suddenly hath cross'd us?
Speak Salisbury; at least, if thou canst, speak:
How far'st thou, Mirror of all Martial men?
One of thy eyes, and thy cheek's side struck off?
Accursed tower, accursed fatal hand,
That hath contriv'd this woeful Tragedy.
In thirteen battles, Salisbury o'ercame:
Henry the Fifth he first train'd to the wars.
Whilst any trump did sound, or drum struck up,
His sword did ne'er leave striking in the field.
Yet liv'st thou Salisbury? though thy speech doth fail
One eye thou hast to look to Heaven for grace.
The Sun with one eye vieweth all the World.
Heaven be thou gracious to none alive,
If Salisbury wants mercy at thy hands.
Bear hence his body, I will help to bury it.
Sir Thomas Gargrave, hast thou any life?
Speak unto Talbot, nay, look up to him.
Salisbury cheer thy spirit with this comfort,
Thou shalt not die whiles —
He beckons with his hand, and smiles on me:
As who should say, When I am dead and gone,
Remember to avenge me on the French.
Plantagenet I will, and like thee, Nero,
Play on the lute, beholding the towns burn:
Wretched shall France be only in my name.
> *Here an alarum, and it thunders and lightens.*
What stir is this? what tumult 's in the Heavens?
Whence cometh this alarum, and the noise?

Enter a Messenger.

MESSENGER: My Lord, my Lord, the French have gather'd head.

The Dolphin, with one Joan de Puzel join'd,
A holy Prophetess, new risen up,
Is come with a great power, to raise the siege.

Here Salisbury lifteth himself up, and groans.

TALBOT: Hear, hear, how dying Salisbury doth groan,
It irks his heart he cannot be reveng'd.
Frenchmen, I'll be a Salisbury to you.
Puzel or Pussel, Dolphin or Dogfish,
Your hearts I'll stamp out with my horse's heels,
And make a quagmire of your mingled brains.
Convey me Salisbury into his tent,
And then we 'll try what these dastard Frenchmen dare.

Alarum. Exeunt.

I. 5

*Here an alarum again, and Talbot pursueth the Dolphin,
and driveth him: Then enter Joan de Puzel, driving
Englishmen before her. Then enter Talbot.*

TALBOT: Where is my strength, my valour, and my force?
Our English troops retire, I cannot stay them,
A Woman clad in armour chaseth them.

Enter Puzel.

Here, here she comes. I'll have a bout with thee:
Devil, or Devil's Dam, I'll conjure thee:
Blood will I draw on thee, thou art a Witch,
And straightway give thy soul to him thou serv'st.

JOAN: Come, come, 'tis only I that must disgrace thee.

Here they fight.

TALBOT: Heavens, can you suffer Hell so to prevail?
My breast I'll burst with straining of my courage,

And from my shoulders crack my arms asunder,
But I will chastise this high-minded strumpet.
                    They fight again.
JOAN: Talbot farewell, thy hour is not yet come,
I must go victual Orleans forthwith:
    A short alarum: then enter the town with soldiers.
O'ertake me if thou canst, I scorn thy strength.
Go, go, cheer up thy hungry-starved men,
Help Salisbury to make his testament,
This day is ours, as many more shall be.
                    Exit.
TALBOT: My thoughts are whirled like a potter's wheel,
I know not where I am, nor what I do:
A Witch by fear, not force, like Hannibal,
Drives back our troops, and conquers as she lists:
So bees with smoke, and doves with noisome stench,
Are from their hives and houses driven away.
They call'd us, for our fierceness, English dogs,
Now like to whelps, we crying run away.
                    A short Alarum.
Hark Countrymen, either renew the fight,
Or tear the lions out of England's coat;
Renounce your soil, give sheep in lions' stead:
Sheep run not half so treacherous from the wolf,
Or horse or oxen from the leopard,
As you fly from your oft-subdued slaves.
                    Alarum. Here another skirmish.
It will not be, retire into your trenches:
You all consented unto Salisbury's death,
For none would strike a stroke in his revenge.
Puzel is enter'd into Orleans,
In spite of us, or aught that we could do.
O would I were to die with Salisbury,
The shame hereof, will make me hide my head.

Exit Talbot.
Alarum, Retreat, Flourish.

I.6

Enter on the walls, Puzel, Dolphin, Reignier, Alan-
son, and Soldiers.

JOAN: Advance our waving colours on the walls,
  Rescu'd is Orleans from the English.
  Thus Joan de Puzel hath perform'd her word.

DOLPHIN: Divinest Creature, Astraea's Daughter,
  How shall I honour thee for this success?
  Thy promises are like Adonis' Garden,
  That one day bloom'd, and fruitful were the next.
  France, triumph in thy glorious Prophetess,
  Recover'd is the Town of Orleans,
  More blessed hap did ne'er befall our State.

REIGNIER: Why ring not out the bells aloud,
  Throughout the Town?
  Dolphin command the citizens make bonfires,
  And feast and banquet in the open streets,
  To celebrate the joy that God hath given us.

ALANSON: All France will be replete with mirth and joy,
  When they shall hear how we have play'd the men.

DOLPHIN: 'Tis Joan, not we, by whom the day is won:
  For which, I will divide my Crown with her,
  And all the Priests and Friars in my Realm,
  Shall in procession sing her endless praise.
  A statelier pyramis to her I'll rear,
  Than Rhodope's or Memphis' ever was.
  In memory of her, when she is dead,
  Her ashes, in an urn more precious
  Than the rich-jewel'd coffer of Darius,
  Transported, shall be at high festivals

Before the Kings and Queens of France.
No longer on Saint Denis will we cry,
But Joan de Puzel shall be France's Saint.
Come in, and let us banquet royally,
After this Golden Day of Victory.
                    Flourish. Exeunt.

II.1

Enter a Sergeant of a band, with two Sentinels.

SERGEANT: Sirs, take your places, and be vigilant:
   If any noise or soldier you perceive
   Near to the walls, by some apparent sign
   Let us have knowledge at the Court of Guard.

SENTINEL: Sergeant you shall. [*Exit Sergeant.*] Thus are
      poor servitors
   (When others sleep upon their quiet beds)
   Constrain'd to watch in darkness, rain, and cold.
      *Enter Talbot, Bedford, and Burgundy, with scaling-
      ladders: Their drums beating a Dead March.*

TALBOT: Lord Regent, and redoubted Burgundy,
   By whose approach, the regions of Artois,
   Wallon, and Picardy, are friends to us:
   This happy night, the Frenchmen are secure,
   Having all day carous'd and banqueted,
   Embrace we then this opportunity,
   As fitting best to quittance their deceit,
   Contriv'd by Art, and baleful sorcery.

BEDFORD: Coward of France, how much he wrongs his
      fame,
   Despairing of his own arm's fortitude,
   To join with Witches, and the help of Hell.

BURGUNDY: Traitors have never other company.
   But what's that Puzell whom they term so pure?

TALBOT: A Maid, they say.

BEDFORD: A Maid? And be so martial?

BURGUNDY: Pray God she prove not masculine ere long:
   If underneath the Standard of the French
   She carry armour, as she hath begun.

TALBOT: Well, let them practise and converse with spirits.
   God is our Fortress, in whose conquering name
   Let us resolve to scale their flinty bulwarks.

BEDFORD: Ascend brave Talbot, we will follow thee.

TALBOT: Not all together: Better far I guess,
   That we do make our entrance several ways:
   That if it chance the one of us do fail,
   The other yet may rise against their force.

BEDFORD: Agreed; I 'll to yond corner.

BURGUNDY: And I to this.

TALBOT: And here will Talbot mount, or make his grave.
   Now Salisbury, for thee and for the right
   Of English Henry, shall this night appear
   How much in duty, I am bound to both.

SENTINEL: Arm, arm, the enemy doth make assault.

   Cry, S. George, A Talbot.

   *The French leap over the walls in their shirts. Enter several
      ways, Bastard, Alanson, Reignier, half ready, and half
      unready.*

ALANSON: How now my Lords? what all unready so?

BASTARD: Unready? ay and glad we 'scap'd so well.

REIGNIER: 'Twas time (I trow) to wake, and leave our
      beds,
   Hearing alarums at our chamber doors.

ALANSON: Of all exploits since first I follow'd arms,
   Ne'er heard I of a warlike enterprise
   More venturous, or desperate than this.

BASTARD: I think this Talbot be a Fiend of Hell.

REIGNIER: If not of Hell, the Heavens sure favour him.

ALANSON: Here cometh Charles, I marvel how he sped.
        Enter Charles and Joan.
BASTARD: Tut, holy Joan was his defensive guard.
CHARLES: Is this thy cunning, thou deceitful Dame?
  Didst thou at first, to flatter us withal,
  Make us partakers of a little gain,
  That now our loss might be ten times so much?
JOAN: Wherefore is Charles impatient with his friend?
  At all times will you have my power alike?
  Sleeping or waking, must I still prevail,
  Or will you blame and lay the fault on me?
  Improvident soldiers, had your watch been good,
  This sudden mischief never could have fall'n.
CHARLES: Duke of Alanson, this was your default,
  That being Captain of the Watch tonight,
  Did look no better to that weighty charge.
ALANSON: Had all your quarters been as safely kept,
  As that whereof I had the government,
  We had not been thus shamefully surpris'd.
BASTARD: Mine was secure.
REIGNIER: And so was mine, my Lord.
CHARLES: And for myself, most part of all this night
  Within her quarter, and mine own precinct,
  I was employ'd in passing to and fro,
  About relieving of the sentinels.
  Then how, or which way, should they first break in?
JOAN: Question (my Lords) no further of the case,
  How or which way; 'tis sure they found some place,
  But weakly guarded, where the breach was made:
  And now there rests no other shift but this,
  To gather our soldiers, scatter'd and dispers'd,
  And lay new platforms to endamage them.
    Alarum. Enter an English Soldier, crying a Talbot,
    a Talbot: they fly, leaving their clothes behind.

SOLDIER: I 'll be so bold to take what they have left:
    The cry of Talbot serves me for a sword,
    For I have loaden me with many spoils,
    Using no other weapon but his name.
                Exit.

II.2

    Enter Talbot, Bedford, Burgundy, a Captain.
BEDFORD: The Day begins to break, and Night is fled,
    Whose pitchy mantle over-veil'd the Earth.
    Here sound retreat, and cease our hot pursuit.
                Retreat.
TALBOT: Bring forth the body of old Salisbury,
    And here advance it in the Market-Place,
    The middle centre of this cursed Town.
    Now have I paid my vow unto his soul:
    For every drop of blood was drawn from him,
    There hath at least five Frenchmen died tonight.
    And that hereafter Ages may behold
    What ruin happen'd in revenge of him,
    Within their chiefest Temple I 'll erect
    A Tomb, wherein his corpse shall be interr'd:
    Upon the which, that every one may read,
    Shall be engrav'd the sack of Orleans,
    The treacherous manner of his mournful death,
    And what a terror he had been to France.
    But Lords, in all our bloody massacre,
    I muse we met not with the Dolphin's Grace,
    His new-come Champion, virtuous Joan of Arc,
    Nor any of his false confederates.
BEDFORD: 'Tis thought Lord Talbot, when the fight
    began,
    Rous'd on the sudden from their drowsy beds,

C

They did amongst the troops of armed men,
Leap o'er the walls for refuge in the field.
BURGUNDY: Myself, as far as I could well discern,
For smoke, and dusky vapours of the night,
Am sure I scar'd the Dolphin and his trull,
When arm in arm they both came swiftly running,
Like to a pair of loving turtle-doves,
That could not live asunder day or night.
After that things are set in order here,
We 'll follow them with all the power we have.

Enter a Messenger.

MESSENGER: All hail, my Lords: which of this princely
train
Call ye the warlike Talbot, for his acts
So much applauded through the Realm of France?
TALBOT: Here is the Talbot, who would speak with him?
MESSENGER: The virtuous Lady, Countess of Auvergne,
With modesty admiring thy renown,
By me entreats (great Lord) thou would'st vouchsafe
To visit her poor Castle where she lies,
That she may boast she hath beheld the man,
Whose glory fills the World with loud report.
BURGUNDY: Is it even so? Nay, then I see our wars
Will turn unto a peaceful comic sport,
When Ladies crave to be encounter'd with.
You may not (my Lord) despise her gentle suit.
TALBOT: Ne'er trust me then: for when a world of men
Could not prevail with all their oratory,
Yet hath a woman's kindness over-rul'd:
And therefore tell her, I return great thanks,
And in submission will attend on her.
Will not your Honours bear me company?
BEDFORD: No, truly, it is more than manners will:
And I have heard it said, Unbidden guests

Are often welcomest when they are gone.
TALBOT: Well then, alone (since there's no remedy)
    I mean to prove this Lady's courtesy.
    Come hither Captain, you perceive my mind? (*Whispers.*)
CAPTAIN: I do my Lord, and mean accordingly.

Exeunt.

II. 3

Enter Countess and Porter.

COUNTESS: Porter, remember what I gave in charge,
    And when you have done so, bring the keys to me.
PORTER: Madame, I will.

Exit.

COUNTESS: That plot is laid, if all things fall out right,
    I shall as famous be by this exploit,
    As Scythian Tomyris by Cyrus' death.
    Great is the rumour of this dreadful Knight,
    And his achievements of no less account:
    Fain would mine eyes be witness with mine ears,
    To give their censure of these rare reports.

Enter Messenger and Talbot.

MESSENGER: Madame, according as your Ladyship desir'd,
    By message crav'd, so is Lord Talbot come.
COUNTESS: And he is welcome: what? is this the man?
MESSENGER: Madame, it is.
COUNTESS: Is this the Scourge of France?
    Is this the Talbot, so much fear'd abroad?
    That with his Name the Mothers still their babes?
    I see Report is fabulous and false.
    I thought I should have seen some Hercules,
    A second Hector, for his grim aspect,
    And large proportion of his strong knit limbs.
    Alas, this is a child, a silly dwarf:

It cannot be, this weak and writhled shrimp
Should strike such terror to his enemies.

TALBOT: Madame, I have been bold to trouble you:
But since your Ladyship is not at leisure,
I'll sort some other time to visit you.

COUNTESS: What means he now?
Go ask him, whither he goes.

MESSENGER: Stay my Lord Talbot, for my Lady craves,
To know the cause of your abrupt departure?

TALBOT: Marry, for that she's in a wrong belief,
I go to certify her Talbot's here.

Enter Porter with keys.

COUNTESS: If thou be he, then art thou prisoner.

TALBOT: Prisoner? to whom?

COUNTESS: To me, blood-thirsty Lord:
And for that cause I train'd thee to my house.
Long time thy shadow hath been thrall to me,
For in my gallery thy picture hangs:
But now the substance shall endure the like,
And I will chain these legs and arms of thine,
That hast by tyranny these many years
Wasted our Country, slain our Citizens,
And sent our sons and husbands captivate.

TALBOT: Ha, ha, ha.

COUNTESS: Laughest thou Wretch?
Thy mirth shall turn to moan.

TALBOT: I laugh to see your Ladyship so fond,
To think, that you have aught but Talbot's shadow,
Whereon to practise your severity.

COUNTESS: Why? art not thou the man?

TALBOT: I am indeed.

COUNTESS: Then have I substance too.

TALBOT: No, no, I am but shadow of myself:
You are deceiv'd, my substance is not here;

For what you see, is but the smallest part,
And least proportion of humanity:
I tell you Madame, were the whole frame here,
It is of such a spacious lofty pitch,
Your roof were not sufficient to contain't.

COUNTESS: This is a riddling merchant for the nonce,
He will be here, and yet he is not here:
How can these contrarieties agree?

TALBOT: That will I show you presently.

Winds his horn. Drums strike up, a peal of ordnance:
Enter Soldiers.

How say you Madame? are you now persuaded,
That Talbot is but shadow of himself?
These are his substance, sinews, arms, and strength,
With which he yoketh your rebellious necks,
Razeth your Cities, and subverts your Towns,
And in a moment makes them desolate.

COUNTESS: Victorious Talbot, pardon my abuse,
I find thou art no less than Fame hath bruited,
And more than may be gather'd by thy shape.
Let my presumption not provoke thy wrath,
For I am sorry, that with reverence
I did not entertain thee as thou art.

TALBOT: Be not dismay'd, fair Lady, nor misconster
The mind of Talbot, as you did mistake
The outward composition of his body.
What you have done, hath not offended me:
Nor other satisfaction do I crave,
But only with your patience, that we may
Taste of your wine, and see what cates you have,
For soldiers' stomachs always serve them well.

COUNTESS: With all my heart, and think me honoured,
To feast so great a Warrior in my House.

Exeunt.

II. 4

Enter Richard Plantagenet, Warwick, Somerset, Pole
and others.

RICHARD: Great Lords and Gentlemen,
  What means this silence?
  Dare no man answer in a case of truth?

SUFFOLK: Within the Temple Hall we were too loud,
  The garden here is more convenient.

RICHARD: Then say at once, if I maintain'd the truth:
  Or else was wrangling Somerset in th' error?

SUFFOLK: Faith I have been a truant in the Law,
  And never yet could frame my will to it,
  And therefore frame the Law unto my will.

SOMERSET: Judge you, my Lord of Warwick, then between us.

WARWICK: Between two hawks, which flies the higher
    pitch,
  Between two dogs, which hath the deeper mouth,
  Between two blades, which bears the better temper,
  Between two horses, which doth bear him best,
  Between two girls, which hath the merriest eye,
  I have perhaps some shallow spirit of judgement:
  But in these nice sharp quillets of the Law,
  Good faith, I am no wiser than a daw.

RICHARD: Tut, tut, here is a mannerly forbearance:
  The truth appears so naked on my side,
  That any purblind eye may find it out.

SOMERSET: And on my side it is so well apparell'd,
  So clear, so shining, and so evident,
  That it will glimmer through a blind-man's eye.

RICHARD: Since you are tongue-tied, and so loath to
    speak,

In dumb significants proclaim your thoughts:
Let him that is a true-born Gentleman,
And stands upon the honour of his birth,
If he suppose that I have pleaded truth,
From off this briar pluck a white rose with me.

SOMERSET: Let him that is no coward, nor no flatterer,
But dare maintain the party of the truth,
Pluck a red rose from off this thorn with me.

WARWICK: I love no colours: and without all colour
Of base insinuating flattery,
I pluck this white rose with Plantagenet.

SUFFOLK: I pluck this red rose, with young Somerset,
And say withal, I think he held the right.

VERNON: Stay Lords and Gentlemen, and pluck no more
Till you conclude, that he upon whose side
The fewest roses are cropp'd from the tree,
Shall yield the other in the right opinion.

SOMERSET: Good Master Vernon, it is well objected:
If I have fewest, I subscribe in silence.

RICHARD: And I.

VERNON: Then for the truth, and plainness of the case,
I pluck this pale and maiden blossom here,
Giving my verdict on the white rose side.

SOMERSET: Prick not your finger as you pluck it off,
Lest bleeding, you do paint the white rose red,
And fall on my side so against your will.

VERNON: If I, my Lord, for my opinion bleed,
Opinion shall be surgeon to my hurt,
And keep me on the side where still I am.

SOMERSET: Well, well, come on, who else?

LAWYER: Unless my study and my books be false,
The argument you held, was wrong in you;
In sign whereof, I pluck a white rose too.

RICHARD: Now Somerset, where is your argument?

SOMERSET: Here in my scabbard, meditating, that
Shall dye your white rose in a bloody red.

RICHARD: Meantime your cheeks do counterfeit our roses:
For pale they look with fear, as witnessing
The truth on our side.

SOMERSET: No Plantagenet:
'Tis not for fear, but anger, that thy cheeks
Blush for pure shame, to counterfeit our roses,
And yet thy tongue will not confess thy error.

RICHARD: Hath not thy rose a canker, Somerset?

SOMERSET: Hath not thy rose a thorn, Plantagenet?

RICHARD: Ay, sharp and piercing to maintain his truth,
Whiles thy consuming canker eats his falsehood.

SOMERSET: Well, I'll find friends to wear my bleeding
roses,
That shall maintain what I have said is true,
Where false Plantagenet dare not be seen.

RICHARD: Now by this maiden blossom in my hand,
I scorn thee and thy fashion, peevish Boy.

SUFFOLK: Turn not thy scorns this way, Plantagenet.

RICHARD: Proud Pole, I will, and scorn both him and thee.

SUFFOLK: I'll turn my part thereof into thy throat.

SOMERSET: Away, away, good William de la Pole,
We grace the yeoman, by conversing with him.

WARWICK: Now by God's will thou wrong'st him, Som-
erset:
His grandfather was Lionel Duke of Clarence,
Third Son to the third Edward King of England:
Spring crestless yeomen from so deep a root?

RICHARD: He bears him on the place's privilege,
Or durst not for his craven heart say thus.

SOMERSET: By him that made me, I'll maintain my
words
On any plot of ground in Christendom.

Was not thy Father, Richard, Earl of Cambridge,
For treason executed in our late King's days?
And by his treason, stand'st not thou attainted,
Corrupted, and exempt from ancient Gentry?
His trespass yet lives guilty in thy blood,
And till thou be restor'd, thou art a yeoman.
RICHARD: My Father was attached, not attainted,
Condemn'd to die for treason, but no traitor;
And that I'll prove on better men than Somerset,
Were growing time once ripen'd to my will.
For your partaker Pole, and you yourself,
I'll note you in my Book of Memory,
To scourge you for this apprehension:
Look to it well, and say you are well warn'd.
SOMERSET: Ah, thou shalt find us ready for thee still:
And know us by these colours for thy foes,
For these, my friends in spite of thee shall wear.
RICHARD: And by my soul, this pale and angry rose,
As cognizance of my blood-thinking hate,
Will I for ever, and my faction wear,
Until it wither with me to my grave,
Or flourish to the height of my degree.
SUFFOLK: Go forward, and be chok'd with thy ambition:
And so farewell, until I meet thee next.
Exit.
SOMERSET: Have with thee Pole: Farewell ambitious
Richard.
Exit.
RICHARD: How I am brav'd, and must perforce endure it?
WARWICK: This blot that they object against your House,
Shall be whipp'd out in the next Parliament,
Call'd for the truce of Winchester and Gloucester:
And if thou be not then created York,
I will not live to be accounted Warwick.

Meantime, in signal of my love to thee,
Against proud Somerset, and William Pole,
Will I upon thy party wear this rose.
And here I prophesy: this brawl today,
Grown to this faction in the Temple Garden,
Shall send between the Red Rose and the White,
A thousand souls to Death and deadly Night.

RICHARD: Good Master Vernon, I am bound to you,
That you on my behalf would pluck a flower.

VERNON: In your behalf still will I wear the same.

LAWYER: And so will I.

RICHARD: Thanks gentle sir.
Come, let us four to dinner: I dare say
This quarrel will drink blood another day.

Exeunt.

II. 5

Enter Mortimer, brought in a chair, and Jailers.

MORTIMER: Kind keepers of my weak decaying age,
Let dying Mortimer here rest himself.
Even like a man new haled from the rack,
So fare my limbs with long imprisonment:
And these grey locks, the pursuivants of death,
Nestor-like aged, in an age of care,
Argue the end of Edmund Mortimer.
These eyes, like lamps, whose wasting oil is spent,
Wax dim, as drawing to their exigent.
Weak shoulders, overborne with burthening grief,
And pithless arms, like to a wither'd vine,
That droops his sapless branches to the ground.
Yet are these feet, whose strengthless stay is numb,
(Unable to support this lump of clay)
Swift-winged with desire to get a grave,

As witting I no other comfort have.
But tell me, Keeper, will my Nephew come?

1 JAILER: Richard Plantagenet, my Lord, will come:
We sent unto the Temple, unto his chamber,
And answer was return'd, that he will come.

MORTIMER: Enough: my soul shall then be satisfied.
Poor Gentleman, his wrong doth equal mine.
Since Henry Monmouth first began to reign,
Before whose glory I was great in arms,
This loathsome sequestration have I had;
And even since then, hath Richard been obscur'd,
Depriv'd of honour and inheritance.
But now, the Arbitrator of Despairs,
Just Death, kind Umpire of men's miseries,
With sweet enlargement doth dismiss me hence:
I would his troubles likewise were expir'd,
That so he might recover what was lost.

Enter Richard.

KEEPER: My Lord, your loving Nephew now is come.

MORTIMER: Richard Plantagenet, my friend, is he come?

RICHARD: Ay, noble Uncle, thus ignobly us'd,
Your Nephew, late despised Richard, comes.

MORTIMER: Direct mine arms, I may embrace his neck,
And in his bosom spend my latter gasp.
Oh tell me when my lips do touch his cheeks,
That I may kindly give one fainting kiss.
And now declare sweet stem from York's great stock,
Why didst thou say of late thou wert despis'd?

RICHARD: First, lean thine aged back against mine arm,
And in that ease, I'll tell thee my disease.
This day in argument upon a case,
Some words there grew 'twixt Somerset and me:
Among which terms, he us'd his lavish tongue,
And did upbraid me with my Father's death;

Which obloquy set bars before my tongue,
Else with the like I had requited him.
Therefore good Uncle, for my Father's sake,
In honour of a true Plantagenet,
And for alliance sake, declare the cause
My Father, Earl of Cambridge, lost his head.

MORTIMER: That cause (fair Nephew) that imprison'd me,
And hath detain'd me all my flow'ring youth,
Within a loathsome dungeon, there to pine,
Was cursed instrument of his decease.

RICHARD: Discover more at large what cause that was,
For I am ignorant, and cannot guess.

MORTIMER: I will, if that my fading breath permit,
And Death approach not, ere my tale be done.
Henry the Fourth, Grandfather to this King,
Depos'd his Nephew Richard, Edward's Son,
The first begotten, and the lawful Heir
Of Edward King, the Third of that descent.
During whose Reign, the Percies of the North,
Finding his usurpation most unjust,
Endeavour'd my advancement to the Throne.
The reason mov'd these warlike Lords to this,
Was, for that (young Richard thus remov'd,
Leaving no Heir begotten of his body)
I was the next by birth and parentage:
For by my Mother, I derived am
From Lionel Duke of Clarence, third Son
To King Edward the Third; whereas he,
From John of Gaunt doth bring his pedigree,
Being but fourth of that Heroic Line.
But mark: as in this haughty great attempt,
They laboured, to plant the rightful Heir,
I lost my liberty, and they their lives.
Long after this, when Henry the Fifth

(Succeeding his Father Bolingbroke) did reign;
Thy Father, Earl of Cambridge, then deriv'd
From famous Edmund Langley, Duke of York,
Marrying my Sister, that thy Mother was;
Again, in pity of my hard distress,
Levied an army, weening to redeem,
And have install'd me in the Diadem:
But as the rest, so fell that noble Earl,
And was beheaded. Thus the Mortimers,
In whom the Title rested, were suppress'd.

RICHARD: Of which, my Lord, your Honour is the last.

MORTIMER: True; and thou seest, that I no issue have,
And that my fainting words do warrant death:
Thou art my Heir; the rest, I wish thee gather:
But yet be wary in thy studious care.

RICHARD: Thy grave admonishments prevail with me:
But yet methinks, my Father's execution
Was nothing less than bloody tyranny.

MORTIMER: With silence, Nephew, be thou politic,
Strong fixed is the House of Lancaster,
And like a mountain, not to be remov'd.
But now thy Uncle is removing hence,
As Princes do their Courts, when they are cloy'd
With long continuance in a settled place.

RICHARD: O Uncle, would some part of my young years
Might but redeem the passage of your age.

MORTIMER: Thou dost then wrong me, as that slaughterer
    doth,
Which giveth many wounds, when one will kill.
Mourn not, except thou sorrow for my good,
Only give order for my funeral.
And so farewell, and fair be all thy hopes,
And prosperous be thy life in Peace and War.
                    Dies.

RICHARD: And Peace, no War, befall thy parting soul.
  In prison hast thou spent a pilgrimage,
  And like a hermit overpass'd thy days.
  Well, I will lock his counsel in my breast,
  And what I do imagine, let that rest.
  Keepers convey him hence, and I myself
  Will see his burial better than his life.
                    Exeunt Jailers.
  Here dies the dusky torch of Mortimer,
  Chok'd with ambition of the meaner sort.
  And for those wrongs, those bitter injuries,
  Which Somerset hath offer'd to my House,
  I doubt not, but with honour to redress.
  And therefore haste I to the Parliament,
  Either to be restored to my Blood,
  Or make my ill th' advantage of my good.
                    Exit.

III. 1

Flourish. Enter King, Exeter, Gloucester, Winchester, War-
wick, Somerset, Suffolk, Richard Plantagenet, and others.
Gloucester offers to put up a Bill; Winchester snatches it,
                    tears it.

WINCHESTER: Com'st thou with deep premeditated lines?
  With written pamphlets, studiously devis'd?
  Humphrey of Gloucester, if thou canst accuse,
  Or aught intend'st to lay unto my charge,
  Do it without invention, suddenly,
  As I with sudden, and extemporal speech,
  Purpose to answer what thou canst object.
GLOUCESTER: Presumptuous Priest, this place commands
    my patience,

Or thou shouldst find thou hast dishonour'd me.
Think not, although in writing I preferr'd
The manner of thy vile outrageous crimes,
That therefore I have forg'd, or am not able
Verbatim to rehearse the method of my pen.
No Prelate, such is thy audacious wickedness,
Thy lewd, pestiferous, and dissentious pranks,
As very infants prattle of thy pride.
Thou art a most pernicious usurer,
Froward by nature, enemy to Peace,
Lascivious, wanton, more than well beseems
A man of thy profession, and degree.
And for thy treachery, what's more manifest?
In that thou laid'st a trap to take my life,
As well as London Bridge, as at the Tower.
Beside, I fear me, if thy thoughts were sifted,
The King, thy Sovereign, is not quite exempt
From envious malice of thy swelling heart.

WINCHESTER: Gloucester, I do defy thee. Lords vouch-
     safe
To give me hearing what I shall reply.
If I were covetous, ambitious, or perverse,
As he will have me: how am I so poor?
Or how haps it, I seek not to advance
Or raise myself? but keep my wonted calling.
And for dissension, who preferreth peace
More than I do? except I be provok'd.
No, my good Lords, it is not that offends,
It is not that, that hath incens'd the Duke:
It is because no one should sway but he,
No one, but he, should be about the King;
And that engenders thunder in his breast,
And makes him roar these accusations forth.
But he shall know I am as good –

GLOUCESTER: As good?
Thou Bastard of my Grandfather.

WINCHESTER: Ay, Lordly Sir; for what are you, I pray,
But one imperious in another's Throne?

GLOUCESTER: Am I not Protector, saucy Priest?

WINCHESTER: And am not I a Prelate of the Church?

GLOUCESTER: Yes, as an outlaw in a Castle keeps,
And useth it, to patronage his theft.

WINCHESTER: Unreverent Gloster.

GLOUCESTER: Thou art reverent,
Touching thy spiritual function, not thy life.

WINCHESTER: Rome shall remedy this.

WARWICK: Roam thither then.
My Lord, it were your duty to forbear.

SOMERSET: Ay, see the Bishop be not overborne.
Methinks my Lord should be religious,
And know the office that belongs to such.

WARWICK: Methinks his lordship should be humbler,
It fitteth not a Prelate so to plead.

SOMERSET: Yes, when his holy state is touch'd so near.

WARWICK: State holy, or unhallow'd, what of that?
Is not his Grace Protector to the King?

RICHARD: Plantagenet I see must hold his tongue,
Lest it be said, Speak sirrah when you should:
Must your bold verdict enter talk with Lords?
Else would I have a fling at Winchester.

KING: Uncles of Gloucester, and of Winchester,
The special Watchmen of our English Weal,
I would prevail, if prayers might prevail,
To join your hearts in love and amity.
Oh, what a scandal is it to our Crown,
That two such noble Peers as ye should jar?
Believe me, Lords, my tender years can tell,
Civil dissension is a viperous worm,

That gnaws the bowels of the Commonwealth.
> *A noise within, Down with the tawny-coats.*
What tumult 's this?

WARWICK: An uproar, I dare warrant,
Begun through malice of the Bishop's men.
> *A noise again, Stones, stones.*
> *Enter Mayor.*

MAYOR: Oh my good Lords, and virtuous Henry,
Pity the City of London, pity us:
The Bishop, and the Duke of Gloucester's men,
Forbidden late to carry any weapon,
Have fill'd their pockets full of pebble stones;
And banding themselves in contrary parts,
Do pelt so fast at one another's pate,
That many have their giddy brains knock'd out:
Our windows are broke down in every street,
And we, for fear, compell'd to shut our shops.
> *Enter Serving-men in skirmish with bloody pates.*

KING: We charge you, on allegiance to ourself,
To hold your slaughtering hands, and keep the peace:
Pray Uncle Gloucester mitigate this strife.

I SERVING-MAN: Nay, if we be forbidden stones, we 'll
fall to it with our teeth.

2 SERVING-MAN: Do what ye dare, we are as resolute.
> *Skirmish again.*

GLOUCESTER: You of my household, leave this peevish
broil,
And set this unaccustom'd fight aside.

3 SERVING-MAN: My Lord, we know your Grace to be a
man
Just, and upright; and for your royal birth,
Inferior to none, but to his Majesty:
And ere that we will suffer such a Prince,
So kind a Father of the Commonweal,

To be disgraced by an ink-horn mate,
We and our wives and children all will fight,
And have our bodies slaughter'd by thy foes.

1 SERVING-MAN: Ay, and the very parings of our nails
Shall pitch a field when we are dead.

Begin again.

GLOUCESTER: Stay, stay, I say:
And if you love me, as you say you do,
Let me persuade you to forbear a while.

KING: Oh, how this discord doth afflict my soul.
Can you, my Lord of Winchester, behold
My sighs and tears, and will not once relent?
Who should be pitiful, if you be not?
Or who should study to prefer a peace,
If holy Church-men take delight in broils?

WARWICK: Yield my Lord Protector, yield Winchester,
Except you mean with obstinate repulse
To slay your Sovereign, and destroy the Realm.
You see what mischief, and what murther too,
Hath been enacted through your enmity:
Then be at peace, except ye thirst for blood.

WINCHESTER: He shall submit, or I will never yield.

GLOUCESTER: Compassion on the King commands me
     stoop,
Or I would see his heart out, ere the Priest
Should ever get that privilege of me.

WARWICK: Behold my Lord of Winchester, the Duke
Hath banish'd moody discontented fury,
As by his smoothed brows it doth appear:
Why look you still so stern, and tragical?

GLOUCESTER: Here Winchester, I offer thee my hand.

KING: Fie Uncle Beaufort, I have heard you preach,
That malice was a great and grievous sin:
And will not you maintain the thing you teach?

But prove a chief offender in the same.

WARWICK: Sweet King: the Bishop hath a kindly gird:
    For shame my Lord of Winchester relent;
    What, shall a Child instruct you what to do?

WINCHESTER: Well, Duke of Gloucester, I will yield to
    thee
    Love for thy love, and hand for hand I give.

GLOUCESTER: Ay, but I fear me with a hollow heart.
    See here my friends and loving countrymen,
    This token serveth for a flag of truce,
    Betwixt ourselves, and all our followers:
    So help me God, as I dissemble not.

WINCHESTER: So help me God, as I intend it not.

KING: Oh loving Uncle, kind Duke of Gloucester,
    How joyful am I made by this contract.
    Away my masters, trouble us no more,
    But join in friendship, as your Lords have done.

1 SERVING-MAN: Content, I'll to the surgeon's.

2 SERVING-MAN: And so will I.

3 SERVING-MAN: And I will see what physic the tavern
    affords.

Exeunt.

WARWICK: Accept this scroll, most gracious Sovereign,
    Which in the right of Richard Plantagenet,
    We do exhibit to your Majesty.

GLOUCESTER: Well urg'd, my Lord of Warwick: for
    sweet Prince,
    And if your Grace mark every circumstance,
    You have great reason to do Richard right,
    Especially for those occasions
    At Eltham Place I told your Majesty.

KING: And those occasions, Uncle, were of force:
    Therefore my loving Lords, our pleasure is,
    That Richard be restored to his Blood.

WARWICK: Let Richard be restored to his Blood,
　　So shall his Father's wrongs be recompens'd.
WINCHESTER: As will the rest, so willeth Winchester.
KING: If Richard will be true, not that alone,
　　But all the whole inheritance I give,
　　That doth belong unto the House of York,
　　From whence you spring, by lineal descent.
RICHARD: Thy humble servant vows obedience,
　　And humble service, till the point of death.
KING: Stoop then, and set your knee against my foot,
　　And in reguerdon of that duty done,
　　I gird thee with the valiant sword of York:
　　Rise Richard, like a true Plantagenet,
　　And rise created princely Duke of York.
RICHARD: And so thrive Richard, as thy foes may fall,
　　And as my duty springs, so perish they,
　　That grudge one thought against your Majesty.
ALL: Welcome high Prince, the mighty Duke of York.
SOMERSET: Perish base Prince, ignoble Duke of York.
GLOUCESTER: Now will it best avail your Majesty,
　　To cross the seas, and to be crown'd in France:
　　The presence of a King engenders love
　　Amongst his subjects, and his loyal friends,
　　As it dis-animates his enemies.
KING: When Gloucester says the word, King Henry goes,
　　For friendly counsel cuts off many foes.
GLOUCESTER: Your ships already are in readiness.
　　　　　Sennet. Flourish. Exeunt.
　　　　　Manet Exeter.
EXETER: Ay, we may march in England, or in France,
　　Not seeing what is likely to ensue:
　　This late dissension grown betwixt the Peers,
　　Burns under feigned ashes of forg'd love,
　　And will at last break out into a flame,

As fester'd members rot but by degree,
Till bones and flesh and sinews fall away,
So will this base and envious discord breed.
And now I fear that fatal Prophecy,
Which in the time of Henry, nam'd the Fifth,
Was in the mouth of every sucking babe,
That Henry born at Monmouth should win all,
And Henry born at Windsor, lose all:
Which is so plain, that Exeter doth wish,
His days may finish, ere that hapless time.

Exit.

III. 2

Enter Pucell disguis'd, with four Soldiers with sacks upon their backs.

JOAN: These are the City gates, the gates of Roan,
   Through which our policy must make a breach.
   Take heed, be wary how you place your words,
   Talk like the vulgar sort of market men,
   That come to gather money for their corn.
   If we have entrance, as I hope we shall,
   And that we find the slothful watch but weak,
   I'll by a sign give notice to our friends,
   That Charles the Dolphin may encounter them.
SOLDIER: Our sacks shall be a mean to sack the City,
   And we be lords and rulers over Roan,
   Therefore we'll knock.

Knock.

WATCH: *Che la?*
JOAN: *Paysans la pauvre gens de France,*
   Poor market folks that come to sell their corn.
WATCH: Enter, go in, the market bell is rung.
JOAN: Now, Roan, I'll shake thy bulwarks to the ground.

Exeunt.
Enter Charles, Bastard, Alanson, Reignier, and forces.

CHARLES: Saint Denis bless this happy stratagem,
　And once again we 'll sleep secure in Roan.

BASTARD: Here enter'd Pucell, and her practisants:
　Now she is there, how will she specify?
　Here is the best and safest passage in.

REIGNIER: By thrusting out a torch from yonder Tower,
　Which once discern'd, shows that her meaning is,
　No way to that (for weakness) which she enter'd.

Enter Pucell on the top, thrusting out a torch burning.

JOAN: Behold, this is the happy wedding torch,
　That joineth Roan unto her countrymen,
　But burning fatal to the Talbonites.

BASTARD: See noble Charles, the beacon of our friend,
　The burning torch in yonder turret stands.

CHARLES: Now shine it like a Comet of Revenge,
　A Prophet to the fall of all our foes.

REIGNIER: Defer no time, delays have dangerous ends,
　Enter, and cry, the Dolphin, presently,
　And then do execution on the watch.

Alarum. Exeunt.
An alarum. Enter Talbot in an excursion.

TALBOT: France, thou shalt rue this treason with thy
　　tears,
　If Talbot but survive thy treachery.
　Pucell that Witch, that damned Sorceress,
　Hath wrought this hellish mischief unawares,
　That hardly we escap'd the pride of France.

Exit.
An alarum: Excursions. Bedford brought in sick in a
chair.
Enter Talbot and Burgundy without: within, Pucell,
Charles, Bastard, Alanson, and Reignier on the walls.

JOAN: God morrow Gallants, want ye corn for bread?
  I think the Duke of Burgundy will fast,
  Before he 'll buy again at such a rate.
  'Twas full of darnel: do you like the taste?

BURGUNDY: Scoff on vile Fiend, and shameless Court-
    ezan,
  I trust ere long to choke thee with thine own,
  And make thee curse the harvest of that corn.

CHARLES: Your Grace may starve (perhaps) before that
    time.

BEDFORD: Oh let no words, but deeds, revenge this
    treason.

JOAN: What will you do, good grey-beard?
  Break a lance, and run a tilt at Death,
  Within a chair?

TALBOT: Foul Fiend of France, and Hag of all despite,
  Encompass'd with thy lustful paramours,
  Becomes it thee to taunt his valiant age,
  And twit with cowardice a man half dead?
  Damsel, I'll have a bout with you again,
  Or else let Talbot perish with this shame.

JOAN: Are ye so hot, sir: yet Pucell hold thy peace,
  If Talbot do but thunder, rain will follow.
        They whisper together in counsel.
  God speed the Parliament: who shall be the Speaker?

TALBOT: Dare ye come forth, and meet us in the field?

JOAN: Belike your Lordship takes us then for fools,
  To try if that our own be ours, or no.

TALBOT: I speak not to that railing Hecate,
  But unto thee Alanson, and the rest.
  Will ye, like soldiers, come and fight it out?

ALANSON: Seignior no.

TALBOT: Seignior hang: base muleters of France,
  Like peasant foot-boys do they keep the walls,

And dare not take up arms, like Gentlemen.

JOAN: Away Captains, let's get us from the walls,
For Talbot means no goodness by his looks.
God b'uy my Lord, we came but to tell you
That we are here.

Exeunt from the walls.

TALBOT: And there will we be too, ere it be long,
Or else reproach be Talbot's greatest fame.
Vow Burgundy, by honour of thy House,
Prick'd on by public wrongs sustain'd in France,
Either to get the Town again, or die.
And I, as sure as English Henry lives,
And as his Father here was Conqueror;
As sure as in this late-betrayed Town,
Great Cordelion's heart was buried;
So sure I swear, to get the Town, or die.

BURGUNDY: My vows are equal partners with thy vows.

TALBOT: But ere we go, regard this dying Prince,
The valiant Duke of Bedford: Come my Lord,
We will bestow you in some better place,
Fitter for sickness, and for crazy age.

BEDFORD: Lord Talbot, do not so dishonour me:
Here will I sit, before the walls of Roan,
And will be partner of your weal or woe.

BURGUNDY: Courageous Bedford, let us now persuade
you.

BEDFORD: Not to be gone from hence: for once I read,
That stout Pendragon, in his litter sick,
Came to the field, and vanquished his foes.
Methinks I should revive the soldiers' hearts,
Because I ever found them as myself.

TALBOT: Undaunted spirit in a dying breast,
Then be it so: Heavens keep old Bedford safe.
And now no more ado, brave Burgundy,

But gather we our forces out of hand,
And set upon our boasting enemy.

Exeunt.

*An alarum: Excursions. Enter Sir John Falstaffe, and
a Captain.*

CAPTAIN: Whither away Sir John Falstaffe, in such
haste?

FALSTAFFE: Whither away? to save myself by flight,
We are like to have the overthrow again.

CAPTAIN: What? will you fly, and leave Lord Talbot?

FALSTAFFE: Ay, all the Talbots in the World, to save my
life.

Exit.

CAPTAIN: Cowardly Knight, ill fortune follow thee.

Exit.

Retreat. Excursions. Pucell, Alanson, and Charles fly.

BEDFORD: Now quiet soul, depart when Heaven please,
For I have seen our enemies' overthrow.
What is the trust or strength of foolish man?
They that of late were daring with their scoffs,
Are glad and fain by flight to save themselves.

Bedford dies, and is carried in by two in his chair.
An alarum. Enter Talbot, Burgundy, and the rest.

TALBOT: Lost, and recover'd in a day again,
This is a double honour, Burgundy:
Yet Heavens have glory for this victory.

BURGUNDY: Warlike and martial Talbot, Burgundy
Enshrines thee in his heart, and there erects
Thy noble deeds, as Valour's monuments.

TALBOT: Thanks gentle Duke: but where is Pucell now?
I think her old familiar is asleep:
Now where 's the Bastard's braves. and Charles his
gleeks?
What all amort? Roan hangs her head for grief,

That such a valiant company are fled.
Now will we take some order in the Town,
Placing therein some expert Officers,
And then depart to Paris, to the King,
For there young Henry with his Nobles lie.
BURGUNDY: What wills Lord Talbot, pleaseth Burgundy.
TALBOT: But yet before we go, let's not forget
The noble Duke of Bedford, late deceas'd,
But see his exequies fulfill'd in Roan.
A braver soldier never couched lance,
A gentler heart did never sway in Court.
But Kings and mightiest Potentates must die,
For that's the end of human misery.

Exeunt.

III. 3

Enter Charles, Bastard, Alanson, Pucell.

JOAN: Dismay not (Princes) at this accident,
Nor grieve that Roan is so recovered:
Care is no cure, but rather corrosive,
For things that are not to be remedied.
Let frantic Talbot triumph for a while,
And like a peacock sweep along his tail,
We'll pull his plumes, and take away his train,
If Dolphin and the rest will be but rul'd.
CHARLES: We have been guided by thee hitherto,
And of thy cunning had no diffidence,
One sudden foil shall never breed distrust.
BASTARD: Search out thy wit for secret policies,
And we will make thee famous through the World.
ALANSON: We'll set thy statue in some holy place,
And have thee reverenc'd like a blessed Saint.
Employ thee then, sweet Virgin, for our good.

JOAN: Then thus it must be, this doth Joan devise:
  By fair persuasions, mix'd with sugar'd words,
  We will entice the Duke of Burgundy
  To leave the Talbot, and to follow us.

CHARLES: Ay marry Sweeting, if we could do that,
  France were no place for Henry's warriors,
  Nor should that Nation boast it so with us,
  But be extirped from our Provinces.

ALANSON: For ever should they be expuls'd from France,
  And not have title of an Earldom here.

JOAN: Your Honours shall perceive how I will work,
  To bring this matter to the wished end.
        Drum sounds afar off.
  Hark, by the sound of drum you may perceive
  Their powers are marching unto Paris-ward.
        Here sound an English march.
  There goes the Talbot, with his colours spread,
  And all the troops of English after him.
    French march. Enter the Duke of Burgundy and forces.
  Now in the rearward comes the Duke and his:
  Fortune in favour makes him lag behind.
  Summon a parley, we will talk with him.
        Trumpets sound a parley.

CHARLES: A parley with the Duke of Burgundy.

BURGUNDY: Who craves a parley with the Burgundy?

JOAN: The princely Charles of France, thy countryman.

BURGUNDY: What say'st thou Charles? for I am marching
      hence.

CHARLES: Speak Pucell, and enchant him with thy words.

JOAN: Brave Burgundy, undoubted hope of France,
  Stay, let thy humble handmaid speak to thee.

BURGUNDY: Speak on, but be not over-tedious.

JOAN: Look on thy Country, look on fertile France,
  And see the Cities and the Towns defac'd,

By wasting ruin of the cruel foe,
As looks the mother on her lowly babe,
When Death doth close his tender-dying eyes.
See, see the pining Malady of France:
Behold the wounds, the most unnatural wounds,
Which thou thyself hast given her woeful breast.
Oh turn thy edged sword another way,
Strike those that hurt, and hurt not those that help:
One drop of blood drawn from thy Country's bosom,
Should grieve thee more than streams of foreign gore.
Return thee therefore with a flood of tears,
And wash away thy Country's stained spots.

BURGUNDY: Either she hath bewitch'd me with her
      words,
Or Nature makes me suddenly relent.

JOAN: Besides, all French and France exclaims on thee,
Doubting thy birth and lawful progeny.
Who join'st thou with, but with a lordly Nation,
That will not trust thee, but for profit's sake?
When Talbot hath set footing once in France,
And fashion'd thee that instrument of ill,
Who then, but English Henry, will be Lord,
And thou be thrust out, like a fugitive?
Call we to mind, and mark but this for proof:
Was not the Duke of Orleans thy foe?
And was he not in England prisoner?
But when they heard he was thine enemy,
They set him free, without his ransom paid,
In spite of Burgundy and all his friends.
See then, thou fight'st against thy countrymen,
And join'st with them will be thy slaughter-men.
Come, come, return; return thou wandering Lord,
Charles and the rest will take thee in their arms.

BURGUNDY: I am vanquished:

These haughty words of hers
Have batter'd me like roaring cannon-shot,
And made me almost yield upon my knees.
Forgive me Country, and sweet Countrymen:
And Lords accept this hearty kind embrace.
My forces and my power of men are yours.
So farewell Talbot, I 'll no longer trust thee.

JOAN: Done like a Frenchman: turn and turn again.

CHARLES: Welcome brave Duke, thy friendship makes us
fresh.

BASTARD: And doth beget new courage in our breasts.

ALANSON: Pucell hath bravely play'd her part in this,
And doth deserve a Coronet of gold.

CHARLES: Now let us on, my Lords,
And join our powers,
And seek how we may prejudice the foe.
Exeunt.

III. 4

*Enter the King, Gloucester, Winchester, York, Suffolk,
Somerset, Warwick, Exeter, Vernon, Basset, and others:
To them with his Soldiers, Talbot.*

TALBOT: My gracious Prince, and honourable Peers,
Hearing of your arrival in this Realm,
I have a while given truce unto my wars,
To do my duty to my Sovereign.
In sign whereof, this arm, that hath reclaim'd
To your obedience, fifty fortresses,
Twelve Cities, and seven walled Towns of strength,
Beside five hundred prisoners of esteem;
Lets fall his sword before your Highness' feet:
And with submissive loyalty of heart
Ascribes the glory of his conquest got,

First to my God, and next unto your Grace.

KING: Is this the Lord Talbot, Uncle Gloucester,
That hath so long been resident in France?

GLOUCESTER: Yes, if it please your Majesty, my Liege.

KING: Welcome brave Captain, and victorious Lord.
When I was young (as yet I am not old)
I do remember how my Father said,
A stouter Champion never handled sword.
Long since we were resolved of your truth,
Your faithful service, and your toil in war:
Yet never have you tasted our reward,
Or been reguerdon'd with so much as thanks,
Because till now, we never saw your face.
Therefore stand up, and for these good deserts,
We here create you Earl of Shrewsbury,
And in our Coronation take your place.

Sennet. Flourish. Exeunt.
Manet Vernon and Basset.

VERNON: Now Sir, to you that were so hot at sea,
Disgracing of these colours that I wear,
In honour of my noble Lord of York:
Dar'st thou maintain the former words thou spak'st?

BASSET: Yes Sir, as well as you dare patronage
The envious barking of your saucy tongue,
Against my Lord the Duke of Somerset.

VERNON: Sirrah, thy Lord I honour as he is.

BASSET: Why, what is he? as good a man as York.

VERNON: Hark ye: not so: in witness take ye that.

Strikes him.

BASSET: Villain, thou know'st
The Law of Arms is such,
That whoso draws a sword, 'tis present death,
Or else this blow should broach thy dearest blood.
But I'll unto his Majesty, and crave,

I may have liberty to venge this wrong,
When thou shalt see, I 'll meet thee to thy cost.
VERNON: Well miscreant, I 'll be there as soon as you,
And after meet you, sooner than you would.
Exeunt.

IV. 1

Enter King, Gloucester, Winchester, York, Suffolk,
Somerset, Warwick, Talbot, Exeter, the Governor of Paris,
and others.

GLOUCESTER: Lord Bishop set the Crown upon his head.
WINCHESTER: God save King Henry of that name the
sixth.
GLOUCESTER: Now Governor of Paris take your oath,
That you elect no other King but him;
Esteem none friends, but such as are his friends,
And none your foes, but such as shall pretend
Malicious practices against his State:
This shall ye do, so help you righteous God.
Enter Falstaffe.
FALSTAFFE: My gracious Sovereign, as I rode from Calice,
To haste unto your Coronation:
A letter was deliver'd to my hands,
Writ to your Grace, from th' Duke of Burgundy.
TALBOT: Shame to the Duke of Burgundy, and thee:
I vow'd (base Knight) when I did meet thee next,
To tear the Garter from thy craven's leg,
Which I have done, because (unworthily)
Thou wast installed in that High Degree.
Pardon me, Princely Henry, and the rest:
This dastard, at the battle of Patay,
When (but in all) I was six thousand strong,
And that the French were almost ten to one,

Before we met, or that a stroke was given,
Like to a trusty Squire, did run away.
In which assault, we lost twelve hundred men.
Myself, and divers Gentlemen beside,
Were there surpris'd, and taken prisoners.
Then judge (great Lords) if I have done amiss:
Or whether that such cowards ought to wear
This Ornament of Knighthood, yea or no?

GLOUCESTER: To say the truth, this fact was infamous,
And ill beseeming any common man;
Much more a Knight, a Captain, and a Leader.

TALBOT: When first this Order was ordain'd my Lords,
Knights of the Garter were of noble birth;
Valiant, and virtuous, full of haughty courage,
Such as were grown to credit by the wars:
Not fearing death, nor shrinking for distress,
But always resolute, in most extremes.
He then, that is not furnish'd in this sort,
Doth but usurp the sacred name of Knight,
Profaning this most Honourable Order,
And should (if I were worthy to be judge)
Be quite degraded, like a hedge-born swain,
That doth presume to boast of gentle blood.

KING: Stain to thy countrymen, thou hear'st thy doom:
Be packing therefore, thou that wast a knight:
Henceforth we banish thee on pain of death.
                    Exit Falstaffe.
And now Lord Protector, view the letter
Sent from our Uncle Duke of Burgundy.

GLOUCESTER: What means his Grace, that he hath chang'd
       his style?
No more but plain and bluntly? (*To the King.*)
Hath he forgot he is his Sovereign?
Or doth this churlish superscription

Pretend some alteration in good will?
What 's here? *I have upon especial cause,*
Mov'd with compassion of my Country's wrack,
Together with the pitiful complaints
Of such as your oppression feeds upon,
Forsaken your pernicious Faction,
And join'd with Charles, the rightful King of France.
O monstrous treachery: Can this be so?
That in alliance, amity, and oaths,
There should be found such false dissembling guile?
KING: What? doth my Uncle Burgundy revolt?
GLOUCESTER: He doth my Lord, and is become your foe.
KING: Is that the worst this letter doth contain?
GLOUCESTER: It is the worst, and all (my Lord) he writes.
KING: Why then Lord Talbot there shall talk with him,
　　And give him chastisement for this abuse.
　　How say you (my Lord) are you not content?
TALBOT: Content, my Liege? Yes: But that I am pre-
　　vented,
　　I should have begg'd I might have been employ'd.
KING: Then gather strength, and march unto him straight:
　　Let him perceive how ill we brook his treason,
　　And what offence it is to flout his friends.
TALBOT: I go my Lord, in heart desiring still
　　You may behold confusion of your foes.
Exit.
Enter Vernon and Basset.
VERNON: Grant me the combat, gracious Sovereign.
BASSET: And me (my Lord) grant me the combat too.
YORK: This is my servant, hear him Noble Prince.
SOMERSET: And this is mine (sweet Henry) favour him.
KING: Be patient Lords, and give them leave to speak.
　　Say Gentlemen, what makes you thus exclaim,
　　And wherefore crave you combat? Or with whom?

D

VERNON: With him (my Lord) for he hath done me
     wrong.
BASSET: And I with him, for he hath done me wrong.
KING: What is that wrong, whereof you both complain?
     First let me know, and then I'll answer you.
BASSET: Crossing the sea, from England into France,
     This fellow here with envious carping tongue,
     Upbraided me about the Rose I wear,
     Saying, the sanguine colour of the leaves
     Did represent my Master's blushing cheeks:
     When stubbornly he did repugn the truth,
     About a certain question in the Law,
     Argu'd betwixt the Duke of York, and him:
     With other vile and ignominious terms.
     In confutation of which rude reproach,
     And in defence of my Lord's worthiness,
     I crave the benefit of Law of Arms.
VERNON: And that is my petition (noble Lord):
     For though he seem with forged quaint conceit
     To set a gloss upon his bold intent,
     Yet know (my Lord) I was provok'd by him,
     And he first took exceptions at this badge,
     Pronouncing that the paleness of this flower,
     Bewray'd the faintness of my Master's heart.
YORK: Will not this malice Somerset be left?
SOMERSET: Your private grudge my Lord of York,
     will out,
     Though ne'er so cunningly you smother it.
KING: Good Lord, what madness rules in brainsick men,
     When for so slight and frivolous a cause,
     Such factious emulations shall arise?
     Good Cousins both of York and Somerset,
     Quiet yourselves (I pray) and be at peace.
YORK: Let this dissension first be tried by fight,

And then your Highness shall command a peace.

SOMERSET: The quarrel toucheth none but us alone,
Betwixt ourselves let us decide it then.

YORK: There is my pledge, accept it Somerset.

VERNON: Nay, let it rest where it began at first.

BASSET: Confirm it so, mine honourable Lord.

GLOUCESTER: Confirm it so? Confounded be your strife,
And perish ye with your audacious prate,
Presumptuous vassals, are you not asham'd
With this immodest clamorous outrage,
To trouble and disturb the King, and us?
And you my Lords, methinks you do not well
To bear with their perverse objections:
Much less to take occasion from their mouths,
To raise a mutiny betwixt yourselves.
Let us persuade you take a better course.

EXETER: It grieves his Highness,
Good my Lords, be friends.

KING: Come hither you that would be combatants:
Henceforth I charge you, as you love our favour,
Quite to forget this quarrel, and the cause.
And you my Lords: Remember where we are,
In France, amongst a fickle wavering Nation:
If they perceive dissension in our looks,
And that within ourselves we disagree;
How will their grudging stomachs be provok'd
To wilful disobedience, and rebel?
Beside, what infamy will there arise,
When Foreign Princes shall be certified,
That for a toy, a thing of no regard,
King Henry's Peers, and chief Nobility,
Destroy'd themselves, and lost the Realm of France?
Oh think upon the conquest of my Father,
My tender years, and let us not forgo

That for a trifle, that was bought with blood.
Let me be umpire in this doubtful strife:
I see no reason if I wear this Rose,
That any one should therefore be suspicious
I more incline to Somerset, than York:
Both are my kinsmen, and I love them both.
As well they may upbraid me with my Crown,
Because (forsooth) the King of Scots is crown'd.
But your discretions better can persuade,
Than I am able to instruct or teach:
And therefore, as we hither came in peace,
So let us still continue peace, and love.
Cousin of York, we institute your Grace
To be our Regent in these parts of France:
And good my Lord of Somerset, unite
Your troops of horsemen, with his bands of foot,
And like true subjects, sons of your progenitors,
Go cheerfully together, and digest
Your angry choler on your enemies.
Our Self, my Lord Protector, and the rest,
After some respite, will return to Calice;
From thence to England, where I hope ere long
To be presented by your victories,
With Charles, Alanson, and that traitorous rout.

        Exeunt. Manet York, Warwick, Exeter, Vernon.

WARWICK: My Lord of York, I promise you the King
  Prettily (methought) did play the orator.

YORK: And so he did, but yet I like it not,
  In that he wears the badge of Somerset.

WARWICK: Tush, that was but his fancy, blame him **not**,
  I dare presume (sweet Prince) he thought no harm.

YORK: And if I wish he did. But let it rest,
  Other affairs must now be managed. *Exeunt.*

        Flourish. Manet Exeter.

EXETER: Well didst thou Richard to suppress thy voice:
  For had the passions of thy heart burst out,
  I fear we should have seen decipher'd there
  More rancorous spite, more furious raging broils,
  Than yet can be imagin'd or suppos'd:
  But howsoe'er, no simple man that sees
  This jarring discord of Nobility,
  This shouldering of each other in the Court,
  This factious bandying of their favourites,
  But that it doth presage some ill event.
  'Tis much, when sceptres are in children's hands:
  But more, when Envy breeds unkind division,
  There comes the ruin, there begins confusion.

                  Exit.

IV. 2

   Enter Talbot with trump and drum, before Bourdeaux.
TALBOT: Go to the gates of Bourdeaux trumpeter,
  Summon their General unto the wall.
                Sounds.
        Enter General aloft.
  English John Talbot (Captains) calls you forth,
  Servant in arms to Harry King of England,
  And thus he would. Open your City gates,
  Be humble to us, call my Sovereign yours,
  And do him homage as obedient subjects,
  And I'll withdraw me, and my bloody power.
  But if you frown upon this proffer'd peace,
  You tempt the fury of my three attendants,
  Lean Famine, quartering Steel, and climbing Fire,
  Who in a moment, even with the earth,
  Shall lay your stately, and air-braving towers,
  If you forsake the offer of their love.

GENERAL: Thou ominous and fearful Owl of death,
    Our Nation's terror, and their bloody scourge,
    The period of thy tyranny approacheth,
    On us thou canst not enter but by death:
    For I protest we are well fortified,
    And strong enough to issue out and fight.
    If thou retire, the Dolphin well appointed,
    Stands with the snares of War to tangle thee.
    On either hand thee, there are squadrons pitch'd,
    To wall thee from the liberty of flight;
    And no way canst thou turn thee for redress,
    But death doth front thee with apparent spoil,
    And pale destruction meets thee in the face:
    Ten thousand French have ta'en the Sacrament,
    To rive their dangerous artillery
    Upon no Christian soul but English Talbot:
    Lo, there thou stand'st a breathing valiant man
    Of an invincible unconquer'd spirit:
    This is the latest glory of thy praise,
    That I thy enemy due thee withal:
    For ere the glass that now begins to run,
    Finish the process of his sandy hour,
    These eyes that see thee now well coloured,
    Shall see thee withered, bloody, pale, and dead.
                    Drum afar off.
    Hark, hark, the Dolphin's drum, a warning bell,
    Sings heavy music to thy timorous soul,
    And mine shall ring thy dire departure out.
                    Exit.
TALBOT: He fables not, I hear the enemy:
    Out some light horsemen, and peruse their wings.
    O negligent and heedless discipline,
    How are we park'd and bounded in a pale?
    A little herd of England's timorous deer,

Maz'd with a yelping kennel of French curs.
If we be English deer, be then in blood,
Not rascal-like to fall down with a pinch,
But rather moody mad: And desperate stags,
Turn on the bloody hounds with heads of steel,
And make the cowards stand aloof at bay:
Sell every man his life as dear as mine,
And they shall find dear deer of us my friends.
God, and S. George, Talbot and England's right,
Prosper our colours in this dangerous fight.
                    Exeunt.

IV. 3

Enter a Messenger that meets York. Enter York with
trumpet, and many Soldiers.

YORK: Are not the speedy scouts return'd again,
    That dogg'd the mighty army of the Dolphin?
MESSENGER: They are return'd my Lord, and give it out,
    That he is march'd to Bourdeaux with his power
    To fight with Talbot as he march'd along.
    By your espials were discovered
    Two mightier troops than that the Dolphin led,
    Which join'd with him, and made their march for
    Bourdeaux.
YORK: A plague upon that villain Somerset,
    That thus delays my promised supply
    Of horsemen, that were levied for this siege.
    Renowned Talbot doth expect my aid,
    And I am lowted by a traitor villain,
    And cannot help the noble Chevalier:
    God comfort him in this necessity:
    If he miscarry, farewell wars in France.
                    Enter another Messenger.

2 MESSENGER: Thou Princely Leader of our English
    strength,
  Never so needful on the earth of France,
  Spur to the rescue of the noble Talbot,
  Who now is girdled with a waist of iron,
  And hemm'd about with grim destruction:
  To Bourdeaux warlike Duke, to Bourdeaux York,
  Else farewell Talbot, France, and England's honour.
YORK: O God, that Somerset who in proud heart
  Doth stop my cornets, were in Talbot's place,
  So should we save a valiant Gentleman,
  By forfeiting a traitor, and a coward:
  Mad ire, and wrathful fury makes me weep,
  That thus we die, while remiss traitors sleep.
2 MESSENGER: O send some succour to the distress'd
    Lord.
YORK: He dies, we lose: I break my warlike word:
  We mourn, France smiles: We lose, they daily get,
  All long of this vile traitor Somerset.
2 MESSENGER: Then God take mercy on brave Talbot's
    soul,
  And on his Son young John, who two hours since,
  I met in travel toward his warlike Father;
  This seven years did not Talbot see his son,
  And now they meet where both their lives are done.
YORK: Alas, what joy shall noble Talbot have,
  To bid his young son welcome to his grave:
  Away, vexation almost stops my breath,
  That sunder'd friends greet in the hour of death.
  Lucy farewell, no more my fortune can,
  But curse the cause I cannot aid the man.
  Maine, Blois, Poictiers, and Tours, are won away,
  Long all of Somerset, and his delay.
                    Exit.

2 MESSENGER: Thus while the Vulture of sedition,
  Feeds in the bosom of such great Commanders,
  Sleeping neglection doth betray to loss
  The conquest of our scarce-cold Conqueror,
  That ever living man of Memory,
  Henry the Fifth: Whiles they each other cross,
  Lives, honours, lands, and all, hurry to loss.
                    Exit.

IV. 4

Enter Somerset with his army.

SOMERSET: It is too late, I cannot send them now:
  This expedition was by York and Talbot,
  Too rashly plotted. All our general force,
  Might with a sally of the very Town
  Be buckled with: the over-daring Talbot
  Hath sullied all his gloss of former honour
  By this unheedful, desperate, wild adventure:
  York set him on to fight, and die in shame,
  That Talbot dead, great York might bear the name.
CAPTAIN: Here is Sir William Lucy, who with me
  Set from our o'er-match'd forces forth for aid.
SOMERSET: How now Sir William, whither were you
    sent?
LUCY: Whither my Lord? from bought and sold Lord
    Talbot,
  Who ring'd about with bold adversity,
  Cries out for noble York and Somerset,
  To beat assailing death from his weak regions,
  And whiles the honourable Captain there
  Drops bloody sweat from his war-wearied limbs,
  And, in advantage ling'ring looks for rescue,
  You his false hopes, the trust of England's honour,

Keep off aloof with worthless emulation:
Let not your private discord keep away
The levied succours that should lend him aid,
While he renowned noble Gentleman
Yields up his life unto a world of odds.
Orleans the Bastard, Charles, Burgundy,
Alanson, Reignier, compass him about,
And Talbot perisheth by your default.

SOMERSET: York set him on, York should have sent him
aid.

LUCY: And York as fast upon your Grace exclaims,
Swearing that you withhold his levied host,
Collected for this expedition.

SOMERSET: York lies: He might have sent, and had the
horse:
I owe him little duty, and less love,
And take foul scorn to fawn on him by sending.

LUCY: The fraud of England, not the force of France,
Hath now entrapp'd the noble-minded Talbot:
Never to England shall he bear his life,
But dies betray'd to fortune by your strife.

SOMERSET: Come go, I will dispatch the horsemen
straight:
Within six hours, they will be at his aid.

LUCY: Too late comes rescue, he is ta'en or slain,
For fly he could not, if he would have fled:
And fly would Talbot never though he might.

SOMERSET: If he be dead, brave Talbot then adieu.

LUCY: His fame lives in the world. His shame in you.

Exeunt.

IV. 5

Enter Talbot and his Son.

TALBOT: O young John Talbot, I did send for thee
　　To tutor thee in stratagems of War,
　　That Talbot's name might be in thee reviv'd,
　　When sapless age, and weak unable limbs
　　Should bring thy Father to his drooping chair.
　　But O malignant and ill-boding Stars,
　　Now thou art come unto a feast of death,
　　A terrible and unavoided danger:
　　Therefore dear Boy, mount on my swiftest horse,
　　And I 'll direct thee how thou shalt escape
　　By sudden flight. Come, dally not, be gone.

JOHN: Is my name Talbot? and am I your Son?
　　And shall I fly? O, if you love my Mother,
　　Dishonour not her honourable name,
　　To make a bastard, and a slave of me:
　　The World will say, he is not Talbot's blood,
　　That basely fled, when noble Talbot stood.

TALBOT: Fly, to revenge my death, if I be slain.

JOHN: He that flies so, will ne'er return again.

TALBOT: If we both stay, we both are sure to die.

JOHN: Then let me stay, and Father do you fly:
　　Your loss is great, so your regard should be;
　　My worth unknown, no loss is known in me.
　　Upon my death, the French can little boast;
　　In yours they will, in you all hopes are lost.
　　Flight cannot stain the honour you have won,
　　But mine it will, that no exploit have done.
　　You fled for vantage, every one will swear:
　　But if I bow, they 'll say it was for fear.
　　There is no hope that ever I will stay,

If the first hour I shrink and run away:
Here on my knee I beg mortality,
Rather than life, preserv'd with infamy.

TALBOT: Shall all thy Mother's hopes lie in one tomb?

JOHN: Ay rather than I 'll shame my Mother's womb.

TALBOT: Upon my blessing I command thee go.

JOHN: To fight I will, but not to fly the foe.

TALBOT: Part of thy Father may be sav'd in thee.

JOHN: No part of him, but will be shame in me.

TALBOT: Thou never hadst renown, nor canst not lose it.

JOHN: Yes, your renowned Name: shall flight abuse it?

TALBOT: Thy Father's charge shall clear thee from that stain.

JOHN: You cannot witness for me, being slain.
If Death be so apparent, then both fly.

TALBOT: And leave my followers here to fight and die?
My age was never tainted with such shame.

JOHN: And shall my youth be guilty of such blame?
No more can I be sever'd from your side,
Than can yourself, yourself in twain divide:
Stay, go, do what you will, the like do I;
For live I will not, if my Father die.

TALBOT: Then here I take my leave of thee, fair Son,
Born to eclipse thy life this afternoon:
Come, side by side, together live and die,
And soul with soul from France to Heaven fly.

Exeunt.

IV. 6

*Alarum: Excursions, wherein Talbot's Son is hemmed
about, and Talbot rescues him.*

TALBOT: Saint George, and victory; fight soldiers, fight:
The Regent hath with Talbot broke his word,

And left us to the rage of France his sword.
  Where is John Talbot? pause, and take thy breath,
  I gave thee life, and rescu'd thee from Death.
JOHN: O twice my Father, twice am I thy Son:
  The life thou gav'st me first, was lost and done,
  Till with thy warlike sword, despite of Fate,
  To my determin'd time thou gav'st new date.
TALBOT: When from the Dolphin's crest thy sword struck
    fire,
  It warm'd thy Father's heart with proud desire
  Of bold-fac'd Victory. Then leaden age,
  Quicken'd with youthful spleen, and warlike rage,
  Beat down Alanson, Orleans, Burgundy,
  And from the pride of Gallia rescued thee.
  The ireful Bastard Orleans, that drew blood
  From thee my Boy, and had the maidenhood
  Of thy first fight, I soon encountered,
  And interchanging blows, I quickly shed
  Some of his bastard blood, and in disgrace
  Bespoke him thus: Contaminated, base,
  And misbegotten blood, I spill of thine,
  Mean and right poor, for that pure blood of mine,
  Which thou didst force from Talbot, my brave Boy.
  Here purposing the Bastard to destroy,
  Came in strong rescue. Speak thy Father's care:
  Art thou not weary, John? How dost thou fare?
  Wilt thou yet leave the battle, Boy, and fly,
  Now thou art seal'd the son of Chivalry?
  Fly, to revenge my death when I am dead,
  The help of one stands me in little stead.
  Oh, too much folly is it, well I wot,
  To hazard all our lives in one small boat.
  If I today die not with Frenchmen's rage,
  Tomorrow I shall die with mickle age.

By me they nothing gain, and if I stay,
'Tis but the short'ning of my life one day.
In thee thy Mother dies, our Household's Name,
My death's revenge, thy youth, and England's fame:
All these, and more, we hazard by thy stay;
All these are sav'd, if thou wilt fly away.
JOHN: The sword of Orleans hath not made me smart,
These words of yours draw life-blood from my heart.
On that advantage, bought with such a shame,
To save a paltry life, and slay bright Fame,
Before young Talbot from old Talbot fly,
The coward horse that bears me, fall and die:
And like me to the peasant boys of France,
To be Shame's scorn, and subject of Mischance.
Surely, by all the glory you have won,
And if I fly, I am not Talbot's Son.
Then talk no more of flight, it is no boot,
If Son to Talbot, die at Talbot's foot.
TALBOT: Then follow thou thy desp'rate sire of Crete,
Thou Icarus, thy life to me is sweet:
If thou wilt fight, fight by thy Father's side,
And commendable prov'd, let's die in pride.
Exeunt.

IV. 7

Alarum. Excursions. Enter old Talbot led.
TALBOT: Where is my other life? mine own is gone.
O, where's young Talbot? where is valiant John?
Triumphant Death, smear'd with captivity,
Young Talbot's valour makes me smile at thee.
When he perceiv'd me shrink, and on my knee,
His bloody sword he brandish'd over me,
And like a hungry lion did commence

Rough deeds of rage, and stern impatience:
But when my angry guardant stood alone,
Tendring my ruin, and assail'd of none,
Dizzy-eyed fury, and great rage of heart,
Suddenly made him from my side to start
Into the clustering battle of the French:
And in that sea of blood, my Boy did drench
His over-mounting spirit; and there died,
My Icarus, my blossom, in his pride.

Enter Soldiers, with the body of young Talbot.

SERVANT: O my dear Lord, lo where your Son is borne.
TALBOT: Thou antic Death, which laugh'st us here to scorn,
Anon from thy insulting tyranny,
Coupled in bonds of perpetuity,
Two Talbots winged through the lither sky,
In thy despite shall 'scape mortality.
O thou whose wounds become hard-favour'd death,
Speak to thy father, ere thou yield thy breath,
Brave death by speaking, whether he will or no:
Imagine him a Frenchman, and thy foe.
Poor Boy, he smiles, methinks, as who should say,
Had Death been French, then Death had died today.
Come, come, and lay him in his Father's arms,
My spirit can no longer bear these harms.
Soldiers adieu: I have what I would have,
Now my old arms are young John Talbot's grave.

Dies.

Enter Charles, Alanson, Burgundy, Bastard,
and Pucell.

CHARLES: Had York and Somerset brought rescue in,
We should have found a bloody day of this.
BASTARD: How the young whelp of Talbot's raging
wood,

Did flesh his puny sword in Frenchmen's blood.

JOAN: Once I encounter'd him, and thus I said:
Thou maiden youth, be vanquish'd by a Maid.
But with a proud majestical high scorn
He answer'd thus: Young Talbot was not born
To be the pillage of a giglot wench:
So rushing in the bowels of the French,
He left me proudly, as unworthy fight.

BURGUNDY: Doubtless he would have made a noble
Knight:
See where he lies inhearsed in the arms
Of the most bloody Nurser of his harms.

BASTARD: Hew them to pieces, hack their bones asunder,
Whose life was England's glory, Gallia's wonder.

CHARLES: Oh no forbear: For that which we have fled
During the life, let us not wrong it dead.

Enter Lucy.

LUCY: Herald, conduct me to the Dolphin's tent,
To know who hath obtain'd the glory of the day.

CHARLES: On what submissive message art thou sent?

LUCY: Submission Dolphin? 'Tis a mere French word:
We English warriors wot not what it means.
I come to know what prisoners thou hast ta'en,
And to survey the bodies of the dead.

CHARLES: For prisoners ask'st thou? Hell our prison is.
But tell me whom thou seek'st?

LUCY: But where's the great Alcides of the field,
Valiant Lord Talbot Earl of Shrewsbury?
Created for his rare success in arms,
Great Earl of Washford, Waterford, and Valence,
Lord Talbot of Goodrig and Urchinfield,
Lord Strange of Blackmere, Lord Verdun of Alton,
Lord Cromwell of Wingfield, Lord Furnival of Sheffield,
The trice victorious Lord of Falconbridge,

   Knight of the Noble Order of Saint George,
   Worthy Saint Michael, and the Golden Fleece,
   Great Marshal to Henry the Sixth,
   Of all his wars within the Realm of France.

JOAN: Here is a silly stately style indeed:
   The Turk that two and fifty Kingdoms hath,
   Writes not so tedious a style as this.
   Him that thou magnifi'st with all these titles,
   Stinking and fly-blown lies here at our feet.

LUCY: Is Talbot slain, the Frenchmen's only Scourge,
   Your Kingdom's terror, and black Nemesis?
   Oh were mine eye-balls into bullets turn'd,
   That I in rage might shoot them at your faces.
   Oh, that I could but call these dead to life,
   It were enough to fright the Realm of France.
   Were but his picture left amongst you here,
   It would amaze the proudest of you all.
   Give me their bodies, that I may bear them hence,
   And give them burial, as beseems their worth.

JOAN: I think this upstart is old Talbot's ghost,
   He speaks with such a proud commanding spirit:
   For God's sake let him have him, to keep them here,
   They would but stink, and putrefy the air.

CHARLES: Go take their bodies hence.

LUCY: I'll bear them hence: but from their ashes shall be
   rear'd
   A Phoenix that shall make all France afear'd.

CHARLES: So we be rid of them, do with him what thou
   wilt.
   And now to Paris in this conquering vein,
   All will be ours, now bloody Talbot's slain.
                      Exeunt.

V. 1

Sennet. Enter King, Gloucester, and Exeter.

KING: Have you perus'd the letters from the Pope,
　　The Emperor, and the Earl of Armagnac?
GLOUCESTER: I have my Lord, and their intent is this,
　　They humbly sue unto your Excellence,
　　To have a godly peace concluded of,
　　Between the Realms of England, and of France.
KING: How doth your Grace affect their motion?
GLOUCESTER: Well (my good Lord) and as the only
　　means
　　To stop effusion of our Christian blood,
　　And stablish quietness on every side.
KING: Ay marry Uncle, for I always thought
　　It was both impious and unnatural,
　　That such immanity and bloody strife
　　Should reign among Professors of one Faith.
GLOUCESTER: Beside my Lord, the sooner to effect,
　　And surer bind this knot of amity,
　　The Earl of Armagnac near knit to Charles,
　　A man of great authority in France,
　　Proffers his only daughter to your Grace,
　　In marriage, with a large and sumptuous dowry.
KING: Marriage Uncle? Alas my years are young:
　　And fitter is my study, and my books,
　　Than wanton dalliance with a paramour.
　　Yet call th' Ambassadors, and as you please,
　　So let them have their answers every one:
　　I shall be well content with any choice
　　Tends to God's glory, and my Country's weal.
　　　　　　Enter Winchester, and three Ambassadors.
EXETER: What, is my Lord of Winchester install'd,

And call'd unto a Cardinal's degree?
Then I perceive, that will be verified
Henry the Fifth did sometime prophesy.
If once he come to be a Cardinal,
He 'll make his cap co-equal with the Crown.

KING: My Lords Ambassadors, your several suits
Have been consider'd and debated on,
Your purpose is both good and reasonable:
And therefore are we certainly resolv'd,
To draw conditions of a friendly peace,
Which by my Lord of Winchester we mean
Shall be transported presently to France.

GLOUCESTER: And for the proffer of my Lord your
Master,
I have inform'd his Highness so at large,
As liking of the Lady's virtuous gifts,
Her beauty, and the value of her dower,
He doth intend she shall be England's Queen.

KING: In argument and proof of which contract,
Bear her this jewel, pledge of my affection.
And so my Lord Protector see them guarded,
And safely brought to Dover, wherein shipp'd
Commit them to the fortune of the sea.

Exeunt, all but Winchester and Legate.

WINCHESTER: Stay my Lord Legate, you shall first re-
ceive
The sum of money which I promised
Should be deliver'd to his Holiness,
For clothing me in these grave ornaments.

LEGATE: I will attend upon your Lordship's leisure.

Exit.

WINCHESTER: Now Winchester will not submit, I trow,
Or be inferior to the proudest Peer;
Humphrey of Gloucester, thou shalt well perceive,

That neither in birth, or for authority,
The Bishop will be overborne by thee:
I'll either make thee stoop, and bend thy knee,
Or sack this Country with a mutiny.

Exit.

V.2

Enter Charles, Burgundy, Alanson, Bastard, Reignier,
and Joan.

CHARLES: These news (my Lords) may cheer our droop-
ing spirits:
'Tis said, the stout Parisians do revolt,
And turn again unto the warlike French.

ALANSON: Then march to Paris royal Charles of France,
And keep not back your powers in dalliance.

JOAN: Peace be amongst them if they turn to us,
Else ruin combat with their Palaces.

Enter Scout.

SCOUT: Success unto our valiant General,
And happiness to his accomplices.

CHARLES: What tidings send our scouts? I prithee speak.

SCOUT: The English army that divided was
Into two parties, is now conjoin'd in one,
And means to give you battle presently.

CHARLES: Somewhat too sudden Sirs, the warning is,
But we will presently provide for them.

BURGUNDY: I trust the Ghost of Talbot is not there:
Now he is gone my Lord, you need not fear.

JOAN: Of all base passions, fear is most accurs'd.
Command the conquest Charles, it shall be thine:
Let Henry fret, and all the world repine.

CHARLES: Then on my Lords, and France be fortunate.

Exeunt. Alarum. Excursions.

V. 3

Enter Joan de Pucell.

JOAN: The Regent conquers, and the Frenchmen fly.
　Now help ye charming spells and periapts,
　And ye choice spirits that admonish me,
　And give me signs of future accidents.
　　　　　Thunder.
　You speedy helpers, that are substitutes,
　Under the Lordly Monarch of the North,
　Appear, and aid me in this enterprise.
　　　　　Enter Fiends.
　This speedy and quick appearance argues proof
　Of your accustom'd diligence to me.
　Now ye Familiar Spirits, that are cull'd
　Out of the powerful Regions under earth,
　Help me this once, that France may get the field.
　　　　　They walk, and speak not.
　Oh hold me with silence over-long:
　Where I was wont to feed you with my blood,
　I'll lop a member off, and give it you,
　In earnest of a further benefit:
　So you do condescend to help me now.
　　　　　They hang their heads.
　No hope to have redress? My body shall
　Pay recompense, if you will grant my suit.
　　　　　They shake their heads.
　Cannot my body, nor blood-sacrifice,
　Entreat you to your wonted furtherance?
　Then take my soul; my body, soul, and all,
　Before that England give the French the foil.
　　　　　They depart.
　See, they forsake me. Now the time is come,

That France must vail her lofty-plumed crest,
And let her head fall into England's lap.
My ancient incantations are too weak,
And hell too strong for me to buckle with:
Now France, thy glory droopeth to the dust.
Exit.
Excursions. Joan and York fight hand to hand.
French fly.

YORK: Damsel of France, I think I have you fast,
Unchain your spirits now with spelling charms,
And try if they can gain your liberty.
A goodly prize, fit for the devil's grace.
See how the ugly Witch doth bend her brows,
As if with Circe, she would change my shape.

JOAN: Chang'd to a worser shape thou canst not be.

YORK: Oh, Charles the Dolphin is a proper man,
No shape but his can please your dainty eye.

JOAN: A plaguing mischief light on Charles, and thee,
And may ye both be suddenly surpris'd
By bloody hands, in sleeping on your beds.

YORK: Fell banning Hag, Enchantress hold thy tongue.

JOAN: I prithee give me leave to curse awhile.

YORK: Curse miscreant, when thou com'st to the stake.
Exeunt.
Alarum. Enter Suffolk, with Margaret in his hand.

SUFFOLK: Be what thou wilt, thou art my prisoner.
Gazes on her.
O Fairest Beauty, do not fear, nor fly:
For I will touch thee but with reverent hands,
I kiss these fingers for eternal peace,
And lay them gently on thy tender side.
Who art thou, say? that I may honour thee.

MARGARET: Margaret my name, and daughter to a King,
The King of Naples, whosoe'er thou art.

SUFFOLK: An Earl I am, and Suffolk am I call'd.
  Be not offended Nature's miracle,
  Thou art allotted to be ta'en by me:
  So doth the swan her downy cygnets save,
  Keeping them prisoner underneath her wings:
  Yet if this servile usage once offend,
  Go, and be free again, as Suffolk's friend.
                    She is going.
  Oh stay: I have no power to let her pass,
  My hand would free her, but my heart says no.
  As plays the Sun upon the glassy streams,
  Twinkling another counterfeited beam,
  So seems this gorgeous beauty to mine eyes.
  Fain would I woo her, yet I dare not speak:
  I'll call for pen and ink, and write my mind:
  Fie de la Pole, disable not thyself:
  Hast not a tongue? Is she not here?
  Wilt thou be daunted at a Woman's sight?
  Ay: Beauty's princely Majesty is such,
  Confounds the tongue, and makes the senses rough.
MARGARET: Say Earl of Suffolk, if thy name be so,
  What ransom must I pay before I pass?
  For I perceive I am thy prisoner.
SUFFOLK: How canst thou tell she will deny thy suit,
  Before thou make a trial of her love?
MARGARET: Why speak'st thou not? What ransom must
    I pay?
SUFFOLK: She's beautiful; and therefore to be woo'd:
  She is a woman; therefore to be won.
MARGARET: Wilt thou accept of ransom, yea nor no?
SUFFOLK: Fond man, remember that thou hast a wife,
  Then how can Margaret be thy paramour?
MARGARET: I were best to leave him, for he will not hear.
SUFFOLK: There all is marr'd: there lies a cooling card.

MARGARET: He talks at random: sure the man is mad.

SUFFOLK: And yet a dispensation may be had.

MARGARET: And yet I would that you would answer me.

SUFFOLK: I'll win this Lady Margaret. For whom?
    Why for my King: Tush, that's a wooden thing.

MARGARET: He talks of wood: It is some carpenter.

SUFFOLK: Yet so my fancy may be satisfied,
    And peace established between these Realms.
    But there remains a scruple in that too:
    For though her Father be the King of Naples,
    Duke of Anjou and Maine, yet is he poor,
    And our Nobility will scorn the match.

MARGARET: Hear ye Captain? Are you not at leisure?

SUFFOLK: It shall be so, disdain they ne'er so much:
    Henry is youthful, and will quickly yield.
    Madam, I have a secret to reveal.

MARGARET: What though I be enthrall'd, he seems a
    knight
    And will not any way dishonour me.

SUFFOLK: Lady, vouchsafe to listen what I say.

MARGARET: Perhaps I shall be rescu'd by the French,
    And then I need not crave his courtesy.

SUFFOLK: Sweet Madam, give me hearing in a cause.

MARGARET: Tush, women have been captivate ere now.

SUFFOLK: Lady, wherefore talk you so?

MARGARET: I cry you mercy, 'tis but *Quid* for *Quo*.

SUFFOLK: Say gentle Princess, would you not suppose
    Your bondage happy, to be made a Queen?

MARGARET: To be a Queen in bondage, is more vile,
    Than is a slave, in base servility:
    For Princes should be free.

SUFFOLK: And so shall you,
    If happy England's Royal King be free.

MARGARET: Why what concerns his freedom unto me?

SUFFOLK: I 'll undertake to make thee Henry's Queen,
  To put a Golden Sceptre in thy hand,
  And set a precious Crown upon thy head,
  If thou wilt condescend to be my –

MARGARET: What?

SUFFOLK: His love.

MARGARET: I am unworthy to be Henry's wife.

SUFFOLK: No gentle Madam, I unworthy am
  To woo so fair a Dame to be his wife,
  And have no portion in the choice myself.
  How say you Madam, are ye so content?

MARGARET: And if my Father please, I am content.

SUFFOLK: Then call our Captains and our colours forth,
  And Madam, at your Father's castle walls,
  We'll crave a parley, to confer with him.
          Sound. Enter Reignier on the walls.
  See Reignier see, thy daughter prisoner.

REIGNIER: To whom?

SUFFOLK: To me.

REIGNIER: Suffolk, what remedy?
  I am a soldier, and unapt to weep,
  Or to exclaim on Fortune's fickleness.

SUFFOLK: Yes, there is remedy enough my Lord,
  Consent, and for thy honour give consent,
  Thy daughter shall be wedded to my King,
  Whom I with pain have woo'd and won thereto:
  And this her easy-held imprisonment,
  Hath gain'd thy daughter princely liberty.

REIGNIER: Speaks Suffolk as he thinks?

SUFFOLK: Fair Margaret knows,
  That Suffolk doth not flatter, face, or feign.

REIGNIER: Upon thy princely warrant, I descend,
  To give thee answer of thy just demand.

SUFFOLK: And here I will expect thy coming.

Trumpets sound. Enter Reignier.

REIGNIER: Welcome brave Earl into our Territories,
Command in Anjou what your Honour pleases.

SUFFOLK: Thanks Reignier, happy for so sweet a child,
Fit to be made companion with a King:
What answer makes your Grace unto my suit?

REIGNIER: Since thou dost deign to woo her little worth,
To be the Princely Bride of such a Lord:
Upon condition I may quietly
Enjoy mine own, the Country Maine and Anjou,
Free from oppression, or the stroke of War,
My daughter shall be Henry's, if he please.

SUFFOLK: That is her ransom, I deliver her,
And those two Counties I will undertake
Your Grace shall well and quietly enjoy.

REIGNIER: And I again in Henry's royal name,
As Deputy unto that gracious King,
Give thee her hand for sign of plighted faith.

SUFFOLK: Reignier of France, I give thee kingly thanks,
Because this is in traffic of a King.
And yet methinks I could be well content
To be mine own Attorney in this case.
I'll over then to England with this news,
And make this marriage to be solemniz'd:
So farewell Reignier, set this diamond safe
In golden palaces as it becomes.

REIGNIER: I do embrace thee, as I would embrace
The Christian Prince King Henry were he here.

MARGARET: Farewell my Lord, good wishes, praise, and
prayers,
Shall Suffolk ever have of Margaret.
She is going.

SUFFOLK: Farewell sweet Madam: but hark you Margaret,

No princely commendations to my King?
MARGARET: Such commendations as becomes a maid,
  A virgin, and his servant, say to him.
SUFFOLK: Words sweetly plac'd, and modestly directed,
  But Madam, I must trouble you again,
  No loving token to his Majesty?
MARGARET: Yes, my good Lord, a pure unspotted heart,
  Never yet taint with love, I send the King.
SUFFOLK: And this withal.
                    Kiss her.
MARGARET: That for thyself, I will not so presume,
  To send such peevish token to a King.
                    Exeunt Reignier and Margaret.
SUFFOLK: Oh wert thou for myself: but Suffolk stay,
  Thou mayst not wander in that labyrinth,
  There Minotaurs and ugly treasons lurk,
  Solicit Henry with her wondrous praise.
  Bethink thee on her virtues that surmount,
  And natural Graces that extinguish Art,
  Repeat their semblance often on the seas,
  That when thou com'st to kneel at Henry's feet,
  Thou mayst bereave him of his wits with wonder.
                    Exit.

V. 4

Enter York, Warwick, Shepherd, Pucell.
YORK: Bring forth that Sorceress condemn'd to burn.
SHEPHERD: Ah Joan, this kills thy Father's heart out-right,
  Have I sought every country far and near,
  And now it is my chance to find thee out,
  Must I behold thy timeless cruel death:
  Ah Joan, sweet daughter Joan, I'll die with thee.
JOAN: Decrepit miser, base ignoble wretch,

I am descended of a gentler blood.
Thou art no father, nor no friend of mine.

SHEPHERD: Out, out: My Lords, and please you, 'tis not
so:
I did beget her, all the parish knows:
Her mother liveth yet, can testify
She was the first fruit of my bachelorship.

WARWICK: Graceless, wilt thou deny thy parentage?

YORK: This argues what her kind of life hath been,
Wicked and vile, and so her death concludes.

SHEPHERD: Fie Joan, that thou wilt be so obstacle:
God knows, thou art a collop of my flesh,
And for thy sake have I shed many a tear:
Deny me not, I prithee, gentle Joan.

JOAN: Peasant avaunt. You have suborn'd this man
Of purpose, to obscure my noble birth.

SHEPHERD: 'Tis true, I gave a noble to the Priest,
The morn that I was wedded to her mother.
Kneel down and take my blessing, good my girl.
Wilt thou not stoop? Now cursed be the time
Of thy nativity: I would the milk
Thy mother gave thee when thou suck'st her breast,
Had been a little ratsbane for thy sake.
Or else, when thou didst keep my lambs a-field,
I wish some ravenous wolf had eaten thee.
Dost thou deny thy father, cursed drab?
O burn her, burn her, hanging is too good.
Exit.

YORK: Take her away, for she hath liv'd too long.
To fill the world with vicious qualities.

JOAN: First let me tell you whom you have condemn'd;
Not me, begotten of a shepherd swain
But issued from the Progeny of Kings.
Virtuous and holy, chosen from above,

By inspiration of Celestial Grace,
To work exceeding miracles on earth.
I never had to do with wicked spirits.
But you that are polluted with your lusts,
Stain'd with the guiltless blood of innocents,
Corrupt and tainted with a thousand vices:
Because you want the grace that others have,
You judge it straight a thing impossible
To compass wonders, but by help of devils.
No misconceived, Joan of Arc hath been
A virgin from her tender infancy,
Chaste, and immaculate in very thought,
Whose maiden-blood thus rigorously effus'd,
Will cry for Vengeance, at the Gates of Heaven.

YORK: Ay, ay: away with her to execution.

WARWICK: And hark ye sirs: because she is a Maid,
Spare for no faggots, let there be enow:
Place barrels of pitch upon the fatal stake,
That so her torture may be shortened.

JOAN: Will nothing turn your unrelenting hearts?
Then Joan discover thine infirmity,
That warranteth by Law, to be thy privilege.
I am with child ye bloody homicides:
Murther not then the fruit within my womb,
Although ye hale me to a violent death.

YORK: Now heaven forfend, the holy Maid with child?

WARWICK: The greatest miracle that e'er ye wrought,
Is all your strict preciseness come to this?

YORK: She and the Dolphin have been juggling,
I did imagine what would be her refuge.

WARWICK: Well go to, we'll have no bastards live,
Especially since Charles must father it.

JOAN: You are deceiv'd, my child is none of his,
It was Alanson that enjoy'd my love.

YORK: Alanson that notorious Machiavel?
  It dies, and if it had a thousand lives.
JOAN: Oh give me leave, I have deluded you,
  'Twas neither Charles, nor yet the Duke I nam'd,
  But Reignier King of Naples that prevail'd.
WARWICK: A married man, that's most intolerable.
YORK: Why here's a girl: I think she knows not well
  (There were so many) whom she may accuse.
WARWICK: It's sign she hath been liberal and free.
YORK: And yet forsooth, she is a Virgin pure.
  Strumpet, thy words condemn thy brat, and thee.
  Use no entreaty, for it is in vain.
JOAN: Then lead me hence: with whom I leave my curse.
  May never glorious Sun reflex his beams
  Upon the country where you make abode:
  But darkness, and the gloomy shade of death
  Environ you, till Mischief and Despair,
  Drive you to break your necks, or hang yourselves.

Exit.
Enter Cardinal.

YORK: Break thou in pieces, and consume to ashes,
  Thou foul accursed minister of Hell.
CARDINAL: Lord Regent, I do greet your Excellence
  With letters of commission from the King.
  For know my Lords, the States of Christendom,
  Mov'd with remorse of these outrageous broils,
  Have earnestly implor'd a general peace,
  Betwixt our Nation, and the aspiring French;
  And here at hand, the Dolphin and his train
  Approacheth, to confer about some matter.
YORK: Is all our travail turn'd to this effect,
  After the slaughter of so many Peers,
  So many Captains, Gentlemen, and soldiers,
  That in this quarrel have been overthrown,

And sold their bodies for their Country's benefit,
Shall we at last conclude effeminate peace?
Have we not lost most part of all the Towns,
By treason, falsehood, and by treachery,
Our great progenitors had conquered:
Oh Warwick, Warwick, I foresee with grief
The utter loss of all the Realm of France.

WARWICK: Be patient York, if we conclude a peace
It shall be with such strict and severe covenants,
As little shall the Frenchmen gain thereby.

Enter Charles, Alanson, Bastard, Reignier.

CHARLES: Since Lords of England, it is thus agreed,
That peaceful truce shall be proclaim'd in France,
We come to be informed by yourselves,
What the conditions of that league must be.

YORK: Speak Winchester, for boiling choler chokes
The hollow passage of my poison'd voice,
By sight of these our baleful enemies.

CARDINAL: Charles, and the rest, it is enacted thus:
That in regard King Henry gives consent,
Of mere compassion, and of lenity,
To ease your country of distressful war,
And suffer you to breathe in fruitful peace,
You shall become true liegemen to his Crown.
And Charles, upon condition thou wilt swear
To pay him tribute, and submit thyself,
Thou shalt be plac'd as Viceroy under him,
And still enjoy thy regal dignity.

ALANSON: Must he be then as shadow of himself?
Adorn his temples with a coronet,
And yet, in substance and authority,
Retain but privilege of a private man?
This proffer is absurd, and reasonless.

CHARLES: 'Tis known already that I am possess'd

With more than half the Gallian Territories,
And therein reverenc'd for their lawful King.
Shall I for lucre of the rest unvanquish'd,
Detract so much from that prerogative,
As to be call'd but Viceroy of the whole?
No Lord Ambassador, I'll rather keep
That which I have, than coveting for more
Be cast from possibility of all.

YORK: Insulting Charles, hast thou by secret means
Us'd intercession to obtain a league,
And now the matter grows to compromise,
Stand'st thou aloof upon comparison.
Either accept the title thou usurp'st,
Or benefit proceeding from our King,
And not of any challenge of desert,
Or we will plague thee with incessant wars.

REIGNIER: My Lord, you do not well in obstinacy,
To cavil in the course of this contract:
If once it be neglected, ten to one
We shall not find like opportunity.

ALANSON: To say the truth, it is your policy,
To save your subjects from such massacre
And ruthless slaughters as are daily seen
By our proceeding in hostility,
And therefore take this compact of a Truce,
Although you break it, when your pleasure serves.

WARWICK: How say'st thou, Charles?
Shall our condition stand?

CHARLES: It shall;
Only reserv'd, you claim no interest
In any of our Towns of Garrison.

YORK: Then swear allegiance to his Majesty,
As thou art Knight, never to disobey,
Nor be rebellious to the Crown of England,

Thou nor thy Nobles, to the Crown of England.
So, now dimiss your army when ye please:
Hang up your ensigns, let your drums be still,
For here we entertain a solemn peace.

Exeunt.

V. 5

Enter Suffolk in conference with the King,
Gloucester, and Exeter.

KING: Your wondrous rare description (noble Earl)
    Of beauteous Margaret hath astonish'd me:
    Her virtues graced with external gifts,
    Do breed Love's settled passions in my heart,
    And like as rigour of tempestuous gusts
    Provokes the mightiest hulk against the tide,
    So am I driven by breath of her renown,
    Either to suffer shipwrack, or arrive
    Where I may have fruition of her love.
SUFFOLK: Tush my good Lord, this superficial tale,
    Is but a preface of her worthy praise:
    The chief perfections of that lovely Dame,
    (Had I sufficient skill to utter them)
    Would make a volume of enticing lines,
    Able to ravish any dull conceit.
    And which is more, she is not so divine,
    So full replete with choice of all delights,
    But with as humble lowliness of mind,
    She is content to be at your command:
    Command I mean, of virtuous chaste intents,
    To love, and honour Henry as her Lord.
KING: And otherwise, will Henry ne'er presume:
    Therefore my Lord Protector, give consent,
    That Marg'ret may be England's Royal Queen.

E

GLOUCESTER: So should I give consent to flatter sin,
    You know (my Lord) your Highness is betroth'd
    Unto another Lady of esteem,
    How shall we then dispense with that contract,
    And not deface your Honour with reproach?
SUFFOLK: As doth a Ruler with unlawful oaths,
    Or one that at a Triumph, having vow'd
    To try his strength, forsaketh yet the lists
    By reason of his adversary's odds.
    A poor Earl's daughter is unequal odds,
    And therefore may be broke without offence.
GLOUCESTER: Why what (I pray) is Margaret more than
      that?
    Her Father is no better than an Earl,
    Although in glorious titles he excel.
SUFFOLK: Yes my Lord, her Father is a King,
    The King of Naples, and Jerusalem,
    And of such great authority in France,
    As his alliance will confirm our peace,
    And keep the Frenchman in allegiance.
GLOUCESTER: And so the Earl of Armagnac may do,
    Because he is near kinsman unto Charles.
EXETER: Beside, his wealth doth warrant a liberal dower,
    Where Reignier sooner will receive, than give.
SUFFOLK: A dower my Lords? Disgrace not so your King,
    That he should be so abject, base, and poor,
    To choose for wealth, and not for perfect love.
    Henry is able to enrich his Queen,
    And not to seek a Queen to make him rich,
    So worthless peasants bargain for their wives,
    As market-men for oxen, sheep, or horse.
    Marriage is a matter of more worth,
    Than to be dealt in by attorney-ship:
    Not whom we will, but whom his Grace affects,

Must be companion of his nuptial bed.
And therefore Lords, since he affects her most,
Most of all these reasons bindeth us,
In our opinions she should be preferr'd.
For what is wedlock forced? but a Hell,
An age of discord and continual strife,
Whereas the contrary bringeth bliss,
And is a pattern of celestial peace.
Whom should we match with Henry being a King,
But Margaret, that is daughter to a King:
Her peerless feature, joined with her birth,
Approves her fit for none, but for a King.
Her valiant courage, and undaunted spirit,
(More than in women commonly is seen)
Will answer our hope in issue of a King.
For Henry, son unto a Conqueror,
Is likely to beget more Conquerors,
If with a Lady of so high resolve,
(As is fair Margaret) he be link'd in love.
Then yield my Lords, and here conclude with me,
That Margaret shall be Queen, and none but she.
KING: Whether it be through force of your report,
My noble Lord of Suffolk: Or for that
My tender youth was never yet attaint
With any passion of inflaming love,
I cannot tell: but this I am assur'd,
I feel such sharp dissension in my breast,
Such fierce alarums both of Hope and Fear,
As I am sick with working of my thoughts.
Take therefore shipping, post my Lord to France,
Agree to any covenants, and procure
That Lady Margaret do vouchsafe to come
To cross the seas to England, and be crown'd
King Henry's faithful and anointed Queen.

For your expenses and sufficient charge,
Among the people gather up a tenth.
Be gone I say, for till you do return,
I rest perplexed with a thousand cares.
And you (good Uncle) banish all offence:
If you do censure me, by what you were,
Not what you are, I know it will excuse
This sudden execution of my will.
And so conduct me, where from company,
I may revolve and ruminate my grief.

Exit.

GLOUCESTER: Ay grief I fear me, both at first at last.

Exeunt Gloucester and Exeter.

SUFFOLK: Thus Suffolk hath prevail'd, and thus he goes
As did the youthful Paris once to Greece,
With hope to find the like event in love,
But prosper better than the Trojan did:
Margaret shall now be Queen, and rule the King:
But I will rule both her, the King, and Realm.

Exit.

The Second Part of Henry the Sixth

WITH THE DEATH OF THE GOOD DUKE HUMPHREY

THE ACTORS' NAMES

KING HENRY THE SIXTH

HUMPHREY, the Duke of Gloucester, his uncle

CARDINAL BEAUFORT, Bishop of Winchester, great-uncle to the King

RICHARD PLANTAGENET, Duke of York

EDWARD and RICHARD, his sons

DUKE OF SOMERSET

DUKE OF SUFFOLK

DUKE OF BUCKINGHAM

LORD CLIFFORD

YOUNG CLIFFORD, his son

EARL OF SALISBURY

EARL OF WARWICK

LORD SCALES

LORD SAY

SIR HUMPHREY STAFFORD, and WILLIAM STAFFORD, his brother

SIR JOHN STANLEY

VAUX

MATTHEW GOFFE

A Sea-Captain, Master, and Master's-Mate, and WALTER WHITMORE

Two Gentlemen, prisoners with Suffolk

JOHN HUME and JOHN SOUTHWELL, priests

BOLINGBROKE, a conjurer   ALEXANDER IDEN,

THOMAS HORNER, an armourer   a Kentish gentleman

PETER, his man

Clerk of Chatham

SIMPCOX, an impostor

Mayor of Saint Alban's

JACK CADE, a rebel

GEORGE BEVIS, JOHN HOLLAND, DICK the butcher, SMITH the weaver, MICHAEL, &c., followers of Cade

Two Murderers

MARGARET, Queen to King Henry

ELEANOR, Duchess of Gloucester

MARGARET JORDAN, a witch, wife to Simpcox

Lords, Ladies, and Attendants, Petitioners, Aldermen, a Herald, a Beadle, Sheriff, and Officers, Citizens, 'Prentices, Falconers, Guards, Soldiers, Messengers, &c.

A Spirit

I. 1

SUFFOLK: As by your high Imperial Majesty,
  I had in charge at my depart for France,
  As Procurator to your Excellence,
  To marry Princess Margaret for your Grace;
  So in the famous ancient City, Tours,
  In presence of the Kings of France and Sicil,
  The Dukes of Orleans, Calaber, Bretagne and Alanson,
  Seven Earls, twelve Barons, and twenty reverend Bish-
    ops,
  I have perform'd my task, and was espous'd,
  And humbly now upon my bended knee,
  In sight of England, and her Lordly Peers,
  Deliver up my Title in the Queen
  To your most gracious hands, that are the substance
  Of that great shadow I did represent:
  The happiest gift, that ever Marquess gave,
  The fairest Queen, that ever King receiv'd.
KING: Suffolk arise. Welcome Queen Margaret,
  I can express no kinder sign of love
  Than this kind kiss: O Lord, that lends me life,
  Lend me a heart replete with thankfulness:
  For thou hast given me in this beauteous face
  A world of earthly blessings to my soul,
  If sympathy of love unite our thoughts.
QUEEN: Great King of England, and my gracious Lord,

The mutual conference that my mind hath had,
By day, by night; waking, and in my dreams,
In Courtly company, or at my beads,
With you mine alder liefest Sovereign,
Makes me the bolder to salute my King,
With ruder terms, such as my wit affords,
And over-joy of heart doth minister.

KING: Her sight did ravish, but her grace in speech,
Her words yclad with wisdom's majesty,
Makes me from wondring, fall to weeping joys,
Such is the fulness of my heart's content.
Lords, with one cheerful voice, Welcome my Love.

All kneel: Long live Queen Margaret, England's happiness.

QUEEN: We thank you all.

Flourish.

SUFFOLK: My Lord Protector, so it please your Grace,
Here are the Articles of contracted peace,
Between our Sovereign, and the French King Charles,
For eighteen months concluded by consent.

GLOUCESTER (*reads*): Imprimis, *It is agreed between the French King Charles, and William de la Pole Marquess of Suffolk, Ambassador for Henry King of England, That the said Henry shall espouse the Lady Margaret, daughter unto Reignier King of Naples, Sicilia, and Jerusalem, and crown her Queen of England, ere the thirtieth of May next ensuing.*

Item, that the Duchy of Anjou, and the County of Maine, shall be released and delivered to the King her father.

KING: Uncle, how now?

GLOUCESTER: Pardon me gracious Lord,
Some sudden qualm hath struck me at the heart,
And dimm'd mine eyes, that I can read no further.

KING: Uncle of Winchester, I pray read on.

CARDINAL: Item, *It is further agreed between them, That the Duchies of Anjou and Maine, shall be released and delivered* over to the King her Father, and she sent over of the King of England's own proper cost and charges, without having any dowry.

KING: They please us well. Lord Marquess kneel down,
We here create thee the first Duke of Suffolk,
And gird thee with the sword. Cousin of York,
We here discharge your Grace from being Regent
I' th' parts of France, till term of eighteen months
Be full expir'd. Thanks Uncle Winchester,
Gloucester, York, Buckingham, Somerset,
Salisbury, and Warwick.
We thank you all for this great favour done,
In entertainment of my Princely Queen.
Come, let us in, and with all speed provide
To see her Coronation be perform'd.
Exeunt King, Queen, and Suffolk.
Manet the rest.

GLOUCESTER: Brave Peers of England, Pillars of the State,
To you Duke Humphrey must unload his grief:
Your grief, the common grief of all the Land.
What? did my brother Henry spend his youth,
His valour, coin, and people in the wars?
Did he so often lodge in open field:
In winter's cold, and summer's parching heat,
To conquer France, his true inheritance?
And did my brother Bedford toil his wits,
To keep by policy what Henry got:
Have you yourselves, Somerset, Buckingham,
Brave York, Salisbury, and victorious Warwick,
Receiv'd deep scars in France and Normandy:
Or hath mine Uncle Beaufort, and myself,
With all the learned Council of the Realm,
Studied so long, sat in the Council house,

Early and late, debating to and fro
How France and Frenchmen might be kept in awe,
And had his Highness in his infancy,
Crowned in Paris in despite of foes,
And shall these labours, and these honours die?
Shall Henry's conquest, Bedford's vigilance,
Your deeds of war, and all our counsel die?
O Peers of England, shameful is this League,
Fatal this marriage, cancelling your fame,
Blotting your names from Books of memory,
Racing the characters of your renown,
Defacing monuments of conquer'd France,
Undoing all as all had never been.

CARDINAL: Nephew, what means this passionate discourse?
This peroration with such circumstance:
For France, 'tis ours; and we will keep it still.

GLOUCESTER: Ay Uncle, we will keep it, if we can:
But now it is impossible we should.
Suffolk, the new made Duke that rules the roast,
Hath given the Duchy of Anjou and Maine,
Unto the poor King Reignier, whose large style
Agrees not with the leanness of his purse.

SALISBURY: Now, by the death of him that died for all,
These Counties were the keys of Normandy:
But wherefore weeps Warwick, my valiant son?

WARWICK: For grief that they are past recovery.
For were there hope to conquer them again,
My sword should shed hot blood, mine eyes no tears.
Anjou and Maine? Myself did win them both:
Those Provinces, these arms of mine did conquer,
And are the Cities that I got with wounds,
Deliver'd up again with peaceful words?
Mort Dieu.

YORK: For Suffolk's Duke, may he be suffocate,
    That dims the honour of this Warlike Isle:
    France should have torn and rent my very heart,
    Before I would have yielded to this League.
    I never read but England's Kings have had
    Large sums of gold, and dowries with their wives,
    And our King Henry gives away his own,
    To match with her that brings no vantages.

GLOUCESTER: A proper jest, and never heard before,
    That Suffolk should demand a whole fifteenth,
    For costs and charges in transporting her:
    She should have stay'd in France, and starv'd in France,
    Before –

CARDINAL: My Lord of Gloucester, now ye grow too hot,
    It was the pleasure of my Lord the King.

GLOUCESTER: My Lord of Winchester I know your mind.
    'Tis not my speeches that you do mislike:
    But 'tis my presence that doth trouble ye,
    Rancour will out, proud Prelate, in thy face
    I see thy fury: If I longer stay,
    We shall begin our ancient bickerings:
    Lordings, farewell, and say when I am gone,
    I prophesied, France will be lost ere long.
                  Exit Humphrey.

CARDINAL: So, there goes our Protector in a rage:
    'Tis known to you he is mine enemy:
    Nay more, an enemy unto you all,
    And no great friend, I fear me to the King;
    Consider Lords, he is the next of blood,
    And heir apparent to the English Crown:
    Had Henry got an Empire by his marriage,
    And all the wealthy Kingdoms of the West,
    There's reason he should be displeas'd at it:

Look to it Lords, let not his smoothing words
Bewitch your hearts, be wise and circumspect.
What though the common people favour him,
Calling him, *Humphrey the good Duke of Gloucester,*
Clapping their hands, and crying with loud voice,
Jesu maintain your Royal Excellence,
With God preserve the good Duke Humphrey:
I fear me Lords, for all this flattering gloss,
He will be found a dangerous Protector.

BUCKINGHAM: Why should he then protect our Sovereign?
　He being of age to govern of himself.
　Cousin of Somerset, join you with me,
　And all together, with the Duke of Suffolk,
　We'll quickly hoise Duke Humphrey from his seat.

CARDINAL: This weighty business will not brook delay,
　I'll to the Duke of Suffolk presently.

Exit Cardinal.

SOMERSET: Cousin of Buckingham, though Humphrey's pride
　And greatness of his place be grief to us,
　Yet let us watch the haughty Cardinal,
　His insolence is more intolerable
　Than all the Princes in the Land beside,
　If Gloucester be displac'd, he'll be Protector.

BUCKINGHAM: Or thou, or I Somerset will be Protectors,
　Despite Duke Humphrey, or the Cardinal.

Exeunt Buckingham and Somerset.

SALISBURY: Pride went before, Ambition follows him.
　While these do labour for their own preferment,
　Behoves it us to labour for the Realm.
　I never saw but Humphrey Duke of Gloucester,
　Did bear him like a noble Gentleman:
　Oft have I seen the haughty Cardinal,

More like a soldier than a man o' th' Church,
As stout and proud as he were Lord of all,
Swear like a ruffian, and demean himself
Unlike the Ruler of a Common-weal.
Warwick my son, the comfort of my age,
Thy deeds, thy plainness, and thy house-keeping,
Hath won the greatest favour of the Commons,
Excepting none but good Duke Humphrey.
And Brother York, thy acts in Ireland,
In bringing them to civil discipline:
Thy late exploits done in the heart of France,
When thou wert Regent for our Sovereign,
Have made thee fear'd and honour'd of the people,
Join we together for the public good,
In what we can, to bridle and suppress
The pride of Suffolk, and the Cardinal,
With Somerset's and Buckingham's ambition,
And as we may, cherish Duke Humphrey's deeds,
While they do tend the profit of the Land.

WARWICK: So God help Warwick, as he loves the Land,
And common profit of his Country.

YORK: And so says York,
For he hath greatest cause.

SALISBURY: Then let's make haste away,
And look unto the main.

WARWICK: Unto the main?
Oh Father, Maine is lost,
That Maine which by main force Warwick did win,
And would have kept, so long as breath did last:
Main-chance father you meant, but I meant Maine,
Which I will win from France, or else be slain.

Exeunt Warwick and Salisbury.
Manet York.

YORK: Anjou and Maine are given to the French,

Paris is lost, the state of Normandy
Stands on a tickle point, now they are gone:
Suffolk concluded on the Articles,
The Peers agreed, and Henry was well pleas'd,
To change two Dukedoms for a Duke's fair daughter.
I cannot blame them all, what is 't to them?
'Tis thine they give away, and not their own.
Pirates may make cheap pennyworths of their pillage,
And purchase friends, and give to courtezans,
Still revelling like Lords till all be gone,
While as the silly owner of the goods
Weeps over them, and wrings his hapless hands,
And shakes his head, and trembling stands aloof,
While all is shar'd, and all is borne away,
Ready to starve, and dare not touch his own.
So York must sit, and fret, and bite his tongue,
While his own lands are bargain'd for, and sold:
Methinks the Realms of England, France, and Ireland,
Bear that proportion to my flesh and blood,
As did the fatal brand Althaea burnt,
Unto the Prince's heart of Calydon.
Anjou and Maine both given unto the French?
Cold news for me: for I had hope of France,
Even as I have of fertile England's soil.
A day will come, when York shall claim his own,
And therefore I will take the Nevils' parts,
And make a show of love to proud Duke Humphrey,
And when I spy advantage, claim the Crown,
For that 's the golden mark I seek to hit:
Nor shall proud Lancaster usurp my right,
Nor hold the Sceptre in his childish fist,
Nor wear the Diadem upon his head,
Whose church-like humours fits not for a Crown.
Then York be still awhile, till time do serve:

Watch thou, and wake when others be asleep,
To pry into the secrets of the State,
Till Henry surfeiting in joys of love,
With his new Bride, and England's dear bought Queen,
And Humphrey with the Peers be fall'n at jars:
Then will I raise aloft the milk-white Rose,
With whose sweet smell the air shall be perfum'd,
And in my standard bear the arms of York,
To grapple with the house of Lancaster,
And force perforce I'll make him yield the Crown,
Whose bookish rule, hath pull'd fair England down.
Exit York.

I. 2

Enter Duke Humphrey and his wife Eleanor.

ELEANOR: Why droops my Lord like over-ripen'd corn,
Hanging the head at Ceres' plenteous load?
Why doth the Great Duke Humphrey knit his brows,
As frowning at the favours of the world?
Why are thine eyes fix'd to the sullen earth,
Gazing on that which seems to dim thy sight?
What seest thou there? King Henry's Diadem,
Enchas'd with all the honours of the world?
If so, gaze on, and grovel on thy face,
Until thy head be circled with the same.
Put forth thy hand, reach at the glorious gold.
What, is't too short? I'll lengthen it with mine,
And having both together heav'd it up,
We'll both together lift our heads to heaven,
And never more abase our sight so low,
As to vouchsafe one glance unto the ground.
GLOUCESTER: O Nell, sweet Nell, if thou dost love thy
    Lord,

Banish the canker of ambitious thoughts:
And may that thought, when I imagine ill
Against my King and Nephew, virtuous Henry,
Be my last breathing in this mortal world.
My troublous dreams this night, doth make me sad.

ELEANOR: What dream'd my Lord, tell me, and I 'll requite it
With sweet rehearsal of my morning's dream?

GLOUCESTER: Methought this staff mine office-badge in Court
Was broke in twain; by whom, I have forgot,
But as I think, it was by th' Cardinal,
And on the pieces of the broken wand
Were plac'd the heads of Edmund Duke of Somerset,
And William de la Pole first Duke of Suffolk.
This was my dream, what it doth bode God knows.

ELEANOR: Tut, this was nothing but an argument,
That he that breaks a stick of Gloucester's grove,
Shall lose his head for his presumption.
But list to me my Humphrey, my sweet Duke:
Methought I sat in Seat of Majesty,
In the Cathedral Church of Westminster,
And in that Chair where Kings and Queens are crown'd,
Where Henry and Dame Margaret kneel'd to me,
And on my head did set the Diadem.

GLOUCESTER: Nay Eleanor, then must I chide outright:
Presumptuous Dame, ill-nurtur'd Eleanor,
Art thou not second Woman in the Realm?
And the Protector's wife belov'd of him?
Hast thou not worldly pleasure at command,
Above the reach or compass of thy thought?
And wilt thou still be hammering treachery,
To tumble down thy husband, and thyself,
From top of Honour, to Disgrace's feet?

Away from me, and let me hear no more.

ELEANOR: What, what, my Lord? Are you so choleric
With Eleanor, for telling but her dream?
Next time I'll keep my dream unto myself,
And not be check'd.

GLOUCESTER: Nay be not angry, I am pleas'd again
Enter Messenger.

MESSENGER: My Lord Protector, 'tis his Highness'
pleasure,
You do prepare to ride unto S. Alban's,
Whereas the King and Queen do mean to hawk.

GLOUCESTER: I go. Come Nell thou wilt ride with us?

ELEANOR: Yes my good Lord, I'll follow presently.
Exeunt Gloucester and Messenger.

Follow I must, I cannot go before,
While Gloucester bears this base and humble mind.
Were I a man, a Duke, and next of blood,
I would remove these tedious stumbling blocks,
And smooth my way upon their headless necks.
And being a woman, I will not be slack
To play my part in Fortune's Pageant.
Where are you there? Sir John; nay fear not man,
We are alone, here's none but thee, and I.
Enter Hume.

HUME: Jesus preserve your Royal Majesty.

ELEANOR: What say'st thou? Majesty: I am but Grace.

HUME: But by the grace of God, and Hume's advice,
Your Grace's title shall be multiplied.

ELEANOR: What say'st thou man? Hast thou as yet
conferr'd
With Margery Jourdain the cunning Witch,
With Roger Bolingbroke the Conjurer?
And will they undertake to do me good?

HUME: This they have promised to show your Highness

A spirit rais'd from depth of under ground,
That shall make answer to such questions,
As by your Grace shall be propounded him.
ELEANOR: It is enough, I'll think upon the questions:
When from Saint Alban's we do make return,
We'll see these things effected to the full.
Here Hume, take this reward, make merry man
With thy confederates in this weighty cause.

Exit Eleanor.

HUME: Hume must make merry with the Duchess' gold:
Marry and shall: but how now, Sir John Hume?
Seal up your lips, and give no words but Mum,
The business asketh silent secrecy.
Dame Eleanor gives gold, to bring the Witch:
Gold cannot come amiss, were she a devil.
Yet have I gold flies from another coast:
I dare not say, from the rich Cardinal,
And from the great and new-made Duke of Suffolk;
Yet I do find it so: for to be plain,
They (knowing Dame Eleanor's aspiring humour)
Have hired me to undermine the Duchess,
And buzz these conjurations in her brain.
They say, A crafty knave does need no broker,
Yet am I Suffolk and the Cardinal's broker.
Hume, if you take not heed, you shall go near
To call them both a pair of crafty knaves.
Well, so it stands; and thus I fear at last,
Hume's knavery will be the Duchess' wrack,
And her attainture, will be Humphrey's fall:
Sort how it will, I shall have gold for all.

Exit.

I. 3

*Enter three or four Petitioners, Peter the Armourer's
Man being one.*

1 PETITIONER: My Masters, let 's stand close, my Lord
Protector will come this way by and by, and then we
may deliver our supplications in the quill.

2 PETITIONER: Marry the Lord protect him, for he 's a
good man, Jesu bless him.

Enter Suffolk, and Queen.

PETER: Here a' comes methinks, and the Queen with him:
I 'll be the first sure.

2 PETITIONER: Come back fool, this is the Duke of
Suffolk, and not my Lord Protector.

SUFFOLK: How now fellow: would'st any thing with me?

1 PETITIONER: I pray my Lord pardon me, I took ye for
my Lord Protector.

QUEEN: To my Lord Protector? Are your supplications to
his Lordship? Let me see them: what is thine?

1 PETITIONER: Mine is, and 't please your Grace, against
John Goodman, my Lord Cardinal's Man, for keeping
my house, and lands, and wife and all, from me.

SUFFOLK: Thy wife too? that 's some wrong indeed.
What 's yours? What 's here? Against the Duke of
Suffolk, for enclosing the Commons of Melford. How
now, Sir Knave?

2 PETITIONER: Alas Sir, I am but a poor petitioner of our
whole township.

PETER: Against my Master Thomas Horner, for saying,
That the Duke of York was rightful Heir to the
Crown.

QUEEN: What say'st thou? Did the Duke of York say, he
was rightful Heir to the Crown?

PETER: That my Mistress was? No forsooth: my Master
said, That he was, and that the King was an Usurper.

SUFFOLK: Who is there?

Enter Servant.

Take this fellow in, and send for his Master with a
pursuivant presently: we 'll hear more of your matter
before the King.

Exit Servant with Peter.

QUEEN: And as for you that love to be protected
Under the wings of our Protector's Grace,
Begin your suits anew, and sue to him.

Tear the supplication.

Away, base cullions: Suffolk let them go.

ALL: Come, let 's be gone.

Exeunt.

QUEEN: My Lord of Suffolk, say, is this the guise?
Is this the fashions in the Court of England?
Is this the Government of Britain's Isle?
And this the Royalty of Albion's King?
What, shall King Henry be a pupil still,
Under the surly Gloucester's governance?
Am I a Queen in Title and in Style,
And must be made a subject to a Duke?
I tell thee Pole, when in the City Tours
Thou ran'st a tilt in honour of my love,
And stol'st away the Ladies' hearts of France;
I thought King Henry had resembled thee,
In courage, courtship, and proportion:
But all his mind is bent to holiness,
To number *Ave-Maries* on his beads:
His champions, are the Prophets and Apostles,
His weapons, holy saws of sacred Writ,
His study is his Tilt-yard, and his loves
Are brazen images of Canonized Saints.

I would the College of the Cardinals
    Would choose him Pope, and carry him to Rome,
    And set the Triple Crown upon his head;
    That were a State fit for his Holiness.
SUFFOLK: Madam be patient: as I was cause
    Your Highness came to England, so will I
    In England work your Grace's full content.
QUEEN: Beside the haughty Protector, have we Beaufort,
    The imperious Churchman; Somerset, Buckingham,
    And grumbling York: and not the least of these,
    But can do more in England than the King.
SUFFOLK: And he of these, that can do most of all,
    Cannot do more in England than the Nevils:
    Salisbury and Warwick are no simple Peers.
QUEEN: Not all these Lords do vex me half so much,
    As that proud Dame, the Lord Protector's Wife:
    She sweeps it through the Court with troops of Ladies,
    More like an Empress, than Duke Humphrey's Wife:
    Strangers in Court, do take her for the Queen:
    She bears a Duke's revenues on her back,
    And in her heart she scorns our poverty:
    Shall I not live to be aveng'd on her?
    Contemptuous base-born callet as she is,
    She vaunted 'mongst her minions t' other day,
    The very train of her worst wearing gown,
    Was better worth than all my Father's lands,
    Till Suffolk gave two Dukedoms for his Daughter.
SUFFOLK: Madame, myself have lim'd a bush for her,
    And plac'd a quire of such enticing birds,
    That she will light to listen to the lays,
    And never mount to trouble you again.
    So let her rest: and Madam list to me,
    For I am bold to counsel you in this;
    Although we fancy not the Cardinal,

Yet must we join with him and with the Lords,
Till we have brought Duke Humphrey in disgrace.
As for the Duke of York, this late complaint
Will make but little for his benefit:
So one by one we'll weed them all at last,
And you yourself shall steer the happy helm.

Exit.

Sound a Sennet.

*Enter the King, Duke Humphrey, Cardinal,
Buckingham, York, Somerset, Salisbury, Warwick,
and the Duchess.*

KING: For my part, noble Lords, I care not which,
Or Somerset, or York, all's one to me.

YORK: If York have ill demean'd himself in France,
Then let him be denay'd the Regentship.

SOMERSET: If Somerset be unworthy of the place,
Let York be Regent, I will yield to him.

WARWICK: Whether your Grace be worthy, yea or no,
Dispute not that, York is the worthier.

CARDINAL: Ambitious Warwick, let thy betters speak.

WARWICK: The Cardinal's not my better in the field.

BUCKINGHAM: All in this presence are thy betters, Warwick.

WARWICK: Warwick may live to be the best of all.

SALISBURY: Peace Son, and show some reason Buckingham,
Why Somerset should be preferr'd in this?

QUEEN: Because the King forsooth will have it so.

GLOUCESTER: Madame, the King is old enough himself
To give his censure: These are no women's matters.

QUEEN: If he be old enough, what needs your Grace
To be Protector of his Excellence?

GLOUCESTER: Madam, I am Protector of the Realm,
And at his pleasure will resign my place.

SUFFOLK: Resign it then, and leave thine insolence.
  Since thou wert King; as who is King, but thou?
  The Common-wealth hath daily run to wrack,
  The Dolphin hath prevail'd beyond the Seas,
  And all the Peers and Nobles of the Realm
  Have been as bondmen to thy Sovereignty.
CARDINAL: The Commons hast thou rack'd, the Clergy's
    bags
  Are lank and lean with thy extortions.
SOMERSET: Thy sumptuous buildings, and thy Wife's
    attire
  Have cost a mass of public Treasury.
BUCKINGHAM: Thy cruelty in execution
  Upon offenders, hath exceeded Law,
  And left thee to the mercy of the Law.
QUEEN: Thy sale of offices and Towns in France,
  If they were known, as the suspect is great,
  Would make thee quickly hop without thy head.
                    Exit Gloucester.
  Give me my fan: what, minion, can ye not?
            She gives the Duchess a box on the ear.
  I cry you mercy, Madam: was it you?
ELEANOR: Was 't I? yea, I it was, proud Frenchwoman:
  Could I come near your beauty with my nails,
  I could set my ten Commandments in your face.
KING: Sweet Aunt be quiet, 'twas against her will.
ELEANOR: Against her will, good King? look to 't in time,
  She 'll hamper thee, and dandle thee like a baby:
  Though in this place most Master wear no breeches,
  She shall not strike Dame Eleanor unreveng'd.
                    Exit Eleanor.
BUCKINGHAM: Lord Cardinal, I will follow Eleanor,
  And listen after Humphrey, how he proceeds:
  She 's tickled now, her fume needs no spurs,

She 'll gallop far enough to her destruction.

Exit Buckingham.

Enter Gloucester.

GLOUCESTER: Now Lords, my choler being over-blown,
　With walking once about the quadrangle,
　I come to talk of Common-wealth affairs.
　As for your spiteful false objections,
　Prove them, and I lie open to the Law:
　But God in mercy so deal with my soul,
　As I in duty love my King and Country.
　But to the matter that we have in hand:
　I say, my Sovereign, York is meetest man
　To be your Regent in the Realm of France.

SUFFOLK: Before we make election, give me leave
　To show some reason, of no little force,
　That York is most unmeet of any man.

YORK: I 'll tell thee, Suffolk, why I am unmeet.
　First, for I cannot flatter thee in pride:
　Next, if I be appointed for the place,
　My Lord of Somerset will keep me here,
　Without discharge, money, or furniture,
　Till France be won into the Dolphin's hands:
　Last time I danc'd attendance on his will,
　Till Paris was beseig'd, famish'd, and lost.

WARWICK: That can I witness, and a fouler fact
　Did never Traitor in the Land commit.

SUFFOLK: Peace headstrong Warwick.

WARWICK: Image of Pride, why should I hold my peace?

Enter Armourer and his Man Peter.

SUFFOLK: Because here is a man accus'd of treason,
　Pray God the Duke of York excuse himself.

YORK: Doth any one accuse York for a Traitor?

KING: What mean'st thou, Suffolk? tell me, what are
　these?

SUFFOLK: Please it your Majesty, this is the man
  That doth accuse his Master of high treason;
  His words were these: That Richard, Duke of York,
  Was rightful Heir unto the English Crown,
  And that your Majesty was an Usurper.
KING: Say man, were these thy words?
ARMOURER: And 't shall please your Majesty, I never said
  nor thought any such matter: God is my witness, I am
  falsely accus'd by the villain.
PETER: By these ten bones, my Lords, he did speak them
  to me in the garret one night, as we were scouring my
  Lord of York's armour.
YORK: Base dunghill villain, and mechanical,
  I'll have thy head for this thy Traitor's speech.
  I do beseech your Royal Majesty,
  Let him have all the rigour of the Law.
ARMOURER: Alas, my Lord, hang me if ever I spake the
  words: my accuser is my 'prentice, and when I did cor-
  rect him for his fault the other day, he did vow upon
  his knees he would be even with me: I have good
  witness of this; therefore I beseech your Majesty, do not
  cast away an honest man for a villain's accusation.
KING: Uncle, what shall we say to this in law?
GLOUCESTER: This doom, my Lord, if I may judge:
  Let Somerset be Regent o'er the French,
  Because in York this breeds suspicion;
  And let these have a day appointed them
  For single combat, in convenient place,
  For he hath witness of his servant's malice:
  This is the Law, and this Duke Humphrey's doom.
SOMERSET: I humbly thank your Royal Majesty.
ARMOURER: And I accept the combat willingly.
PETER: Alas, my Lord, I cannot fight; for God's sake pity
  my case: the spite of man prevaileth against me. O Lord

have mercy upon me, I shall never be able to fight a
blow: O Lord my heart.

GLOUCESTER: Sirrah, or you must fight, or else be hang'd.

KING: Away with them to prison: and the day of combat,
shall be the last of the next month. Come Somerset,
we 'll see thee sent away.

Flourish. Exeunt.

I. 4

*Enter the Witch, the two Priests, Hume and
Southwell, and Bolingbroke.*

HUME: Come my Masters, the Duchess I tell you expects
performance of your promises.

BOLINGBROKE: Master Hume, we are therefore provided:
will her Ladyship behold and hear our exorcisms?

HUME: Ay, what else? fear you not her courage.

BOLINGBROKE: I have heard her reported to be a Woman
of an invincible spirit: but it shall be convenient, Master
Hume, that you be by her aloft, while we be busy
below; and so I pray you go in God's Name, and leave
us.

Exit Hume.

Mother Jordan, be you prostrate, and grovel on the
earth; John Southwell read you, and let us to our work.

Enter Eleanor aloft.

ELEANOR: Well said my Masters, and welcome all: To
this gear, the sooner the better.

BOLINGBROKE: Patience, good Lady, Wizards know their
times:

Deep night, dark night, the silent of the night,

The time of night when Troy was set on fire,

The time when screech-owls cry, and ban-dogs howl,

And spirits walk, and ghosts break up their graves;

That time best fits the work we have in hand.

Madame, sit you, and fear not: whom we raise,

We will make fast within a hallow'd verge.

> *Here do the ceremonies belonging, and make the circle,*
> *Bolingbroke or Southwell reads,* Conjuro te, &c. *It*
> *thunders and lightens terribly; then the Spirit riseth.*

SPIRIT: Adsum.

JORDAN: Asmath, by the eternal God,

Whose name and power thou tremblest at,

Answer that I shall ask: for till thou speak,

Thou shalt not pass from hence.

SPIRIT: Ask what thou wilt; that I had said, and done.

BOLINGBROKE: First of the King: What shall of him
become?

SPIRIT: The Duke yet lives, that Henry shall depose;

But him outlive, and die a violent death.

BOLINGBROKE: What fates await the Duke of Suffolk?

SPIRIT: By water shall he die, and take his end.

BOLINGBROKE: What shall befall the Duke of Somerset?

SPIRIT: Let him shun Castles,

Safer shall he be upon the sandy plains,

Than where Castles mounted stand.

Have done, for more I hardly can endure.

BOLINGBROKE: Descend to darkness, and the burning
Lake:

False Fiend avoid.

> *Thunder and lightning. Exit Spirit.*
> *Enter the Duke of York, and the Duke of Buckingham*
> *with their Guard, and break in.*

YORK: Lay hands upon these traitors, and their trash:

Beldam I think we watch'd you at an inch.

What Madame, are you there? the King and Common-
weal

Are deeply indebted for this piece of pains;

My Lord Protector will, I doubt it not,
See you well guerdon'd for these good deserts.

ELEANOR: Not half so bad as thine to England's King,
Injurious Duke, that threatest where 's no cause.

BUCKINGHAM: True Madame, none at all: what call you this?
Away with them, let them be clapp'd up close,
And kept asunder: you Madame shall with us.
Stafford take her to thee.
We 'll see your trinkets here all forthcoming.
All away.

Exeunt except York and Buckingham.

YORK: Lord Buckingham, methinks you watch'd her well:
A pretty plot, well chosen to build upon.
Now pray my Lord, let 's see the Devil's Writ.
What have we here?

Reads.

The Duke yet lives, that Henry shall depose:
But him outlive, and die a violent death.
Why this is just, *Aio Aeacida Romanos vincere posse.*
Well, to the rest:
Tell me what fate awaits the Duke of Suffolk?
By water shall he die, and take his end.
What shall betide the Duke of Somerset?
Let him shun Castles;
Safer shall he be upon the sandy plains,
Than where Castles mounted stand.
Come, come, my Lords,
These oracles are hardly attain'd,
And hardly understood.
The King is now in progress towards Saint Alban's,
With him, the Husband of this lovely Lady:
Thither go these news,

As fast as horse can carry them:
A sorry breakfast for my Lord Protector.

BUCKINGHAM: Your Grace shall give me leave, my Lord
of York,

To be the post, in hope of his reward.

YORK: At your pleasure, my good Lord.
Who 's within there, ho?

Enter a Serving-man.

Invite my Lords of Salisbury and Warwick
To sup with me tomorrow night. Away.

Exeunt.

II. 1

*Enter the King, Queen, Protector, Cardinal, and
Suffolk, with Falconers hallowing.*

QUEEN: Believe me Lords, for flying at the brook,
I saw not better sport these seven years' day:
Yet by your leave, the wind was very high,
And ten to one, old Joan had not gone out.

KING: But what a point, my Lord, your falcon made,
And what a pitch she flew above the rest:
To see how God in all his creatures works,
Yea man and birds are fain of climbing high.

SUFFOLK: No marvel, and it like your Majesty,
My Lord Protector's hawks do tower so well,
They know their Master loves to be aloft,
And bears his thoughts above his falcon's pitch.

GLOUCESTER: My Lord, 'tis but a base ignoble mind,
That mounts no higher than a bird can soar.

CARDINAL: I thought as much, he would be above the
clouds.

GLOUCESTER: Ay my Lord Cardinal, how think you by
that?

Were it not good your Grace could fly to Heaven?

KING: The Treasury of everlasting Joy.

CARDINAL: Thy Heaven is on Earth, thine eyes and
    thoughts
Beat on a Crown, the treasure of thy heart,
Pernicious Protector, dangerous Peer,
That smooth'st it so with King and Common-weal.

GLOUCESTER: What, Cardinal?
Is your priesthood grown peremptory?
    Tantaene animis caelestibus irae, Churchmen so hot?
Good Uncle hide such malice:
With such holiness can you do it?

SUFFOLK: No malice Sir, no more than well becomes
So good a quarrel, and so bad a Peer.

GLOUCESTER: As who, my Lord?

SUFFOLK: Why, as you, my Lord,
An 't like your Lordly Lord's Protectorship.

GLOUCESTER: Why Suffolk, England knows thine inso-
    lence.

QUEEN: And thy ambition, Gloucester.

KING: I prithee peace, good Queen,
And whet not on these furious Peers,
For blessed are the Peacemakers on Earth.

CARDINAL: Let me be blessed for the peace I make
Against this proud Protector with my sword.

GLOUCESTER: Faith holy Uncle, would't were come to
    that.

CARDINAL: Marry, when thou dar'st.

GLOUCESTER: Make up no factious numbers for the
    matter,
In thine own person answer thy abuse.

CARDINAL: Ay, where thou dar'st not peep:
And if thou dar'st, this evening,
On the east side of the Grove.

KING: How now, my Lords?

CARDINAL: Believe me, Cousin Gloucester,
Had not your man put up the fowl so suddenly,
We had had more sport.
Come with thy two-hand sword.

GLOUCESTER: True Uncle, are ye advis'd?
The east side of the Grove:
Cardinal, I am with you.

KING: Why how now, Uncle Gloucester?

GLOUCESTER: Talking of hawking; nothing else, my
Lord.
Now by God's Mother, Priest,
I 'll shave your crown for this,
Or all my fence shall fail.

CARDINAL: *Medice teipsum,* Protector see to 't well, protect yourself.

KING: The winds grow high,
So do your stomachs, Lords:
How irksome is this music to my heart?
When such strings jar, what hope of harmony?
I pray my Lords let me compound this strife.
Enter one crying a Miracle.

GLOUCESTER: What means this noise?
Fellow, what Miracle dost thou proclaim?

ONE: A Miracle, a Miracle.

SUFFOLK: Come to the King, and tell him what Miracle.

ONE: Forsooth, a blind man at Saint Alban's Shrine,
Within this half hour hath receiv'd his sight,
A man that ne'er saw in his life before.

KING: Now God be prais'd, that to believing souls
Gives Light in Darkness, Comfort in Despair.
*Enter the Mayor of Saint Alban's and his
Brethren, bearing the man between two in a chair.*

CARDINAL: Here comes the townsmen, on procession,

To present your Highness with the man.

KING: Great is his comfort in this Earthly Vale,
Although by his sight his sin be multiplied.

GLOUCESTER: Stand by, my Masters, bring him near the King,
His Highness' pleasure is to talk with him.

KING: Good-fellow, tell us here the circumstance,
That we for thee may glorify the Lord.
What, hast thou been long blind, and now restor'd?

SIMPCOX: Born blind, and 't please your Grace.

WIFE: Ay indeed was he.

SUFFOLK: What woman is this?

WIFE: His wife, and 't like your Worship.

GLOUCESTER: Hadst thou been his Mother, thou could'st have better told.

KING: Where wert thou born?

SIMPCOX: At Berwick in the North, and 't like your Grace.

KING: Poor soul,
God's goodness hath been great to thee:
Let never day nor night unhallow'd pass,
But still remember what the Lord hath done.

QUEEN: Tell me, good fellow,
Cam'st thou here by chance, or of devotion,
To this holy Shrine?

SIMPCOX: God knows of pure devotion,
Being call'd a hundred times, and oftener,
In my sleep, by good Saint Alban:
Who said; Simon, come; come offer at my Shrine,
And I will help thee.

WIFE: Most true, forsooth:
And many time and oft myself have heard a Voice,
To call him so.

CARDINAL: What, art thou lame?

SIMPCOX: Ay, God Almighty help me.

SUFFOLK: How cam'st thou so?

SIMPCOX: A fall off of a tree.

WIFE: A plum-tree, Master.

GLOUCESTER: How long hast thou been blind?

SIMPCOX: O born so, Master.

GLOUCESTER: What, and would'st climb a tree?

SIMPCOX: But that in all my life, when I was a youth.

WIFE: Too true, and bought his climbing very dear.

GLOUCESTER: 'Mass, thou lov'st plums well, that would'st venture so.

SIMPCOX: Alas, good Master, my Wife desir'd some damsons, and made me climb, with danger of my life.

GLOUCESTER: A subtle Knave, but yet it shall not serve: Let me see thine eyes; wink now, now open them, In my opinion, yet thou seest not well.

SIMPCOX: Yes Master, clear as day, I thank God and Saint Alban's.

GLOUCESTER: Say'st thou me so: what colour is this cloak of?

SIMPCOX: Red Master, red as blood.

GLOUCESTER: Why that's well said: What colour is my gown of?

SIMPCOX: Black forsooth, coal-black, as jet.

KING: Why then, thou know'st what colour jet is of?

SUFFOLK: And yet I think, jet did he never see.

GLOUCESTER: But cloaks and gowns, before this day, a many.

WIFE: Never before this day, in all his life.

GLOUCESTER: Tell me sirrah, what's my name?

SIMPCOX: Alas Master, I know not.

GLOUCESTER: What's his name?

SIMPCOX: I know not.

GLOUCESTER: Nor his?

F

SIMPCOX: No indeed, Master.

GLOUCESTER: What's thine own name?

SIMPCOX: Saunder Simpcox, and if it please you, Master.

GLOUCESTER: Then Saunder, sit there, the lying'st knave in Christendom. If thou hadst been born blind, thou might'st as well have known all our names, as thus to name the several colours we do wear. Sight may distinguish of colours: but suddenly to nominate them all, it is impossible. My Lords, Saint Alban here hath done a Miracle; and would ye not think it cunning to be great, that could restore this cripple to his legs again?

SIMPCOX: O Master, that you could!

GLOUCESTER: My Masters of Saint Alban's, have you not Beadles in your Town, and things called whips?

MAYOR: Yes, my Lord, if it please your Grace.

GLOUCESTER: Then send for one presently.

MAYOR: Sirrah, go fetch the Beadle hither straight.

Exit an Attendant.

GLOUCESTER: Now fetch me a stool hither by and by. Now sirrah, if you mean to save yourself from whipping, leap me over this stool, and run away.

SIMPCOX: Alas Master, I am not able to stand alone: You go about to torture me in vain.

Enter a Beadle with whips.

GLOUCESTER: Well Sir, we must have you find your legs. Sirrah Beadle, whip him till he leap over that same stool.

BEADLE: I will, my Lord.

Come on sirrah, off with your doublet, quickly.

SIMPCOX: Alas Master, what shall I do? I am not able to stand.

After the Beadle hath hit him once, he leaps over the stool, and runs away: and they follow, and cry, A Miracle.

KING: O God, seest Thou this, and bearest so long?

QUEEN: It made me laugh, to see the villain run.

GLOUCESTER: Follow the knave, and take this drab away.

WIFE: Alas Sir, we did it for pure need.

GLOUCESTER: Let them be whipp'd through every Market Town, till they come to Berwick, from whence they came.

Exeunt Wife, Beadle, Mayor, &c.

CARDINAL: Duke Humphrey has done a miracle today.

SUFFOLK: True: made the lame to leap and fly away.

GLOUCESTER: But you have done more miracles than I: You made in a day, my Lord, whole Towns to fly.

Enter Buckingham.

KING: What tidings with our Cousin Buckingham?

BUCKINGHAM: Such as my heart doth tremble to unfold: A sort of naughty persons, lewdly bent Under the countenance and confederacy Of Lady Eleanor, the Protector's Wife, The ringleader and head of all this rout, Have practis'd dangerously against your State, Dealing with Witches and with Conjurers, Whom we have apprehended in the fact, Raising up wicked Spirits from under ground, Demanding of King Henry's life and death, And other of your Highness' Privy Council, As more at large your Grace shall understand.

CARDINAL: And so my Lord Protector, by this means Your Lady is forthcoming, yet at London. This news I think hath turn'd your weapon's edge; 'Tis like, my Lord, you will not keep your hour.

GLOUCESTER: Ambitious Church-man, leave to afflict my heart: Sorrow and grief have vanquish'd all my powers; And vanquish'd as I am, I yield to thee, Or to the meanest groom.

KING: O God, what mischiefs work the wicked ones?
　Heaping confusion on their own heads thereby.
QUEEN: Gloucester, see here the tainture of thy nest,
　And look thyself be faultless, thou wert best.
GLOUCESTER: Madame, for myself, to Heaven I do appeal,
　How I have lov'd my King, and Common-weal:
　And for my Wife, I know not how it stands,
　Sorry I am to hear what I have heard.
　Noble she is: but if she have forgot
　Honour and virtue, and convers'd with such,
　As like to pitch, defile Nobility;
　I banish her my bed, and company,
　And give her as a prey to Law and Shame,
　That hath dishonour'd Gloucester's honest name.
KING: Well, for this night we will repose us here:
　Tomorrow toward London, back again,
　To look into this business thoroughly,
　And call these foul offenders to their answers;
　And poise the cause in Justice' equal scales,
　Whose beam stands sure, whose rightful cause prevails.
Flourish. Exeunt.

II. 2

Enter York, Salisbury, and Warwick.

YORK: Now my good Lords of Salisbury and Warwick,
　Our simple supper ended, give me leave,
　In this close walk, to satisfy myself,
　In craving your opinion of my Title,
　Which is infallible, to England's Crown.
SALISBURY: My Lord, I long to hear it at full.
WARWICK: Sweet York begin: and if thy claim be good,
　The Nevils are thy subjects to command.

YORK: Then thus:
  Edward the Third, my Lords, had seven Sons:
  The first, Edward the Black Prince, Prince of Wales;
  The second, William of Hatfield; and the third,
  Lionel, Duke of Clarence; next to whom
  Was John of Gaunt, the Duke of Lancaster;
  The fifth, was Edmund Langley, Duke of York;
  The sixth, was Thomas of Woodstock, Duke of Glou-
    cester;
  William of Windsor was the seventh, and last.
  Edward the Black Prince died before his Father,
  And left behind him Richard, his only Son,
  Who after Edward the Third's death, reign'd as King,
  Till Henry Bolingbroke, Duke of Lancaster,
  The eldest Son and Heir of John of Gaunt,
  Crown'd by the name of Henry the Fourth,
  Seiz'd on the Realm, depos'd the rightful King,
  Sent his poor Queen to France, from whence she came,
  And him to Pomfret; where, as all you know,
  Harmless Richard was murther'd traitorously.
WARWICK: Father, the Duke hath told the truth;
  Thus got the House of Lancaster the Crown.
YORK: Which now they hold by force, and not by right:
  For Richard, the first Son's heir, being dead,
  The issue of the next Son should have reign'd.
SALISBURY: But William of Hatfield died without an
  Heir.
YORK: The third son, Duke of Clarence,
  From whose Line I claim the Crown,
  Had issue, Philipp, a daughter,
  Who married Edmund Mortimer, Earl of March:
  Edmund had issue, Roger, Earl of March;
  Roger had issue, Edmund, Anne, and Eleanor.
SALISBURY: This Edmund, in the reign of Bolingbroke,

As I have read, laid claim unto the Crown,
And but for Owen Glendower, had been King;
Who kept him in captivity, till he died.
But, to the rest.

YORK: His eldest Sister, Anne,
My Mother, being Heir unto the Crown,
Married Richard, Earl of Cambridge,
Who was son to Edmund Langley,
Edward the Third's fifth son's son;
By her I claim the Kingdom:
She was heir to Roger, Earl of March,
Who was the son of Edmund Mortimer,
Who married Philipp, sole Daughter
Unto Lionel, Duke of Clarence.
So, if the issue of the elder Son
Succeed before the younger, I am King.

WARWICK: What plain proceedings is more plain than
this?
Henry doth claim the Crown from John of Gaunt,
The fourth Son, York claims it from the third:
Till Lionel's Issue fails, his should not reign.
It fails not yet, but flourishes in thee,
And in thy Sons, fair slips of such a stock.
Then Father Salisbury, kneel we together,
And in this private plot be we the first,
That shall salute our rightful Sovereign
With honour of his Birth-right to the Crown.

BOTH: Long live our Sovereign Richard, England's King.

YORK: We thank you Lords:
But I am not your King, till I be crown'd,
And that my sword be stain'd
With heart-blood of the House of Lancaster:
And that's not suddenly to be perform'd,
But with advice and silent secrecy.

Do you as I do in these dangerous days,
Wink at the Duke of Suffolk's insolence,
At Beaufort's pride, at Somerset's ambition,
At Buckingham, and all the crew of them,
Till they have snar'd the Shepherd of the Flock,
That virtuous Prince, the good Duke Humphrey:
'Tis that they seek; and they, in seeking that,
Shall find their deaths, if York can prophesy.

SALISBURY: My Lord, break we off; we know your mind
  at full.

WARWICK: My heart assures me, that the Earl of Warwick
Shall one day make the Duke of York a King.

YORK: And Nevil, this I do assure myself,
  Richard shall live to make the Earl of Warwick
  The greatest man in England, but the King.
                    Exeunt.

II. 3

Sound Trumpets. Enter the King and State, with
Guard, to banish the Duchess.

KING: Stand forth, Dame Eleanor Cobham,
  Gloucester's wife:
  In sight of God, and us, your guilt is great,
  Receive the Sentence of the Law for sin,
  Such as by God's Book are adjudg'd to death.
  You four from hence to prison, back again;
  From thence, unto the place of execution:
  The Witch in Smithfield shall be burn'd to ashes,
  And you three shall be strangled on the gallows.
  You Madame, for you are more nobly born,
  Despoiled of your honour in your life,
  Shall, after three days' open penance done,

Live in your country here, in banishment,
With Sir John Stanley, in the Isle of Man.

ELEANOR: Welcome is banishment, welcome were my
death.

GLOUCESTER: Eleanor, the Law thou see'st hath judged
thee,
I cannot justify whom the Law condemns:

Exeunt Duchess and other prisoners, guarded.

Mine eyes are full of tears, my heart of grief.
Ah Humphrey, this dishonour in thine age,
Will bring thy head with sorrow to the ground.
I beseech your Majesty give me leave to go;
Sorrow would solace, and mine age would ease.

KING: Stay Humphrey, Duke of Gloucester,
Ere thou go, give up thy staff,
Henry will to himself Protector be,
And God shall be my hope, my stay, my guide,
And Lanthorn to my feet:
And go in peace, Humphrey, no less belov'd,
Than when thou wert Protector to thy King.

QUEEN: I see no reason, why a King of years
Should be to be protected like a child.
God and King Henry govern England's Realm:
Give up your staff, Sir, and the King his Realm.

GLOUCESTER: My staff? Here, noble Henry, is my staff:
As willingly do I the same resign,
As e'er thy Father Henry made it mine;
And even as willingly at thy feet I leave it,
As others would ambitiously receive it.
Farewell good King: when I am dead, and gone,
May honourable peace attend thy Throne.

Exit Gloucester.

QUEEN: Why now is Henry King, and Margaret Queen,
And Humphrey, Duke of Gloucester, scarce himself,

That bears so shrewd a maim: two pulls at once;
His Lady banish'd, and a limb lopp'd off.
This staff of honour raught, there let it stand,
Where it best fits to be, in Henry's hand.

SUFFOLK: Thus droops this lofty pine, and hangs his
    sprays,
Thus Eleanor's pride dies in her youngest days.

YORK: Lords, let him go. Please it your Majesty,
This is the day appointed for the combat,
And ready are the Appellant and Defendant,
The Armourer and his man, to enter the lists,
So please your Highness to behold the fight.

QUEEN: Ay, good my Lord: for purposely therefore
Left I the Court, to see this quarrel tried.

KING: A' God's Name see the lists and all things fit,
Here let them end it, and God defend the right.

YORK: I never saw a fellow worse bested,
Or more afraid to fight, than is the Appellant,
The servant of this Armourer, my Lords.

*Enter at one door the Armourer and his Neighbours, drinking
to him so much, that he is drunk; and he enters with a drum
before him, and his staff, with a sand-bag fastened to it:
and at the other door his Man, with a drum and sand-bag,
and Prentices drinking to him.*

1 NEIGHBOUR: Here Neighbour Horner, I drink to you in
a cup of sack: and fear not Neighbour, you shall do well
enough.

2 NEIGHBOUR: And here Neighbour, here 's a cup of
charneco.

3 NEIGHBOUR: And here 's a pot of good double beer
Neighbour: drink, and fear not your man.

ARMOURER: Let it come i' faith, and I 'll pledge you all,
and a fig for Peter.

1 PRENTICE: Here Peter, I drink to thee, and be not afraid.

2 PRENTICE: Be merry Peter, and fear not thy Master,
Fight for credit of the prentices.

PETER: I thank you all: drink, and pray for me, I pray you,
for I think I have taken my last draught in this world.
Here Robin, and if I die, I give thee my apron; and Will,
thou shalt have my hammer: and here Tom, take all the
money that I have. O Lord bless me, I pray God, for I
am never able to deal with my Master, he hath learnt so
much fence already.

SALISBURY: Come, leave your drinking, and fall to
blows.
Sirrah, what's thy name?

PETER: Peter forsooth.

SALISBURY: Peter? what more?

PETER: Thump.

SALISBURY: Thump? Then see thou thump thy Master
well.

ARMOURER: Masters, I am come hither as it were upon my
Man's instigation, to prove him a knave, and myself an
honest man: and touching the Duke of York, I will take
my death, I never meant him any ill, nor the King, nor
the Queen: and therefore Peter have at thee with a
downright blow.

YORK: Dispatch, this knave's tongue begins to double.
Sound Trumpets, alarum to the combatants.
They fight, and Peter strikes him down.

ARMOURER: Hold Peter, hold, I confess, I confess treason.
Dies.

YORK: Take away his weapon: Fellow thank God, and
the good wine in thy Master's way.

PETER: O God, have I overcome mine enemies in this
presence? O Peter, thou hast prevail'd in right.

KING: Go, take hence that traitor from our sight,
For by his death we do perceive his guilt,

And God in justice hath reveal'd to us
The truth and innocence of this poor fellow,
Which he had thought to have murther'd wrongfully.
Come fellow, follow us for thy reward.
> *Sound a flourish. Exeunt.*

II. 4

Enter Duke Humphrey and his Men in mourning cloaks.

GLOUCESTER: Thus sometimes hath the brightest day a
  cloud:
And after summer, evermore succeeds
Barren winter, with his wrathful nipping cold;
So cares and joys abound, as seasons fleet.
Sirs, what's 'a clock?

SERVING-MAN: Ten, my Lord.

GLOUCESTER: Ten is the hour that was appointed me,
To watch the coming of my punish'd Duchess:
Unneath may she endure the flinty streets,
To tread them with her tender-feeling feet.
Sweet Nell, ill can thy noble mind abrook
The abject people, gazing on thy face,
With envious looks laughing at thy shame,
That erst did follow thy proud chariot-wheels,
When thou didst ride in triumph through the streets.
But soft, I think she comes, and I'll prepare
My tear-stain'd eyes, to see her miseries.
> *Enter the Duchess in a white sheet, and a taper
> burning in her hand, with the Sheriff and Officers.*

SERVING-MAN: So please your Grace, we'll take her from
  the Sheriff.

GLOUCESTER: No, stir not for your lives, let her pass by.

ELEANOR: Come you, my Lord, to see my open shame?
Now thou dost penance too. Look how they gaze,

See how the giddy multitude do point,
And nod their heads, and throw their eyes on thee.
Ah Gloucester, hide thee from their hateful looks,
And in thy closet pent up, rue my shame,
And ban thine enemies, both mine and thine.

GLOUCESTER: Be patient, gentle Nell, forget this grief.

ELEANOR: Ah Gloucester, teach me to forget myself:
For whilst I think I am thy married Wife,
And thou a Prince, Protector of this Land;
Methinks I should not thus be led along,
Mail'd up in shame, with papers on my back,
And follow'd with a rabble, that rejoice
To see my tears, and hear my deep-fet groans.
The ruthless flint doth cut my tender feet,
And when I start, the envious people laugh,
And bid me be advised how I tread.
Ah Humphrey, can I bear this shameful yoke?
Trow'st thou, that e'er I'll look upon the World,
Or count them happy, that enjoy the Sun?
No: Dark shall be my Light, and Night my Day.
To think upon my pomp, shall be my Hell.
Sometime I'll say, I am Duke Humphrey's Wife,
And he a Prince, and Ruler of the Land:
Yet so he rul'd, and such a Prince he was,
As he stood by, whilst I, his forlorn Duchess,
Was made a wonder, and a pointing-stock
To every idle rascal follower.
But be thou mild, and blush not at my shame,
Nor stir at nothing, till the axe of death
Hang over thee, as sure it shortly will.
For Suffolk, he that can do all in all
With her, that hateth thee and hates us all,
And York, and impious Beaufort, that false Priest,
Have all lim'd bushes to betray thy wings,

And fly thou how thou canst, they'll tangle thee.
But fear not thou, until thy foot be snar'd,
Nor never seek prevention of thy foes.

GLOUCESTER: Ah Nell, forbear: thou aimest all awry.
I must offend, before I be attainted:
And had I twenty times so many foes,
And each of them had twenty times their power,
All these could not procure me any scathe,
So long as I am loyal, true, and crimeless.
Would'st have me rescue thee from this reproach?
Why yet thy scandal were not wip'd away,
But I in danger for the breach of Law.
Thy greatest help is quiet, gentle Nell:
I pray thee sort thy heart to patience,
These few days' wonder will be quickly worn.

Enter a Herald.

HERALD: I summon your Grace to his Majesty's Parliament,
Holden at Bury, the first of this next month.

GLOUCESTER: And my consent ne'er ask'd herein before?
This is close dealing. Well, I will be there.

Exit Herald.

My Nell, I take my leave: and Master Sheriff,
Let not her penance exceed the King's Commission.

SHERIFF: And't please your Grace, here my Commission stays:
And Sir John Stanley is appointed now,
To take her with him to the Isle of Man.

GLOUCESTER: Must you, Sir John, protect my Lady here?

STANLEY: So am I given in charge, may't please your Grace.

GLOUCESTER: Entreat her not the worse, in that I pray
You use her well: the World may laugh again,
And I may live to do you kindness, if you do it her.

And so Sir John, farewell.

ELEANOR: What, gone my Lord, and bid me not farewell?

GLOUCESTER: Witness my tears, I cannot stay to speak.

Exit Gloucester.

ELEANOR: Art thou gone too? all comfort go with thee,
For none abides with me: my joy, is death;
Death, at whose name I oft have been afear'd,
Because I wish'd this World's eternity.
Stanley, I prithee go, and take me hence,
I care not whither, for I beg no favour;
Only convey me where thou art commanded.

STANLEY: Why, Madame, that is to the Isle of Man,
There to be us'd according to your state.

ELEANOR: That's bad enough, for I am but reproach:
And shall I then be us'd reproachfully?

STANLEY: Like to a Duchess, and Duke Humphrey's
Lady,
According to that state you shall be us'd.

ELEANOR: Sheriff farewell, and better than I fare,
Although thou hast been conduct of my shame.

SHERIFF: It is my office, and Madame pardon me.

ELEANOR: Ay, ay, farewell, thy office is discharg'd:
Come Stanley, shall we go?

STANLEY: Madame, your penance done,
Throw off this sheet,
And go we to attire you for our journey.

ELEANOR: My shame will not be shifted with my sheet:
No, it will hang upon my richest robes,
And show itself, attire me how I can.
Go, lead the way, I long to see my prison.

Exeunt.

III. 1

Sound a Sennet. Enter King, Queen, Cardinal,
Suffolk, York, Buckingham, Salisbury, and
Warwick, to the Parliament.

KING: I muse my Lord of Gloucester is not come:
'Tis not his wont to be the hindmost man,
Whate'er occasion keeps him from us now.

QUEEN: Can you not see? or will ye not observe
The strangeness of his alter'd countenance?
With what a Majesty he bears himself,
How insolent of late he is become,
How proud, how peremptory, and unlike himself.
We know the time since he was mild and affable,
And if we did but glance a far-off look,
Immediately he was upon his knee,
That all the Court admir'd him for submission.
But meet him now, and be it in the morn,
When every one will give the time of day,
He knits his brow, and shows an angry eye,
And passeth by with stiff unbowed knee,
Disdaining duty that to us belongs.
Small curs are not regarded when they grin,
But great men tremble when the lion roars,
And Humphrey is no little man in England.
First note, that he is near you in descent,
And should you fall, he is the next will mount.
Me seemeth then, it is no policy,
Respecting what a rancorous mind he bears,
And his advantage following your decease,
That he should come about your Royal Person,
Or be admitted to your Highness' Council.
By flattery hath he won the Commons' hearts:

And when he please to make commotion,
'Tis to be fear'd they all will follow him.
Now 'tis the Spring, and weeds are shallow-rooted,
Suffer them now, and they 'll o'ergrow the garden,
And choke the herbs for want of husbandry.
The reverent care I bear unto my Lord,
Made me collect these dangers in the Duke.
If it be fond, call it a woman's fear:
Which fear, if better reasons can supplant,
I will subscribe, and say I wrong'd the Duke.
My Lord of Suffolk, Buckingham, and York,
Reprove my allegation, if you can,
Or else conclude my words effectual.

SUFFOLK: Well hath your Highness seen into this Duke:
And had I first been put to speak my mind,
I think I should have told your Grace's tale.
The Duchess, by his subornation,
Upon my life began her devilish practices:
Or if he were not privy to those faults,
Yet by reputing of his high descent,
As next the King, he was successive Heir,
And such high vaunts of his Nobility,
Did instigate the bedlam brain-sick Duchess,
By wicked means to frame our Sovereign's fall.
Smooth runs the water, where the brook is deep,
And in his simple show he harbours treason.
The fox barks not, when he would steal the lamb.
No, no, my Sovereign, Gloucester is a man
Unsounded yet, and full of deep deceit.

CARDINAL: Did he not, contrary to form of Law,
Devise strange deaths, for small offences done?

YORK: And did he not, in his Protectorship,
Levy great sums of money through the Realm,
For soldiers' pay in France, and never sent it?

By means whereof, the Towns each day revolted.

BUCKINGHAM: Tut, these are petty faults to faults unknown,

Which time will bring to light in smooth Duke Humphrey.

KING: My Lords at once: the care you have of us,

To mow down thorns that would annoy our foot,

Is worthy praise: but shall I speak my conscience,

Our Kinsman Gloucester is as innocent,

From meaning treason to our Royal Person,

As is the sucking lamb, or harmless dove:

The Duke is virtuous, mild, and too well given,

To dream on evil, or to work my downfall.

QUEEN: Ah what 's more dangerous, than this fond
affiance?

Seems he a dove? his feathers are but borrow'd,

For he 's disposed as the hateful raven.

Is he a lamb? his skin is surely lent him,

For he 's inclin'd as is the ravenous wolves.

Who cannot steal a shape, that means deceit?

Take heed, my Lord, the welfare of us all,

Hangs on the cutting short that fraudful man.

Enter Somerset.

SOMERSET: All health unto my gracious Sovereign.

KING: Welcome Lord Somerset: What news from France?

SOMERSET: That all your interest in those Territories,

Is utterly bereft you; all is lost.

KING: Cold news, Lord Somerset: but God's will be
done.

YORK: Cold news for me: for I had hope of France,

As firmly as I hope for fertile England.

Thus are my blossoms blasted in the bud,

And caterpillars eat my leaves away:

But I will remedy this gear ere long,

Or sell my title for a glorious grave.

Enter Gloucester.

GLOUCESTER: All happiness unto my Lord the King:
  Pardon, my Liege, that I have stay'd so long.

SUFFOLK: Nay Gloucester, know that thou art come too
    soon,
  Unless thou wert more loyal than thou art:
  I do arrest thee of High Treason here.

GLOUCESTER: Well Suffolk, thou shalt not see me blush,
  Nor change my countenance for this arrest:
  A heart unspotted, is not easily daunted.
  The purest spring is not so free from mud,
  As I am clear from treason to my Sovereign.
  Who can accuse me? wherein am I guilty?

YORK: 'Tis thought, my Lord,
  That you took bribes of France,
  And being Protector, stay'd the soldiers' pay,
  By means whereof, his Highness hath lost France.

GLOUCESTER: Is it but thought so?
  What are they that think it?
  I never robb'd the soldiers of their pay,
  Nor ever had one penny bribe from France.
  So help me God, as I have watch'd the night,
  Ay, night by night, in studying good for England.
  That doit that e'er I wrested from the King,
  Or any groat I hoarded to my use,
  Be brought against me at my trial day.
  No: many a pound of mine own proper store,
  Because I would not tax the needy Commons,
  Have I dispursed to the garrisons,
  And never ask'd for restitution.

CARDINAL: It serves you well, my Lord, to say so much.

GLOUCESTER: I say no more than truth, so help me God.

YORK: In your Protectorship, you did devise

Strange tortures for offenders, never heard of,
That England was defam'd by tyranny.

GLOUCESTER: Why 'tis well known, that whiles I was Protector,
Pity was all the fault that was in me:
For I should melt at an offender's tears,
And lowly words were ransom for their fault:
Unless it were a bloody murtherer,
Or foul felonious thief, that fleec'd poor passengers,
I never gave them condign punishment.
Murther indeed, that bloody sin, I tortur'd
Above the felon, or what trespass else.

SUFFOLK: My Lord, these faults are easy, quickly answer'd:
But mightier crimes are laid unto your charge,
Whereof you cannot easily purge yourself.
I do arrest you in his Highness' name,
And here commit you to my Lord Cardinal
To keep, until your further time of trial.

KING: My Lord of Gloucester, 'tis my special hope,
That you will clear yourself from all suspect,
My conscience tells me you are innocent.

GLOUCESTER: Ah gracious Lord, these days are dangerous:
Virtue is chok'd with foul ambition,
And charity chas'd hence by rancour's hand;
Foul subornation is predominant,
And equity exil'd your Highness' Land.
I know, their complot is to have my life:
And if my death might make this Island happy,
And prove the period of their tyranny,
I would expend it with all willingness.
But mine is made the Prologue to their Play:
For thousands more, that yet suspect no peril,

Will not conclude their plotted Tragedy.
Beaufort's red sparkling eyes blab his heart's malice,
And Suffolk's cloudy brow his stormy hate;
Sharp Buckingham unburthens with his tongue,
The envious load that lies upon his heart:
And dogged York, that reaches at the Moon,
Whose overweening arm I have pluck'd back,
By false accuse doth level at my life.
And you, my Sovereign Lady, with the rest,
Causeless have laid disgraces on my head,
And with your best endeavour have stirr'd up
My liefest Liege to be mine enemy:
Ay, all of you have laid your heads together,
Myself had notice of your conventicles,
And all to make away my guiltless life.
I shall not want false witness, to condemn me,
Nor store of treasons, to augment my guilt:
The ancient Proverb will be well effected:
A staff is quickly found to beat a dog.

CARDINAL: My Liege, his railing is intolerable.
If those that care to keep your Royal Person
From Treason's secret knife, and Traitors' rage,
Be thus upbraided, chid, and rated at,
And the offender granted scope of speech,
'Twill make them cool in zeal unto your Grace.

SUFFOLK: Hath he not twit our Sovereign Lady here
With ignominious words, though clerkly couch'd?
As if she had suborned some to swear
False allegations, to o'erthrow his state?

QUEEN: But I can give the loser leave to chide.

GLOUCESTER: Far truer spoke than meant: I lose indeed,
Beshrew the winners, for they play'd me false
And well such losers may have leave to speak.

BUCKINGHAM: He 'll wrest the sense, and hold us here all
    day.

    Lord Cardinal, he is your prisoner.

CARDINAL: Sirs, take away the Duke, and guard him sure.

GLOUCESTER: Ah, thus King Henry throws away his
    crutch,

    Before his legs be firm to bear his body.

    Thus is the Shepherd beaten from thy side,

    And wolves are gnarling, who shall gnaw thee first.

    Ah that my fear were false, ah that it were;

    For good King Henry, thy decay I fear.

Exit Gloucester.

KING: My Lords, what to your wisdoms seemeth best,

    Do, or undo, as if ourself were here.

QUEEN: What, will your Highness leave the Parliament?

KING: Ay Margaret: my heart is drown'd with grief,

    Whose flood begins to flow within mine eyes;

    My body round engirt with misery:

    For what 's more miserable than discontent?

    Ah Uncle Humphrey, in thy face I see

    The map of Honour, Truth, and Loyalty:

    And yet, good Humphrey, is the hour to come,

    That e'er I prov'd thee false, or fear'd thy faith.

    What louring star now envies thy estate?

    That these great Lords, and Margaret our Queen,

    Do seek subversion of thy harmless life.

    Thou never didst them wrong, nor no man wrong:

    And as the butcher takes away the calf,

    And binds the wretch, and beats it when it strays,

    Bearing it to the bloody slaughter-house;

    Even so remorseless have they borne him hence:

    And as the dam runs lowing up and down,

    Looking the way her harmless young one went,

    And can do nought but wail her darling's loss;

Even so myself bewails good Gloucester's case
With sad unhelpful tears, and with dimm'd eyes;
Look after him, and cannot do him good:
So mighty are his vowed enemies.
His fortunes I will weep, and 'twixt each groan,
Say, who's a traitor? Gloucester he is none.

Exeunt all but Queen, Cardinal Beaufort, Suffolk,
and York. Somerset remains apart.

QUEEN: Free Lords:
Cold snow melts with the sun's hot beams:
Henry, my Lord, is cold in great affairs,
Too full of foolish pity: and Gloucester's show
Beguiles him, as the mournful crocodile
With sorrow snares relenting passengers;
Or as the snake, roll'd in a flowering bank,
With shining checker'd slough doth sting a child,
That for the beauty thinks it excellent.
Believe me Lords, were none more wise than I,
And yet herein I judge mine own wit good;
This Gloucester should be quickly rid the World,
To rid us from the fear we have of him.

CARDINAL: That he should die, is worthy policy,
But yet we want a colour for his death:
'Tis meet he be condemn'd by course of Law.

SUFFOLK: But in my mind, that were no policy:
The King will labour still to save his life,
The Commons haply rise, to save his life;
And yet we have but trivial argument,
More than mistrust, that shows him worthy death.

YORK: So that by this, you would not have him die.

SUFFOLK: Ah York, no man alive, so fain as I.

YORK: 'Tis York that hath more reason for his death.
But my Lord Cardinal, and you my Lord of Suffolk,
Say as you think, and speak it from your souls:

Were 't not all one, an empty eagle were set,
To guard the chicken from a hungry kite,
As place Duke Humphrey for the King's Protector?
QUEEN: So the poor chicken should be sure of death.
SUFFOLK: Madame 'tis true: and were 't not madness then,
To make the fox surveyor of the fold?
Who being accus'd a crafty murtherer,
His guilt should be but idly posted over,
Because his purpose is not executed.
No: let him die, in that he is a fox,
By nature prov'd an enemy to the flock,
Before his chaps be stain'd with crimson blood,
As Humphrey prov'd by reasons to my Liege.
And do not stand on quillets how to slay him:
Be it by gins, by snares, by subtlety,
Sleeping, or waking, 'tis no matter how,
So he be dead; for that is good deceit
Which mates him first, that first intends deceit.
QUEEN: Thrice-noble Suffolk, 'tis resolutely spoke.
SUFFOLK: Not resolute, except so much were done,
For things are often spoke, and seldom meant,
But that my heart accordeth with my tongue,
Seeing the deed is meritorious,
And to preserve my Sovereign from his foe,
Say but the word, and I will be his priest.
CARDINAL: But I would have him dead, my Lord of
Suffolk,
Ere you can take due orders for a Priest:
Say you consent, and censure well the deed,
And I'll provide his executioner,
I tender so the safety of my Liege.
SUFFOLK: Here is my hand, the deed is worthy doing.
QUEEN: And so say I.
YORK: And I: and now we three have spoke it,

It skills not greatly who impugns our doom.
Enter a Post.

POST: Great Lords, from Ireland am I come amain,
  To signify, that rebels there are up,
  And put the Englishmen unto the sword.
  Send succours (Lords) and stop the rage betime,
  Before the wound do grow uncurable;
  For being green, there is great hope of help.

CARDINAL: A breach that craves a quick expedient stop.
  What counsel give you in this weighty cause?

YORK: That Somerset be sent as Regent thither:
  'Tis meet that lucky Ruler be employ'd,
  Witness the fortune he hath had in France.

SOMERSET: If York, with all his far-fet policy,
  Had been the Regent there, instead of me,
  He never would have stay'd in France so long.

YORK: No, not to lose it all, as thou hast done.
  I rather would have lost my life betimes,
  Than bring a burthen of dishonour home,
  By staying there so long, till all were lost.
  Show me one scar, character'd on thy skin,
  Men's flesh preserv'd so whole, do seldom win.

QUEEN: Nay then, this spark will prove a raging fire,
  If wind and fuel be brought, to feed it with:
  No more, good York; sweet Somerset be still.
  Thy fortune, York, hadst thou been Regent there,
  Might happily have prov'd far worse than his.

YORK: What, worse than nought? nay, then a shame take
  all.

SOMERSET: And in the number, thee, that wishest shame.

CARDINAL: My Lord of York, try what your fortune is:
  Th' uncivil kernes of Ireland are in arms,
  And temper clay with blood of Englishmen.
  To Ireland will you lead a band of men,

Collected choicely, from each county some,
And try your hap against the Irishmen?
YORK: I will, my Lord, so please his Majesty.
SUFFOLK: Why, our authority is his consent,
And what we do establish, he confirms:
Then, noble York, take thou this task in hand.
YORK: I am content: Provide me soldiers, Lords,
Whiles I take order for mine own affairs.
SUFFOLK: A charge, Lord York, that I will see perform'd.
But now return we to the false Duke Humphrey.
CARDINAL: No more of him: for I will deal with him,
That henceforth he shall trouble us no more:
And so break off, the day is almost spent;
Lord Suffolk, you and I must talk of that event.
YORK: My Lord of Suffolk, within fourteen days
At Bristow I expect my soldiers,
For there I 'll ship them all for Ireland.
SUFFOLK: I 'll see it truly done, my Lord of York. *Exeunt.*
Manet York.
YORK: Now York, or never, steel thy fearful thoughts,
And change misdoubt to resolution;
Be that thou hop'st to be, or what thou art;
Resign to death, it is not worth th' enjoying:
Let pale-fac'd fear keep with the mean-born man,
And find no harbour in a royal heart.
Faster than spring-time showers, comes thought on
thought,
And not a thought, but thinks on Dignity.
My brain, more busy than the labouring spider,
Weaves tedious snares to trap mine enemies.
Well Nobles, well; 'tis politicly done,
To send me packing with an host of men:
I fear me, you but warm the starved snake,
Who cherish'd in your breasts, will sting your hearts.

'Twas men I lack'd, and you will give them me;
I take it kindly; yet be well assur'd,
You put sharp weapons in a madman's hands.
Whiles I in Ireland nourish a mighty band,
I will stir up in England some black storm,
Shall blow ten thousand souls to Heaven, or Hell:
And this fell tempest shall not cease to rage,
Until the Golden Circuit on my head,
Like to the glorious sun's transparent beams,
Do calm the fury of this mad-bred flaw.
And for a minister of my intent,
I have seduc'd a headstrong Kentishman,
John Cade of Ashford,
To make commotion, as full well he can,
Under the title of John Mortimer.
In Ireland have I seen this stubborn Cade
Oppose himself against a troop of kernes,
And fought so long, till that his thighs with darts
Were almost like a sharp-quill'd porpentine:
And in the end being rescued, I have seen
Him caper upright, like a wild Morisco,
Shaking the bloody darts, as he his bells.
Full often, like a shag-hair'd crafty kerne,
Hath he conversed with the enemy,
And undiscover'd, come to me again,
And given me notice of their villainies.
This Devil here shall be my substitute;
For that John Mortimer, which now is dead,
In face, in gait, in speech he doth resemble.
By this, I shall perceive the Commons' mind,
How they affect the House and claim of York.
Say he be taken, rack'd, and tortured;
I know, no pain they can inflict upon him,
Will make him say, I mov'd him to those arms.

Say that he thrive, as 'tis great like he will,
Why then from Ireland come I with my strength,
And reap the harvest which that rascal sow'd.
For Humphrey; being dead, as he shall be,
And Henry put apart: the next for me.

Exit.

III. 2

Enter two or three running over the stage,
from the murther of Duke Humphrey.

1 MURTHERER: Run to my Lord of Suffolk: let him know
We have dispatch'd the Duke, as he commanded.

2 MURTHERER: Oh, that it were to do: what have we done?
Didst ever hear a man so penitent?

Enter Suffolk.

1 MURTHERER: Here comes my Lord.

SUFFOLK: Now Sirs, have you dispatch'd this thing?

1 MURTHERER: Ay, my good Lord, he's dead.

SUFFOLK: Why that's well said. Go, get you to my house,
I will reward you for this venturous deed:
The King and all the Peers are here at hand.
Have you laid fair the bed? Is all things well,
According as I gave directions?

1 MURTHERER: 'Tis, my good Lord.

SUFFOLK: Away, be gone.

Exeunt Murtherers.

Sound trumpets. Enter the King, the Queen,
Cardinal, Suffolk, Somerset, with Attendants.

KING: Go call our Uncle to our presence straight:
Say, we intend to try his Grace today,
If he be guilty, as 'tis published.

SUFFOLK: I'll call him presently, my Noble Lord.

Exit.

KING: Lords take your places: and I pray you all
Proceed no straiter 'gainst our Uncle Gloucester,
Than from true evidence, of good esteem,
He be approv'd in practice culpable.

QUEEN: God forbid any malice should prevail,
That faultless may condemn a Nobleman:
Pray God he may acquit him of suspicion.

KING: I thank thee Nell, these words content me much.

Enter Suffolk.

How now? why look'st thou pale? why tremblest thou?
Where is our Uncle? what's the matter, Suffolk?

SUFFOLK: Dead in his bed, my Lord: Gloucester is dead.

QUEEN: Marry God forfend.

CARDINAL: God's secret Judgement: I did dream tonight,
The Duke was dumb, and could not speak a word.

King sounds.

QUEEN: How fares my Lord? Help Lords, the King is
dead.

SOMERSET: Rear up his body, wring him by the nose.

QUEEN: Run, go, help, help: Oh Henry ope thine eyes.

SUFFOLK: He doth revive again, Madame be patient.

KING: Oh Heavenly God.

QUEEN: How fares my gracious Lord?

SUFFOLK: Comfort my Sovereign, gracious Henry comfort.

KING: What, doth my Lord of Suffolk comfort me?
Came he right now to sing a raven's note,
Whose dismal tune bereft my vital powers:
And thinks he, that the chirping of a wren,
By crying comfort from a hollow breast,
Can chase away the first-conceived sound?
Hide not thy poison with such sugar'd words,
Lay not thy hands on me: forbear I say,
Their touch affrights me as a serpent's sting.

Thou baleful messenger, out of my sight:
Upon thy eye-balls, murderous Tyranny
Sits in grim majesty, to fright the World.
Look not upon me, for thine eyes are wounding;
Yet do not go away: come basilisk,
And kill the innocent gazer with thy sight:
For in the shade of death, I shall find joy;
In life, but double death, now Gloucester's dead.

QUEEN: Why do you rate my Lord of Suffolk thus?
Although the Duke was enemy to him,
Yet he most Christian-like laments his death:
And for myself, foe as he was to me,
Might liquid tears, or heart-offending groans,
Or blood-consuming sighs recall his life;
I would be blind with weeping, sick with groans,
Look pale as primrose with blood-drinking sighs,
And all to have the Noble Duke alive.
What know I how the world may deem of me?
For it is known we were but hollow friends:
It may be judg'd I made the Duke away,
So shall my name with Slander's tongue be wounded,
And Princes' Courts be fill'd with my reproach:
This get I by his death: Aye me unhappy,
To be a Queen, and crown'd with infamy.

KING: Ah woe is me for Gloucester, wretched man.

QUEEN: Be woe for me, more wretched than he is.
What? Dost thou turn away, and hide thy face?
I am no loathsome leper, look on me.
What? Art thou like the adder waxen deaf?
Be poisonous too, and kill thy forlorn Queen.
Is all thy comfort shut in Gloucester's tomb?
Why then Dame Margaret was ne'er thy joy.
Erect his statue, and worship it,
And make my image but an ale-house sign.

Was I for this nigh wrack'd upon the sea,
And twice by awkward wind from England's bank
Drove back again unto my native clime?
What boded this? but well forewarning wind
Did seem to say, seek not a scorpion's nest,
Nor set no footing on this unkind shore.
What did I then? But curs'd the gentle gusts,
And he that loos'd them forth their brazen caves,
And bid them blow towards England's blessed shore,
Or turn our stern upon a dreadful rock:
Yet Aeolus would not be a murtherer,
But left that hateful office unto thee.
The pretty vaulting sea refus'd to drown me,
Knowing that thou would'st have me drown'd on shore
With tears as salt as sea, through thy unkindness.
The splitting rocks cower'd in the sinking sands,
And would not dash me with their ragged sides,
Because thy flinty heart more hard than they,
Might in thy Palace, perish Margaret.
As far as I could ken thy chalky cliffs,
When from thy shore, the tempest beat us back,
I stood upon the hatches in the storm:
And when the dusky sky, began to rob
My earnest-gaping sight of thy Land's view,
I took a costly jewel from my neck,
A heart it was bound in with diamonds,
And threw it towards thy Land: The sea receiv'd it,
And so I wish'd thy body might my heart:
And even with this, I lost fair England's view,
And bid mine eyes be packing with my heart,
And call'd them blind and dusky spectacles,
For losing ken of Albion's wished coast.
How often have I tempted Suffolk's tongue,
(The agent of thy foul inconstancy)

To sit and watch me as Ascanius did,
When he to madding Dido would unfold
His Father's acts, commenc'd in burning Troy.
Am I not witch'd like her? Or thou not false like him?
Aye me, I can no more: Die Margaret,
For Henry weeps, that thou dost live so long.
> *Noise within. Enter Warwick, Salisbury, and*
> *many Commons.*

WARWICK: It is reported, mighty Sovereign,
That good Duke Humphrey traitorously is murder'd
By Suffolk, and the Cardinal Beaufort's means:
The Commons like an angry hive of bees
That want their leader, scatter up and down,
And care not who they sting in his revenge.
Myself have calm'd their spleenful mutiny,
Until they hear the order of his death.

KING: That he is dead good Warwick, 'tis too true,
But how he died, God knows, not Henry:
Enter his chamber, view his breathless corpse,
And comment then upon his sudden death.

WARWICK: That shall I do my Liege; Stay Salisbury,
With the rude multitude, till I return.

KING: O Thou that judgest all things, stay my thoughts;
My thoughts, that labour to persuade my soul,
Some violent hands were laid on Humphrey's life:
If my suspect be false, forgive me God,
For judgement only doth belong to thee:
Fain would I go to chafe his paly lips,
With twenty thousand kisses, and to drain
Upon his face on ocean of salt tears,
To tell my love unto his dumb deaf trunk,
And with my fingers feel his hand, unfeeling:
But all in vain are these mean obsequies;
> *Bed put forth.*

And to survey his dead and earthy image:
  What were it but to make my sorrow greater?
WARWICK: Come hither gracious Sovereign, view this
    body.
KING: That is to see how deep my grave is made,
  For with his soul fled all my worldly solace:
  For seeing him, I see my life in death.
WARWICK: As surely as my soul intends to live
  With that dread King that took our state upon him,
  To free us from his Father's wrathful curse,
  I do believe that violent hands were laid
  Upon the life of this thrice-famed Duke.
SUFFOLK: A dreadful oath, sworn with a solemn tongue:
  What instance gives Lord Warwick for his vow.
WARWICK: See how the blood is settled in his face.
  Oft have I seen a timely-parted ghost,
  Of ashy semblance, meagre, pale, and bloodless,
  Being all descended to the labouring heart,
  Who in the conflict that it holds with death,
  Attracts the same for aidance 'gainst the enemy,
  Which with the heart there cools, and ne'er returneth,
  To blush and beautify the cheek again.
  But see, his face is black, and full of blood:
  His eye-balls further out, than when he liv'd,
  Staring full ghastly, like a strangled man:
  His hair uprear'd, his nostrils stretch'd with strugg-
    ling:
  His hands abroad display'd, as one that grasp'd
  And tugg'd for life, and was by strength subdu'd.
  Look on the sheets his hair (you see) is sticking,
  His well-proportion'd beard, made rough and rugged,
  Like to the summer's corn by tempest lodged:
  It cannot be but he was murder'd here,
  The least of all these signs were probable.

SUFFOLK: Why Warwick, who should do the Duke to
    death?
  Myself and Beaufort had him in protection,
  And we I hope sir, are no murtherers.

WARWICK: But both of you were vow'd Duke Hum-
    phrey's foes,
  And you (forsooth) had the good Duke to keep:
  'Tis like you would not feast him like a friend,
  And 'tis well seen, he found an enemy.

QUEEN: Then you belike suspect these Noblemen,
  As guilty of Duke Humphrey's timeless death.

WARWICK: Who finds the heifer dead, and bleeding fresh,
  And sees fast by, a butcher with an axe,
  But will suspect, 'twas he that made the slaughter?
  Who finds the partridge in the puttock's nest,
  But may imagine how the bird was dead,
  Although the kite soar with unbloodied beak?
  Even so suspicious is this Tragedy.

QUEEN: Are you the butcher, Suffolk? where 's your
    knife?
  Is Beaufort term'd a kite? where are his talons?

SUFFOLK: I wear no knife, to slaughter sleeping men,
  But here 's a vengeful sword, rusted with ease,
  That shall be scoured in his rancorous heart,
  That slanders me with Murther's crimson badge.
  Say, if thou dar'st, proud Lord of Warwickshire,
  That I am faulty in Duke Humphrey's death.

WARWICK: What dares not Warwick, if false Suffolk
    dare him?

QUEEN: He dares not calm his contumelious spirit,
  Nor cease to be an arrogant controller,
  Though Suffolk dare him twenty thousand times.

WARWICK: Madame be still: with reverence may I say,
  For every word you speak in his behalf,

G

Is slander to your Royal Dignity.

SUFFOLK: Blunt-witted Lord, ignoble in demeanour,
If ever Lady wrong'd her Lord so much,
Thy Mother took into her blameful bed
Some stern untutor'd churl; and noble stock
Was graft with crab-tree slip, whose fruit thou art,
And never of the Nevils' Noble Race.

WARWICK: But that the guilt of murther bucklers thee,
And I should rob the deaths-man of his fee,
Quitting thee thereby of ten thousand shames,
And that my Sovereign's presence makes me mild,
I would, false murd'rous coward, on thy knee
Make thee beg pardon for thy passed speech,
And say, it was thy Mother that thou meant'st,
That thou thyself wast born in bastardy;
And after all this fearful homage done,
Give thee thy hire, and send thy soul to Hell,
Pernicious blood-sucker of sleeping men.

SUFFOLK: Thou shalt be waking, while I shed thy blood,
If from this presence thou dar'st go with me.

WARWICK: Away even now, or I will drag thee hence:
Unworthy though thou art, I 'll cope with thee,
And do some service to Duke Humphrey's Ghost.
                    Exeunt Suffolk and Warwick.

KING: What stronger breastplate than a heart untainted?
Thrice is he arm'd, that hath his quarrel just;
And he but naked, though lock'd up in steel,
Whose conscience with injustice is corrupted.
                    A noise within.

QUEEN: What noise is this?
          *Enter Suffolk and Warwick, with their weapons
                    drawn.*

KING: Why how now Lords?
Your wrathful weapons drawn,

Here in our presence? Dare you be so bold?
Why what tumultuous clamour have we here?
SUFFOLK: The traitorous Warwick, with the men of Bury,
Set all upon me, mighty Sovereign.
Enter Salisbury.
SALISBURY: Sirs stand apart, the King shall know your
   mind.
Dread Lord, the Commons send you word by me,
Unless Lord Suffolk straight be done to death,
Or banished fair England's territories,
They will by violence tear him from your Palace,
And torture him with grevious ling'ring death.
They say, by him the good Duke Humphrey died:
They say, in him they fear your Highness' death;
And mere instinct of love and loyalty,
Free from a stubborn opposite intent,
As being thought to contradict your liking,
Makes them thus forward in his banishment.
They say, in care of your most Royal Person,
That if your Highness should intend to sleep,
And charge, that no man should disturb your rest,
In pain of your dislike, or pain of death;
Yet notwithstanding such a strait edict,
Were there a serpent seen, with forked tongue,
That slily glided towards your Majesty,
It were but necessary you were wak'd:
Lest being suffer'd in that harmful slumber,
The mortal worm might make the sleep eternal.
And therefore do they cry, though you forbid,
That they will guard you, where you will, or no,
From such fell serpents as false Suffolk is;
With whose envenomed and fatal sting,
Your loving Uncle, twenty times his worth,
They say is shamefully bereft of life.

COMMONS *within*: An answer from the King, my Lord
    of Salisbury.

SUFFOLK: 'Tis like the Commons, rude unpolish'd hinds,
    Could send such message to their Sovereign:
    But you, my Lord, were glad to be employ'd,
    To show how quaint an orator you are.
    But all the honour Salisbury hath won,
    Is, that he was the Lord Ambassador
    Sent from a sort of tinkers to the King.

COMMONS *within*: An answer from the King, or we will
    all break in.

KING: Go Salisbury, and tell them all from me,
    I thank them for their tender loving care;
    And had I not been cited so by them,
    Yet did I purpose as they do entreat:
    For sure, my thoughts do hourly prophesy,
    Mischance unto my State by Suffolk's means.
    And therefore by his Majesty I swear,
    Whose far-unworthy Deputy I am,
    He shall not breathe infection in this air,
    But three days longer, on the pain of death.

QUEEN: Oh Henry, let me plead for gentle Suffolk.

KING: Ungentle Queen, to call him gentle Suffolk.
    No more I say: if thou dost plead for him,
    Thou wilt but add increase unto my wrath.
    Had I but said, I would have kept my word;
    But when I swear, it is irrevocable:
    If after three days' space thou here be'st found,
    On any ground that I am Ruler of,
    The World shall not be ransom for thy life.
    Come Warwick, come good Warwick, go with me
    I have great matters to impart to thee.

        Exeunt all but Queen and Suffolk.

QUEEN: Mischance and Sorrow go along with you,

Heart's Discontent, and sour Affliction,
Be play-fellows to keep you company:
There's two of you, the Devil make a third,
And three-fold Vengeance tend upon your steps.

SUFFOLK: Cease, gentle Queen, these execrations
And let thy Suffolk take his heavy leave.

QUEEN: Fie coward woman, and soft-hearted wretch,
Hast thou not spirit to curse thine enemy.

SUFFOLK: A plague upon them: wherefore should I curse
them?
Would curses kill, as doth the mandrake's groan,
I would invent as bitter searching terms,
As curst, as harsh, and horrible to hear,
Deliver'd strongly through my fixed teeth,
With full as many signs of deadly hate,
As lean-fac'd Envy in her loathsome cave.
My tongue should stumble in mine earnest words,
Mine eyes should sparkle like the beaten flint,
Mine hair be fix'd an end, as one distract:
Ay, every joint should seem to curse and ban,
And even now my burthen'd heart would break
Should I not curse them. Poison be their drink.
Gall, worse than gall, the daintiest that they taste:
Their sweetest shade, a grove of cypress trees:
Their chiefest prospect, murd'ring basilisks:
Their softest touch, as smart as lizards' stings:
Their music, frightful as the serpent's hiss,
And boding screech-owls, make the consort full.
All the foul terrors in dark-seated hell –

QUEEN: Enough sweet Suffolk, thou torment'st thyself,
And these dread curses like the Sun 'gainst glass,
Or like an over-charged gun, recoil,
And turn the force of them upon thyself.

SUFFOLK: You bade me ban, and will you bid me leave?

Now by the ground that I am banish'd from,
Well could I curse away a winter's night,
Though standing naked on a mountain top,
Where biting cold would never let grass grow,
And think it but a minute spent in sport.
QUEEN: Oh, let me entreat thee cease, give me thy hand,
That I may dew it with my mournful tears:
Nor let the rain of heaven wet this place,
To wash away my woeful monuments.
Oh, could this kiss be printed in thy hand,
That thou might'st think upon these by the seal,
Through whom a thousand sighs are breath'd for thee.
So get thee gone, that I may know my grief,
'Tis but surmis'd, whiles thou art standing by,
As one that surfeits, thinking on a want:
I will repeal thee, or be well assur'd,
Adventure to be banished myself;
And banished I am, if but from thee.
Go, speak not to me; even now be gone.
Oh go not yet. Even thus, two friends condemn'd,
Embrace, and kiss, and take ten thousand leaves,
Loather a hundred times to part than die;
Yet now farewell, and farewell Life with thee.
SUFFOLK: Thus is poor Suffolk ten times banished,
Once by the King, and three times thrice by thee.
'Tis not the Land I care for, wert thou thence,
A wilderness is populous enough,
So Suffolk had thy heavenly company:
For where thou art, there is the World itself,
With every several pleasure in the World:
And where thou art not, Desolation.
I can no more: Live thou to joy thy life;
Myself no joy in nought, but that thou liv'st.
                    Enter Vaux.

QUEEN: Whither goes Vaux so fast? What news I prithee?
VAUX: To signify unto his Majesty,
 That Cardinal Beaufort is at point of death:
 For suddenly a grievous sickness took him,
 That makes him gasp, and stare, and catch the air,
 Blaspheming God, and cursing men on earth.
 Sometime he talks, as if Duke Humphrey's Ghost
 Were by his side: Sometime, he calls the King,
 And whispers to his pillow, as to him,
 The secrets of his over-charged soul,
 And I am sent to tell his Majesty,
 That even now he cries aloud for him.
QUEEN: Go tell this heavy message to the King.
     Exit Vaux.
 Aye me! What is this world? What news are these?
 But wherefore grieve I at an hour's poor loss,
 Omitting Suffolk's exile, my soul's Treasure?
 Why only Suffolk mourn I not for thee?
 And with the southern clouds, contend in tears?
 Theirs for the earth's increase, mine for my sorrows.
 Now get thee hence, the King thou know'st is coming,
 If thou be found by me, thou art but dead.
SUFFOLK: If I depart from thee, I cannot live,
 And in thy sight to die, what were it else,
 But like a pleasant slumber in thy lap?
 Here could I breathe my soul into the air,
 As mild and gentle as the cradle-babe,
 Dying with mother's dug between its lips.
 Where from thy sight, I should be raging mad,
 And cry out for thee to close up mine eyes:
 To have thee with thy lips to stop my mouth:
 So should'st thou either turn my flying soul,
 Or I should breathe it so into thy body,
 And then it liv'd in sweet Elysium.

To die by thee, were but to die in jest,
From thee to die, were torture more than death:
O let me stay, befall what may befall.

QUEEN: Away: Though parting be a fretful corrosive,
It is applied to a deathful wound.
To France sweet Suffolk: Let me hear from thee:
For wheresoe'er thou art in this world's globe,
I'll have an Iris that shall find thee out.

SUFFOLK: I go.

QUEEN: And take my heart with thee.

SUFFOLK: A jewel lock'd into the woefull'st cask,
That ever did contain a thing of worth,
Even as a splitted bark, so sunder we:
This way fall I to death.

QUEEN: This way for me.

Exeunt.

III. 3

Enter the King, Salisbury, Warwick, to the
Cardinal in bed.

KING: How fares my Lord? Speak Beaufort to thy
Sovereign.

CARDINAL: If thou be'st death, I 'll give thee England's
Treasure,
Enough to purchase such another Island,
So thou wilt let me live, and feel no pain.

KING: Ah, what a sign it is of evil life,
Where death's approach is seen so terrible.

WARWICK: Beaufort, it is thy Sovereign speaks to thee.

CARDINAL: Bring me unto my trial when you will.
Died he not in his bed? Where should he die?
Can I make men live where they will or no?
Oh torture me no more, I will confess.

Alive again? Then show me where he is,
I'll give a thousand pound to look upon him.
He hath no eyes, the dust hath blinded them.
Comb down his hair; look, look, it stands upright,
Like lime-twigs set to catch my winged soul:
Give me some drink, and bid the Apothecary
Bring the strong poison that I bought of him.

KING: Oh thou eternal mover of the heavens,
Look with a gentle eye upon this Wretch,
Oh beat away the busy meddling Fiend,
That lays strong siege unto this wretch's soul,
And from his bosom purge this black despair.

WARWICK: See how the pangs of death do make him grin.

SALISBURY: Disturb him not, let him pass peaceably.

KING: Peace to his soul, if God's good pleasure be.
Lord Card'nal, if thou think'st on heaven's bliss,
Hold up thy hand, make signal of thy hope.
He dies, and makes no sign: Oh God forgive him.

WARWICK: So bad a death, argues a monstrous life.

KING: Forbear to judge, for we are sinners all.
Close up his eyes, and draw the curtain close.
And let us all to meditation.

Exeunt.

IV. 1

Alarum. Fight at sea. Ordnance goes off.
Enter Lieutenant, Suffolk, and others.

LIEUTENANT: The gaudy blabbing and remorseful day,
Is crept into the bosom of the Sea:
And now loud howling wolves arouse the jades
That drag the tragic melancholy night:
Who with their drowsy, slow, and flagging wings
Clip dead men's graves, and from their misty jaws,

Breathe foul contagious darkness in the air:
Therefore bring forth the soldiers of our prize,
For whilst our pinnace anchors in the Downs,
Here shall they make their ransom on the sand,
Or with their blood stain this discoloured shore.
Master, this prisoner freely give I thee,
And thou that art his mate, make boot of this:
The other Walter Whitmore is thy share.

1 GENTLEMAN: What is my ransom Master, let me know.

MASTER: A thousand crowns, or else lay down your head.

MATE: And so much shall you give, or off goes yours.

LIEUTENANT: What think you much to pay two thousand crowns,
And bear the name and port of Gentlemen?
Cut both the villains' throats, for die you shall:
The lives of those which we have lost in fight,
Be counterpois'd with such a petty sum.

1 GENTLEMAN: I'll give it sir, and therefore spare my life.

2 GENTLEMAN: And so will I, and write home for it straight.

WHITMORE: I lost mine eye in laying the prize aboard,
And therefore to revenge it, shalt thou die,
And so should these, if I might have my will.

LIEUTENANT: Be not so rash, take ransom, let him live.

SUFFOLK: Look on my George, I am a Gentleman,
Rate me at what thou wilt, thou shalt be paid.

WHITMORE: And so am I: my name is Walter Whitmore.
How now? why start'st thou? What doth death affright?

SUFFOLK: Thy name affrights me, in whose sound is death:
A cunning man did calculate my birth,
And told me that by Water I should die:
Yet let not this make thee be bloody-minded,
Thy name is Gaultier, being rightly sounded.

WHITMORE: Gualtier or Walter, which it is I care not,
  Never yet did base dishonour blur our name,
  But with our sword we wip'd away the blot.
  Therefore, when merchant-like I sell revenge,
  Broke be my sword, my arms torn and defac'd,
  And I proclaim'd a coward through the world.
SUFFOLK: Stay Whitmore, for thy prisoner is a Prince,
  The Duke of Suffolk, William de la Pole.
WHITMORE: The Duke of Suffolk, muffled up in rags?
SUFFOLK: Ay, but these rags are no part of the Duke.
LIEUTENANT: But Jove was never slain as thou shalt be,
  Obscure and lousy swain, King Henry's blood.
SUFFOLK: The honourable blood of Lancaster
  Must not be shed by such a jaded groom:
  Hast thou not kiss'd thy hand, and held my stirrup?
  Bare-headed plodded by my foot-cloth mule,
  And thought thee happy when I shook my head.
  How often hast thou waited at my cup,
  Fed from my trencher, kneel'd down at the board,
  When I have feasted with Queen Margaret?
  Remember it, and let it make thee crest-fall'n,
  Ay, and allay this thy abortive pride:
  How in our voiding-lobby hast thou stood,
  And duly waited for my coming forth?
  This hand of mine hath writ in thy behalf,
  And therefore shall it charm thy riotous tongue.
WHITMORE: Speak Captain, shall I stab the forlorn swain?
LIEUTENANT: First let my words stab him, as he hath me.
SUFFOLK: Base slave, thy words are blunt, and so art thou.
LIEUTENANT: Convey him hence, and on our long-boat's
    side
  Strike off his head.
SUFFOLK: Thou dar'st not for thy own.
LIEUTENANT: Pool, Sir Pool? Lord,

Ay kennel, puddle, sink, whose filth and dirt
Troubles the silver spring, where England drinks:
Now will I dam up this thy yawning mouth,
For swallowing the Treasure of the Realm.
Thy lips that kiss'd the Queen, shall sweep the ground:
And thou that smil'dst at good Duke Humphrey's death,
Against the senseless winds shalt grin in vain,
Who in contempt shall hiss at thee again.
And wedded be thou to the Hags of hell,
For daring to affy a mighty Lord
Unto the daughter of a worthless King,
Having neither subject, wealth, nor diadem:
By devilish policy art thou grown great,
And like ambitious Sylla overgorg'd,
With gobbets of thy Mother's bleeding heart.
By thee Anjou and Maine were sold to France.
The false revolting Normans thorough thee,
Disdain to call us Lord, and Picardy
Hath slain their Governors, surpris'd our Forts,
And sent the ragged soldiers wounded home.
The Princely Warwick, and the Nevils all,
Whose dreadful swords were never drawn in vain,
As hating thee, are rising up in arms.
And now the House of York thrust from the Crown,
By shameful murther of a guiltless King,
And lofty proud encroaching tyranny,
Burns with revenging fire, whose hopeful colours
Advance our half-fac'd Sun, striving to shine;
Under the which is writ, *Invitis nubibus.*
The Commons here in Kent are up in arms,
And to conclude, Reproach and Beggary,
Is crept into the Palace of our King,
And all by thee: away, convey him hence.
SUFFOLK: O that I were a God, to shoot forth thunder

Upon these paltry, servile, abject drudges:
Small things make base men proud. This villain here,
Being Captain of a pinnace, threatens more
Than Bargulus the strong Illyrian Pirate.
Drones suck not eagles' blood, but rob bee-hives:
It is impossible that I should die
By such a lowly vassal as thyself.
Thy words move rage, and not remorse in me:
I go of message from the Queen to France;
I charge thee waft me safely cross the Channel.

LIEUTENANT: Walter –

WHITMORE: Come Suffolk, I must waft thee to thy death.

SUFFOLK: *Gelidus timor occupat artus,* it is thee I fear.

WHITMORE: Thou shalt have cause to fear before I leave
  thee.
  What, are ye daunted now? Now will ye stoop.

1 GENTLEMAN: My gracious Lord entreat him, speak him
  fair.

SUFFOLK: Suffolk's imperial tongue is stern and rough:
  Us'd to command, untaught to plead for favour.
  Far be it, we should honour such as these
  With humble suit: no, rather let my head
  Stoop to the block, than these knees bow to any,
  Save to the God of heaven, and to my King:
  And sooner dance upon a bloody pole,
  Than stand uncover'd to the vulgar groom.
  True Nobility, is exempt from fear:
  More can I bear, than you dare execute.

LIEUTENANT: Hale him away, and let him talk no more:

SUFFOLK: Come soldiers, show what cruelty ye can,
  That this my death may never be forgot.
  Great men oft die by vile Bezonians.
  A Roman sworder, and bandetto slave
  Murder'd sweet Tully. Brutus' bastard hand

Stabb'd Julius Caesar. Savage islanders
Pompey the Great, and Suffolk dies by pirates.
Exit Walter with Suffolk.

LIEUTENANT: And as for these whose ransom we have set,
It is our pleasure one of them depart:
Therefore come you with us, and let him go.
Exit Lieutenant, and the rest.
Manet the first Gentleman. Enter Walter with
the body.

WHITMORE: There let his head, and lifeless body lie,
Until the Queen his Mistress bury it.
Exit Walter.

I GENTLEMAN: O barbarous and bloody spectacle,
His body will I bear unto the King:
If he revenge it not, yet will his friends,
So will the Queen, that living, held him dear.
Exeunt.

IV. 2

Enter Bevis, and John Holland.

BEVIS: Come and get thee a sword, though made of a lath,
they have been up these two days.

HOLLAND: They have the more need to sleep now then.

BEVIS: I tell thee, Jack Cade the Clothier, means to dress
the Common-wealth and turn it, and set a new nap
upon it.

HOLLAND: So he had need, for 'tis threadbare. Well, I
say, it was never merry world in England, since Gentlemen came up.

BEVIS: O miserable Age: Virtue is not regarded in handi-
crafts-men.

HOLLAND: The Nobility think scorn to go in leather
aprons.

BEVIS: Nay more, the King's Council are no good work-men.

HOLLAND: True: and yet it is said, Labour in thy voca-tion: which is as much to say, as let the Magistrates be labouring men, and therefore should we be Magistrates.

BEVIS: Thou hast hit it: for there 's no better sign of a brave mind, than a hard hand.

HOLLAND: I see them, I see them: There 's Best's son, the Tanner of Wingham.

BEVIS: He shall have the skins of our enemies, to make dog's-leather of.

HOLLAND: And Dick the Butcher.

BEVIS: Then is sin struck down like an ox, and iniquity's throat cut like a calf.

HOLLAND: And Smith the Weaver.

BEVIS: Argo, their thread of life is spun.

HOLLAND: Come, come, let 's fall in with them.

Drum. Enter Cade, Dick Butcher, Smith the Weaver,
and a Sawyer, with infinite numbers.

CADE: We John Cade, so term'd of our supposed Father.

BUTCHER: Or rather of stealing a cade of herrings.

CADE: For our enemies shall fall before us, inspired with the spirit of putting down Kings and Princes. Command silence.

BUTCHER: Silence.

CADE: My Father was a Mortimer.

BUTCHER: He was an honest man, and a good bricklayer.

CADE: My mother a Plantagenet.

BUTCHER: I knew her well, she was a midwife.

CADE: My wife descended of the Lacies.

BUTCHER: She was indeed a pedlar's daughter, and sold many laces.

WEAVER: But now of late, not able to travel with her furr'd pack, she washes bucks here at home.

CADE: Therefore am I of an honourable house.

BUTCHER: Ay by my faith, the field is honourable, and there was he born, under a hedge: for his father had never a house but the cage.

CADE: Valiant I am.

WEAVER: A' must needs, for beggary is valiant.

CADE: I am able to endure much.

BUTCHER: No question of that: for I have seen him whipp'd three market-days together.

CADE: I fear neither sword, nor fire.

WEAVER: He need not fear the sword, for his coat is of proof.

BUTCHER: But methinks he should stand in fear of fire, being burnt i' th' hand for stealing of sheep.

CADE: Be brave then, for your Captain is brave, and vows reformation. There shall be in England, seven half-penny loaves sold for a penny: the three-hoop'd pot, shall have ten hoops, and I will make it felony to drink small beer. All the Realm shall be in common, and in Cheapside shall my palfry go to grass: and when I am King, as King I will be.

ALL: God save your Majesty.

CADE: I thank you good people. There shall be no money, all shall eat and drink on my score, and I will apparel them all in one Livery, that they may agree like Brothers, and worship me their Lord.

BUTCHER: The first thing we do, let's kill all the Lawyers.

CADE: Nay, that I mean to do. Is not this a lamentable thing, that of the skin of an innocent lamb should be made parchment; that parchment being scribbled o'er, should undo a man. Some say the bee stings, but I say, 'tis the bee's wax: for I did but seal once to a thing, and I was never mine own man since. How now? Who's there?

Enter a Clerk.

WEAVER: The Clerk of Chatham: he can write and read, and cast accompt.

CADE: O monstrous.

WEAVER: We took him setting of boys' copies.

CADE: Here 's a villain.

WEAVER: 'Has a book in his pocket with red letters in 't.

CADE: Nay then he is a Conjurer.

BUTCHER: Nay, he can make Obligations, and write Court-hand.

CADE: I am sorry for't: The man is a proper man of mine honour: unless I find him guilty, he shall not die. Come hither sirrah, I must examine thee: What is thy name?

CLERK: Emmanuel.

BUTCHER: They use to write it on the top of letters: 'Twill go hard with you.

CADE: Let me alone: Dost thou use to write thy name? Or hast thou a mark to thyself, like an honest plain-dealing man?

CLERK: Sir I thank God, I have been so well brought up, that I can write my name.

ALL: He hath confess'd: away with him: he 's a villain and a traitor.

CADE: Away with him I say: Hang him with his pen and ink-horn about his neck.

Exit one with the Clerk.
Enter Michael.

MICHAEL: Where 's our General?

CADE: Here I am thou particular fellow.

MICHAEL: Fly, fly, fly, Sir Humphrey Stafford and his brother are hard by, with the King's Forces.

CADE: Stand villain, stand, or I 'll fell thee down: he shall be encounter'd with a man as good as himself. He is but a knight, is a'?

MICHAEL: No.

CADE: To equal him I will make myself a knight presently;
　　Rise up Sir John Mortimer. Now have at him.
　　　　　Enter Sir Humphrey Stafford and his Brother,
　　　　　　　with drum and soldiers.

STAFFORD: Rebellious hinds, the filth and scum of Kent,
　　Mark'd for the gallows: Lay your weapons down,
　　Home to your cottages; forsake this groom.
　　The King is merciful, if you revolt.

BROTHER: But angry, wrathful, and inclin'd to blood,
　　If you go forward: therefore yield, or die.

CADE: As for these silken-coated slaves I pass not.
　　It is to you good people, that I speak,
　　Over whom (in time to come) I hope to reign:
　　For I am rightful heir unto the Crown.

STAFFORD: Villain, thy father was a plasterer,
　　And thou thyself a shearman, art thou not?

CADE: And Adam was a gardener.

BROTHER: And what of that?

CADE: Marry, this Edmund Mortimer Earl of March,
　　Married the Duke of Clarence's daughter, did he not?

STAFFORD: Ay sir.

CADE: By her he had two children at one birth.

BROTHER: That 's false.

CADE: Ay, there 's the question; But I say, 'tis true:
　　The elder of them being put to nurse,
　　Was by a beggar-woman stol'n away,
　　And ignorant of his birth and parentage,
　　Became a bricklayer, when he came to age.
　　His son am I, deny it if you can.

BUTCHER: Nay, 'tis too true, therefore he shall be King.

WEAVER: Sir, he made a chimney in my Father's house,
　　and the bricks are alive at this day to testify it: therefore
　　deny it not.

STAFFORD: And will you credit this base drudge's words,
that speaks he knows not what?

ALL: Ay marry will we: therefore get ye gone.

BROTHER: Jack Cade, the Duke of York hath taught you
this.

CADE: He lies, for I invented it myself. Go to Sirrah, tell
the King from me, that, for his Father's sake Henry the
fifth, (in whose time, boys went to span-counter for
French crowns) I am content he shall reign but I 'll be
Protector over him.

BUTCHER: And furthermore, we 'll have the Lord Say's
head, for selling the Dukedome of Maine.

CADE: And good reason: for thereby is England main'd,
and fain to go with a staff, but that my puissance holds it
up. Fellow-Kings, I tell you, that that Lord Say hath
gelded the Commonwealth, and made it an eunuch: and
more than that, he can speak French, and therefore he is a
Traitor.

STAFFORD: O gross and miserable ignorance.

CADE: Nay answer if you can: The Frenchmen are our
enemies; go to then, I ask but this: Can he that speaks
with the tongue of an enemy, be a good Councillor, or
no?

ALL: No, no, and therefore we 'll have his head.

BROTHER: Well, seeing gentle words will not prevail,
Assail them with the Army of the King.

STAFFORD: Herald away, and throughout every Town,
Proclaim them Traitors that are up with Cade,
That those which fly before the battle ends,
May even in their wives' and children's sight,
Be hang'd up for example at their doors:
And you that be the King's friends follow me.

Exeunt the two Staffords, and soldiers.

CADE: And you that love the Commons, follow me:

Now show yourselves men, 'tis for Liberty.
We will not leave one Lord, one Gentleman:
Spare none, but such as go in clouted shooen,
For they are thrifty honest men, and such
As would (but that they dare not) take our parts.

BUTCHER: They are all in order, and march toward us.

CADE: But then are we in order, when we are most out of order. Come, march forward.

Exeunt.

IV. 3

Alarums to the fight, wherein both the Staffords
are slain. Enter Cade and the rest.

CADE: Where's Dick, the Butcher of Ashford?

BUTCHER: Here sir.

CADE: They fell before thee like sheep and oxen, and thou behaved'st thyself, as if thou hadst been in thine own slaughter-house: Therefore thus will I reward thee, the Lent shall be as long again as it is, and thou shalt have a licence to kill for a hundred lacking one.

BUTCHER: I desire no more.

CADE: And, to speak truth, thou deserv'st no less. This monument of the victory will I bear, and the bodies shall be dragged at my horse heels, till I do come to London, where we will have the Mayor's sword borne before us.

BUTCHER: If we mean to thrive, and do good, break open the jails, and let out the prisoners.

CADE: Fear not that I warrant thee. Come, let's march towards London.

Exeunt.

IV. 4

*Enter the King with a supplication, and the Queen
with Suffolk's head, the Duke of Buckingham,
and the Lord Say.*

QUEEN: Oft have I heard that grief softens the mind,
And makes it fearful and degenerate.
Think therefore on revenge, and cease to weep.
But who can cease to weep, and look on this.
Here may his head lie on my throbbing breast:
But where 's the body that I should embrace?

BUCKINGHAM: What answer makes your Grace to the
rebels' supplication?

KING: I 'll send some holy Bishop to entreat:
For God forbid, so many simple souls
Should perish by the sword. And I myself,
Rather than bloody war shall cut them short,
Will parley with Jack Cade their General.
But stay, I 'll read it over once again.

QUEEN: Ah barbarous villains: Hath this lovely face,
Rul'd like a wandering Planet over me,
And could it not enforce them to relent,
That were unworthy to behold the same.

KING: Lord Say, Jack Cade hath sworn to have thy head.

SAY: Ay, but I hope your Highness shall have his.

KING: How now Madam?
Still lamenting and mourning for Suffolk's death?
I fear me (Love) if that I had been dead,
Thou would'st not have mourn'd so much for me.

QUEEN: No my Love, I should not mourn, but die for thee.
Enter a Messenger.

KING: How now? What news? Why com'st thou in such
haste?

MESSENGER: The Rebels are in Southwark: Fly my Lord:
  Jack Cade proclaims himself Lord Mortimer,
  Descended from the Duke of Clarence' house,
  And calls your Grace Usurper, openly,
  And vows to crown himself in Westminster.
  His army is a ragged multitude
  Of hinds and peasants, rude and merciless:
  Sir Humphrey Stafford, and his Brother's death,
  Hath given them heart and courage to proceed:
  All Scholars, Lawyers, Courtiers, Gentlemen,
  They call false Caterpillars, and intend their death.

KING: Oh graceless men: they know not what they do.

BUCKINGHAM: My gracious Lord, retire to Killingworth,
  Until a power be rais'd to put them down.

QUEEN: Ah were the Duke of Suffolk now alive,
  These Kentish Rebels would be soon appeas'd.

KING: Lord Say, the traitors hateth thee,
  Therefore away with us to Killingworth.

SAY: So might your Grace's person be in danger.
  The sight of me is odious in their eyes:
  And therefore in this City will I stay,
  And live alone as secret as I may.

Enter another Messenger.

MESSENGER: Jack Cade hath gotten London-bridge.
  The citizens fly and forsake their houses:
  The rascal people, thirsting after prey,
  Join with the Traitor, and they jointly swear
  To spoil the City, and your Royal Court.

BUCKINGHAM: Then linger not my Lord, away, take
  horse.

KING: Come Margaret, God our hope will succour us.

QUEEN: My hope is gone, now Suffolk is deceas'd.

KING: Farewell my Lord, trust not the Kentish Rebels.

BUCKINGHAM: Trust nobody for fear you be betray'd.

SAY: The trust I have, is in mine innocence,
And therefore am I bold and resolute.

Exeunt.

IV. 5

Enter Lord Scales upon the Tower walking.
Then enter two or three Citizens below.

SCALES: How now? Is Jack Cade slain?

1 CITIZEN: No my Lord, nor likely to be slain: for they
have won the Bridge, killing all those that withstand
them: The Lord Mayor craves aid of your Honour
from the Tower to defend the City from the Rebels.

SCALES: Such aid as I can spare you shall command,
But I am troubled here with them myself.
The Rebels have assay'd to win the Tower.
But get you to Smithfield, and gather head,
And thither I will send you Matthew Goffe.
Fight for your King, your Country, and your lives,
And so farewell, for I must hence again.

Exeunt.

IV. 6

Enter Jack Cade and the rest, and strikes his staff
on London Stone.

CADE: Now is Mortimer Lord of this City. And here
sitting upon London Stone, I charge and command,
that of the City's cost the pissing-conduit run nothing
but claret wine this first year of our reign. And now
henceforward it shall be treason for any that calls me
other than Lord Mortimer.

Enter a Soldier running.

SOLDIER: Jack Cade, Jack Cade.

CADE: Knock him down there.
> *They kill him.*

WEAVER: If this fellow be wise, he 'll never call ye Jack Cade more, I think he hath a very fair warning.

BUTCHER: My Lord, there 's an Army gathered together in Smithfield.

CADE: Come, then let 's go fight with them: But first, go and set London Bridge on fire, and if you can, burn down the Tower too. Come, let 's away.
> *Exeunt omnes.*

IV. 7

> *Alarums. Matthew Goffe is slain, and all the rest.*
> *Then enter Jack Cade, with his company.*

CADE: So sirs; now go some and pull down the Savoy: Others to th' Inns of Court, down with them all.

BUTCHER: I have a suit unto your Lordship.

CADE: Be it a Lordship, thou shalt have it for that word.

BUTCHER: Only that the Laws of England may come out of your mouth.

HOLLAND: Mass 'twill be sore Law then, for he was thrust in the mouth with a spear, and 'tis not whole yet.

WEAVER: Nay John, it will be stinking Law, for his breath stinks with eating toasted cheese.

CADE: I have thought upon it, it shall be so. Away, burn all the Records of the Realm, my mouth shall be the Parliament of England.

HOLLAND: Then we are like to have biting Statutes unless his teeth be pull'd out.

CADE: And henceforward all things shall be in common.
> *Enter a Messenger.*

MESSENGER: My Lord, a prize, a prize, here 's the Lord Say, which sold the Towns in France. He that made us pay one and twenty fifteens, and one shilling to the pound, the last Subsidy.

Enter George, with the Lord Say.

CADE: Well, he shall be beheaded for it ten times: Ah thou Say, thou Serge, nay thou Buckram Lord, now art thou within point-blank of our Jurisdiction Regal. What canst thou answer to my Majesty, for giving up of Normandy unto Mounsieur Basimecu, the Dolphin of France? Be it known unto thee by these presence, even the presence of Lord Mortimer, that I am the Besom that must sweep the Court clean of such filth as thou art: Thou hast most traitorously corrupted the youth of the Realm, in erecting a Grammar School: and whereas before, our Forefathers had no other books but the score and the tally, thou hast caused printing to be us'd, and contrary to the King, his Crown, and Dignity, thou hast built a paper-mill. It will be proved to thy face, that thou hast men about thee, that usually talk of a noun and a verb, and such abhominable words, as no Christian ear can endure to hear. Thou hast appointed Justices of Peace, to call poor men before them, about matters they were not able to answer. Moreover, thou hast put them in prison, and because they could not read, thou hast hang'd them, when (indeed) only for that cause they have been most worthy to live. Thou dost ride in a foot-cloth, dost thou not?

SAY: What of that?

CADE: Marry, thou ought'st not to let thy horse wear a cloak, when honester men than thou go in their hose and doublets.

BUTCHER: And work in their shirt too, as myself for example, that am a butcher.

SAY: You men of Kent.

BUTCHER: What say you of Kent?

SAY: Nothing but this; 'Tis *bona terra, mala gens.*

CADE: Away with him, away with him, he speaks Latin.

SAY: Hear me but speak, and bear me where you will:
Kent, in the Commentaries Caesar writ,
Is term'd the civil'st place of all this Isle:
Sweet is the country, because full of riches,
The people liberal, valiant, active, wealthy,
Which makes me hope you are not void of pity.
I sold not Maine, I lost not Normandy,
Yet to recover them would lose my life:
Justice with favour have I always done,
Prayers and tears have mov'd me, gifts could never.
When have I aught exacted at your hands?
Kent to maintain, the King, the Realm and you,
Large gifts have I bestow'd on learned Clerks,
Because my book preferr'd me to the King.
And seeing ignorance is the curse of God,
Knowledge the wing wherewith we fly to heaven.
Unless you be possess'd with devilish spirits,
You cannot but forbear to murther me:
This tongue hath parley'd unto foreign Kings
For your behoof.

CADE: Tut, when struck'st thou one blow in the field?

SAY: Great men have reaching hands: oft have I struck
Those that I never saw, and struck them dead.

GEORGE: O monstrous coward! What, to come behind
folks?

SAY: These cheeks are pale for watching for your good.

CADE: Give him a box o' the ear, and that will make 'em
red again.

SAY: Long sitting to determine poor men's causes
Hath made me full of sickness and diseases.

CADE: Ye shall have a hempen caudle then, and the help
of hatchet.

BUTCHER: Why dost thou quiver man?

SAY: The palsy, and not fear provokes me.

CADE: Nay, he nods at us, as who should say, I 'll be even with you. I 'll see if his head will stand steadier on a pole, or no. Take him away, and behead him.

SAY: Tell me: wherein have I offended most?
Have I affected wealth, or honour? Speak.
Are my chests fill'd up with extorted gold?
Is my apparel sumptuous to behold?
Whom have I injur'd, that ye seek my death?
These hands are free from guiltless blood-shedding,
This breast from harbouring foul deceitful thoughts.
O let me live.

CADE: I feel remorse in myself with his words: but I 'll bridle it: he shall die, and it be but for pleading so well for his life. Away with him, he has a familiar under his tongue, he speaks not a' God's name. Go, take him away I say, and strike off his head presently, and then break into his Son-in-law's house, Sir James Cromer, and strike off his head, and bring them both upon two poles hither.

ALL: It shall be done.

SAY: Ah countrymen: If when you make your pray'rs,
God should be so obdurate as yourselves,
How would it fare with your departed souls,
And therefore yet relent, and save my life.

CADE: Away with him, and do as I command ye: [*Exeunt some with Lord Say*] The proudest Peer in the Realm, shall not wear a head on his shoulders, unless he pay me tribute: there shall not a maid be married, but she shall pay to me her maidenhead ere they have it: Men shall hold of me in Capite: And we charge and command, that their wives be as free as heart can wish, or tongue can tell.

BUTCHER: My Lord, when shall we go to Cheapside, and
take up commodities upon our bills?

CADE: Marry presently.

ALL: O brave.

Enter one with the heads.

CADE: But is not this braver? Let them kiss one another:
for they lov'd well when they were alive. Now part
them again, lest they consult about the giving up of
some more Towns in France. Soldiers, defer the spoil of
the City until night: for with these borne before us,
instead of maces, will we ride through the streets, and at
every corner have them kiss. Away.

Exeunt.

IV. 8

*Alarum, and Retreat. Enter again Cade, and all his
rabblement.*

CADE: Up Fish Street, down Saint Magnus' Corner,
kill and knock down, throw them into Thames:

Sound a parley.

What noise is this I hear? Dare any be so bold to sound
retreat or parley when I command them kill?

Enter Buckingham, and old Clifford.

BUCKINGHAM: Ay here they be, that dare and will disturb
thee:

Know Cade, we come Ambassadors from the King
Unto the Commons, whom thou hast misled,
And here pronounce free pardon to them all,
That will forsake thee, and go home in peace.

CLIFFORD: What say ye Countrymen, will ye relent
And yield to mercy, whilst 'tis offer'd you,
Or let a rabble lead you to your deaths.
Who loves the King, and will embrace his pardon,

Fling up his cap, and say, God save his Majesty.
Who hateth him, and honours not his Father,
Henry the Fifth, that made all France to quake,
Shake he his weapon at us, and pass by.

ALL: God save the King, God save the King.

CADE: What Buckingham and Clifford are ye so brave?
And you base peasants, do ye believe him, will you needs
be hang'd with your pardons about your necks? Hath
my sword therefore broke through London gates, that
you should leave me at the White Hart in Southwark.
I thought ye would never have given out these arms till
you had recovered your ancient freedom. But you are all
recreants and dastards, and delight to live in slavery to
the Nobility. Let them break your backs with burthens,
take your houses over your heads, ravish your Wives
and Daughters before your faces. For me, I will make
shift for one, and so God's Curse light upon you all.

ALL: We 'll follow Cade, we 'll follow Cade.

CLIFFORD: Is Cade the son of Henry the Fifth,
That thus you do exclaim you 'll go with him?
Will he conduct you through the heart of France,
And make the meanest of you Earls and Dukes?
Alas, he hath no home, no place to fly to:
Nor knows he how to live, but by the spoil,
Unless by robbing of your friends, and us.
Were 't not a shame, that whilst you live at jar,
The fearful French, whom you late vanquished
Should make a start o'er-seas, and vanquish you?
Methinks already in this civil broil,
I see them lording it in London streets,
Crying *Villiago* unto all they meet.
Better ten thousand base-born Cades miscarry,
Than you should stoop unto a Frenchman's mercy.
To France, to France, and get what you have lost:

Spare England, for it is your native coast:
Henry hath money, you are strong and manly:
God on our side, doubt not of victory.

ALL: A Clifford, a Clifford, we 'll follow the King, and
Clifford.

CADE: Was ever feather so lightly blown to and fro, as
this multitude? The name of Henry the Fifth, hales
them to an hundred mischiefs, and makes them leave me
desolate. I see them lay their heads together to surprise
me. My sword make way for me, for here is no staying:
in despite of the devils and hell, have through the very
middest of you, and heavens and honour be witness, that
no want of resolution in me, but only my followers' base
and ignominious treasons, makes me betake me to my
heels.

Exit.

BUCKINGHAM: What, is he fled? Go some, and follow
him,
And he that brings his head unto the King,
Shall have a thousand crowns for his reward.

Exeunt some of them.

Follow me soldiers, we'll devise a mean,
To reconcile you all unto the King.

Exeunt omnes.

IV. 9

*Sound trumpets. Enter King, Queen, and
Somerset, on the Tarras.*

KING: Was ever King that joy'd an earthly Throne,
And could command no more content than I?
No sooner was I crept out of my cradle,
But I was made a King, at nine months old.
Was never Subject long'd to be a King,

As I do long and wish to be a Subject.
Enter Buckingham and Clifford.

BUCKINGHAM: Health and glad tidings to your Majesty.

KING: Why Buckingham, is the Traitor Cade surpris'd?
Or is he but retir'd to make him strong?
Enter multitudes with halters about their necks.

CLIFFORD: He is fled my Lord, and all his powers do
yield,
And humbly thus with halters on their necks,
Expect your Highness' doom of life, or death.

KING: Then heaven set ope thy everlasting gates,
To entertain my vows of thanks and praise.
Soldiers, this day have you redeem'd your lives,
And show'd how well you love your Prince and
Country:
Continue still in this so good a mind,
And Henry though he be infortunate,
Assure yourselves will never be unkind:
And so with thanks, and pardon to you all,
I do dismiss you to your several Countries.

ALL: God save the King, God save the King.
Enter a Messenger.

MESSENGER: Please it your Grace to be advertised,
The Duke of York is newly come from Ireland,
And with a puissant and a mighty power
Of gallow-glasses and stout kernes,
Is marching hitherward in proud array,
And still proclaimeth as he comes along,
His arms are only to remove from thee
The Duke of Somerset, whom he terms a Traitor.

KING: Thus stands my state, 'twixt Cade and York dis-
tress'd.
Like to a ship, that having 'scap'd a tempest,
Is straightway calm, and boarded with a pirate.

But now is Cade driven back, his men dispers'd,
And now is York in arms, to second him.
I pray thee Buckingham go and meet him,
And ask him what's the reason of these arms:
Tell him, I'll send Duke Edmund to the Tower,
And Somerset we will commit thee thither,
Until his Army be dismiss'd from him.

SOMERSET: My Lord,
I'll yield myself to prison willingly,
Or unto death, to do my Country good.

KING: In any case, be not too rough in terms,
For he is fierce, and cannot brook hard language.

BUCKINGHAM: I will my Lord, and doubt not so to deal,
As all things shall redound unto your good.

KING: Come wife, let's in, and learn to govern better,
For yet may England curse my wretched reign.

Flourish. Exeunt.

IV. 10

Enter Cade.

CADE: Fie on ambitions: fie on myself, that have a sword,
and yet am ready to famish. These five days have I hid
me in these woods, and durst not peep out, for all the
country is laid for me: but now am I so hungry, that if I
might have a lease of my life for a thousand years, I
could stay no longer. Wherefore on a brick wall have I
climb'd into this garden, to see if I can eat grass, or pick
a sallet another while, which is not amiss to cool a
man's stomach this hot weather: and I think this word
sallet was born to do me good: for many a time but for a
sallet, my brain-pan had been cleft with a brown bill;
and many a time when I have been dry, and bravely
marching, it hath serv'd me instead of a quart pot to

drink in; and now the word sallet must serve me to feed on.

Enter Iden.

IDEN: Lord, who would live turmoiled in the Court,
And may enjoy such quiet walks as these?
This small inheritance my Father left me,
Contenteth me, and worth a Monarchy.
I seek not to wax great by others' waning,
Or gather wealth I care not with what envy:
Sufficeth, that I have maintains my state,
And sends the poor well pleased from my gate.

CADE: Here's the Lord of the soil come to seize me for a stray, for entering his fee-simple without leave. Ah villain, thou wilt betray me, and get a thousand crowns of the King by carrying my head to him, but I'll make thee eat iron like an ostrich, and swallow my sword like a great pin ere thou and I part.

IDEN: Why rude companion, whatsoe'er thou be,
I know thee not, why then should I betray thee?
Is't not enough to break into my garden,
And like a thief to come to rob my grounds:
Climbing my walls in spite of me the owner,
But thou wilt brave me with these saucy terms?

CADE: Brave thee? ay by the best blood that ever was broach'd, and beard thee too. Look on me well, I have eat no meat these five days, yet come thou and thy five men, and if I do not leave you all as dead as a door-nail, I pray God I may never eat grass more.

IDEN: Nay, it shall ne'er be said, while England stands,
That Alexander Iden an Esquire of Kent,
Took odds to combat a poor famish'd man.
Oppose thy steadfast gazing eyes to mine,
See if thou canst outface me with thy looks:
Set limb to limb, and thou art far the lesser:

H

Thy hand is but a finger to my fist,
Thy leg a stick compared with this truncheon,
My foot shall fight with all the strength thou hast,
And if mine arm be heaved in the air,
Thy grave is digg'd already in the earth:
As for words, whose greatness answers words,
Let this my sword report what speech forbears.

CADE: By my valour: the most complete Champion that
ever I heard. Steel, if thou turn the edge, or cut not out
the burly-bon'd clown in chines of beef, ere thou sleep
in thy sheath, I beseech Jove on my knees thou mayst be
turn'd to hobnails.

Here they fight.

O I am slain, Famine and no other hath slain me, let ten
thousand devils come against me, and give me but the
ten meals I have lost, and I 'ld defy them all. Wither
garden, and be henceforth a burying-place to all that do
dwell in this house, because the unconquered soul of
Cade is fled.

IDEN: Is't Cade that I have slain, that monstrous traitor?
Sword, I will hallow thee for this thy deed,
And hang thee o'er my tomb, when I am dead.
Ne'er shall this blood be wiped from thy point,
But thou shalt wear it as a Herald's coat,
To emblaze the honour that thy Master got.

CADE: Iden farewell, and be proud of thy victory: Tell
Kent from me, she hath lost her best man, and exhort
all the World to be cowards; For I that never feared any,
am vanquished by famine, not by valour.

Dies.

IDEN: How much thou wrong'st me, heaven be my judge;
Die damned wretch, the curse of her that bare thee:
And as I thrust thy body in with my sword,
So wish I, I might trust thy soul to hell.

Hence will I drag thee headlong by the heels
Unto a dunghill, which shall be thy grave,
And there cut off thy most ungracious head,
Which I will bear in triumph to the King,
Leaving thy trunk for crows to feed upon.

Exit.

V. 1

*Enter York, and his Army of Irish, with drum
and colours.*

YORK: From Ireland thus comes York to claim his right,
And pluck the Crown from feeble Henry's head.
Ring bells aloud, burn bonfires clear and bright
To entertain great England's lawful King.
Ah *Sancta Maiestas!* who would not buy thee dear?
Let them obey, that know not how to rule.
This hand was made to handle nought but gold.
I cannot give due action to my words,
Except a sword or sceptre balance it.
A sceptre shall it have, have I a soul,
On which I'll toss the fleur-de-luce of France.

Enter Buckingham.

Whom have we here? Buckingham to disturb me?
The King hath sent him sure: I must dissemble.

BUCKINGHAM: York, if thou meanest well, I greet thee
well.

YORK: Humphrey of Buckingham, I accept thy greeting.
Art thou a messenger, or come of pleasure?

BUCKINGHAM: A messenger from Henry, our dread
Liege,
To know the reason of these arms in peace.
Or why, thou being a subject, as I am,
Against thy Oath, and true allegiance sworn,

Should raise so great a power without his leave?
Or dare to bring thy force so near the Court?

YORK: Scarce can I speak, my choler is so great.
  Oh I could hew up rocks, and fight with flint,
  I am so angry at these abject terms,
  And now like Ajax Telamonius,
  On sheep or oxen could I spend my fury.
  I am far better born than is the King:
  More like a King, more kingly in my thoughts.
  But I must make fair weather yet a while,
  Till Henry be more weak, and I more strong.
  Buckingham, I prithee pardon me,
  That I have given no answer all this while:
  My mind was troubled with deep melancholy.
  The cause why I have brought this Amy hither,
  Is to remove proud Somerset from the King,
  Seditious to his Grace, and to the State.

BUCKINGHAM: That is too much presumption on thy part:
  But if thy arms be to no other end,
  The King hath yielded unto thy demand:
  The Duke of Somerset is in the Tower.

YORK: Upon thine honour is he prisoner?

BUCKINGHAM: Upon mine honour he is prisoner.

YORK: Then Buckingham I do dismiss my Powers.
  Soldiers, I thank you all: disperse yourselves:
  Meet me tomorrow in S. George's Field,
  You shall have pay, and every thing you wish.
  And let my Sovereign, virtuous Henry,
  Command my eldest son, nay all my sons,
  As pledges of my fealty and love,
  I'll send them all as willing as I live:
  Lands, goods, horse, armour, any thing I have,
  Is his to use, so Somerset may die.

BUCKINGHAM: York, I commend this kind submission,
 We twain will go into his Highness' tent.
>*Enter King and Attendants.*

KING: Buckingham, doth York intend no harm to us
 That thus he marcheth with thee arm in arm?

YORK: In all submission and humility,
 York doth present himself unto your Highness.

KING: Then what intends these forces thou dost bring?

YORK: To heave the Traitor Somerset from hence,
 And fight against that monstrous Rebel Cade,
 Who since I heard to be discomfited.
>*Enter Iden with Cade's head.*

IDEN: If one so rude, and of so mean condition
 May pass into the presence of a King:
 Lo, I present your Grace a Traitor's head,
 The head of Cade, whom I in combat slew.

KING: The head of Cade? Great God, how just art thou?
 Oh let me view his visage being dead,
 That living wrought me such exceeding trouble.
 Tell me my Friend, art thou the man that slew him?

IDEN: I was, an't like your Majesty.

KING: How art thou call'd? And what is thy degree?

IDEN: Alexander Iden, that's my name,
 A poor Esquire of Kent, that loves his King.

BUCKINGHAM: So please it you my Lord, 'twere not amiss
 He were created Knight for his good service.

KING: Iden, kneel down, rise up a Knight:
 We give thee for reward a thousand marks,
 And will, that thou henceforth attend on us.

IDEN: May Iden live to merit such a bounty,
 And never live but true unto his Liege.
>*Enter Queen and Somerset.*

KING: See Buckingham, Somerset comes with the Queen;
 Go bid her hide him quickly from the Duke.

QUEEN: For thousand Yorks he shall not hide his head,
But boldly stand, and front him to his face.
YORK: How now? is Somerset at liberty?
Then York unloose thy long-imprison'd thoughts,
And let thy tongue be equal with thy heart.
Shall I endure the sight of Somerset?
False King, why hast thou broken faith with me,
Knowing how hardly I can brook abuse?
King did I call thee? No: thou art not King:
Not fit to govern and rule multitudes,
Which dar'st not, no nor canst not rule a Traitor.
That head of thine doth not become a Crown;
Thy hand is made to grasp a palmer's staff,
And not to grace an aweful princely Sceptre.
That Gold, must round engirt these brows of mine,
Whose smile and frown, like to Achilles' spear
Is able with the change, to kill and cure.
Here is a hand to hold a sceptre up,
And with the same to act controlling Laws:
Give place: by heaven thou shalt rule no more
O'er him, whom heaven created for thy Ruler.
SOMERSET: O monstrous Traitor! I arrest thee York
Of Capital Treason 'gainst the King and Crown:
Obey, audacious Traitor, kneel for grace.
YORK: Would'st have me kneel? First let me ask of thee,
If they can brook I bow a knee to man:
Sirrah, call in my sons to be my bail:
I know ere they will have me go to ward,
They 'll pawn their swords at my enfranchisement.
QUEEN: Call hither Clifford, bid him come amain,
To say, if that the bastard boys of York
Shall be the surety for their Traitor Father.
YORK: O blood-bespotted Neapolitan,
Outcast of Naples, England's bloody Scourge,

The sons of York, thy betters in their birth,
Shall be their Father's bail, and bane to those
That for my surety will refuse the boys.
Enter Edward and Richard.
See where they come, I'll warrant they'll make it good.
Enter Clifford and his son.
QUEEN: And here comes Clifford to deny their bail.
CLIFFORD: Health, and all happiness to my Lord the King.
YORK: I thank thee Clifford: Say, what news with thee?
Nay, do not fright us with an angry look:
We are thy Sovereign Clifford, kneel again;
For thy mistaking so, We pardon thee.
CLIFFORD: This is my King York, I do not mistake,
But thou mistakes me much to think I do,
To Bedlam with him, is the man grown mad.
KING: Ay Clifford, a bedlam and ambitious humour
Makes him oppose himself against his King.
CLIFFORD: He is a Traitor, let him to the Tower,
And chop away that factious pate of his.
QUEEN: He is arrested, but will not obey:
His sons (he says) shall give their words for him.
YORK: Will you not Sons?
EDWARD: Ay noble Father, if our words will serve.
RICHARD: And if words will not, then our weapons shall.
CLIFFORD: Why what a brood of Traitors have we here?
YORK: Look in a glass, and call thy image so.
I am thy King, and thou a false-heart Traitor:
Call hither to the stake my two brave bears,
That with the very shaking of their chains,
They may astonish these fell-lurking curs,
Bid Salisbury and Warwick come to me.
Enter the Earls of Warwick, and Salisbury.
CLIFFORD: Are these thy bears? We'll bait thy bears to
death,

And manacle the bear'ard in their chains,
If thou dar'st bring them to the baiting place.
RICHARD: Oft have I seen a hot o'erweening cur,
Run back and bite, because he was withheld,
Who being suffer'd with the bear's fell paw,
Hath clapp'd his tail, between his legs and cried,
And such a piece of service will you do,
If you oppose yourselves to match Lord Warwick.
CLIFFORD: Hence heap of wrath, foul indigested lump,
As crooked in thy manners, as thy shape.
YORK: Nay we shall heat you thoroughly anon.
CLIFFORD: Take heed lest by your heat you burn your-
selves.
KING: Why Warwick, hath thy knee forgot to bow?
Old Salisbury, shame to thy silver hair,
Thou mad misleader of thy brain-sick son,
What wilt thou on thy death-bed play the ruffian?
And seek for sorrow with thy spectacles?
Oh where is Faith? Oh, where is Loyalty?
If it be banish'd from the frosty head,
Where shall it find a harbour in the earth?
Wilt thou go dig a grave to find out War,
And shame thine honourable age with blood?
Why art thou old, and want'st experience?
Or wherefore dost abuse it, if thou hast it?
For shame in duty bend thy knee to me,
That bows unto the grave with mickle age.
SALISBURY: My Lord, I have consider'd with myself
The Title of this most renowned Duke,
And in my conscience, do repute his grace
The rightful heir to England's royal seat.
KING: Hast thou not sworn allegiance unto me?
SALISBURY: I have.
KING: Canst thou dispense with heaven for such an oath?

SALISBURY: It is great sin, to swear unto a sin:
　　But greater sin to keep a sinful oath:
　　Who can be bound by any solemn vow
　　To do a murd'rous deed, to rob a man,
　　To force a spotless virgin's chastity,
　　To reave the orphan of his patrimony,
　　To wring the widow from her custom'd right,
　　And have no other reason for this wrong,
　　But that he was bound by a solemn oath?

QUEEN: A subtle Traitor needs no sophister.

KING: Call Buckingham, and bid him arm himself.

YORK: Call Buckingham, and all the friends thou hast,
　　I am resolv'd for death and dignity.

OLD CLIFFORD: The first I warrant thee, if dreams prove
　　true.

WARWICK: You were best to go to bed, and dream again,
　　To keep thee from the tempest of the field.

OLD CLIFFORD: I am resolv'd to bear a greater storm,
　　Than any thou canst conjure up today;
　　And that I'll write upon thy burgonet,
　　Might I but know thee by thy household badge.

WARWICK: Now by my Father's badge, old Nevil's
　　crest,
　　The rampant bear chain'd to the ragged staff,
　　This day I'll wear aloft my burgonet,
　　As on a mountain top, the cedar shows,
　　That keeps his leaves in spite of any storm,
　　Even to affright thee with the view thereof.

OLD CLIFFORD: And from thy burgonet I'll rend thy
　　bear,
　　And tread it under foot with all contempt,
　　Despite the bear'ard, that protects the Bear.

YOUNG CLIFFORD: And so to arms victorious Father,
　　To quell the Rebels, and their complices.

RICHARD: Fie, charity for shame, speak not in spite,
  For you shall sup with Jesu Christ tonight.
YOUNG CLIFFORD: Foul stigmatic that's more than thou
    canst tell.
RICHARD: If not in heaven, you'll surely sup in hell.
                    Exeunt.

V. 2

Enter Warwick.

WARWICK: Clifford of Cumberland, 'tis Warwick calls:
  And if thou dost not hide thee from the Bear,
  Now when the angry trumpet sounds alarum,
  And dead men's cries do fill the empty air,
  Clifford I say, come forth and fight with me,
  Proud Northern Lord, Clifford of Cumberland,
  Warwick is hoarse with calling thee to arms.
                    Enter York.
  How now, my noble Lord? What all a-foot.
YORK: The deadly-handed Clifford slew my steed:
  But match to match I have encounter'd him,
  And made a prey for carrion kites and crows
  Even of the bonny beast he lov'd so well.
                    Enter Clifford.
WARWICK: Of one or both of us the time is come.
YORK: Hold Warwick: seek thee out some other chase
  For I myself must hunt this deer to death.
WARWICK: Then nobly York, 'tis for a Crown thou
    fight'st:
  As I intend Clifford to thrive today,
  It grieves my soul to leave thee unassail'd.
                    Exit Warwick.
CLIFFORD: What seest thou in me York?
  Why dost thou pause?

YORK: With thy brave bearing should I be in love,
  But that thou art so fast mine enemy.

CLIFFORD: Nor should thy prowess want praise and
    esteem,
  But that 'tis shown ignobly, and in treason.

YORK: So let it help me now against thy sword,
  As I in justice, and true right express it.

CLIFFORD: My soul and body on the action both.

YORK: A dreadful lay, address thee instantly.

                They fight, and Clifford falls.

CLIFFORD: *La fin couronne les œuvres.*

                        Dies.

YORK: Thus War hath given thee peace, for thou art still,
  Peace with his soul, heaven if it be thy will.

                        Exit.
                Enter young Clifford.

YOUNG CLIFFORD: Shame and confusion all is on the
    rout,
  Fear frames disorder, and disorder wounds
  Where it should guard. O War, thou son of hell,
  Whom angry heavens do make their minister,
  Throw in the frozen bosoms of our part,
  Hot coals of vengeance. Let no soldier fly.
  He that is truly dedicate to War
  Hath no self-love: nor he that loves himself,
  Hath not essentially, but by circumstance
  The name of valour. O let the vile world end,
  And the premised flames of the Last day,
  Knit earth and heaven together.
  Now let the general Trumpet blow his blast,
  Particularities, and petty sounds
  To cease. Wast thou ordain'd (dear Father)
  To lose thy youth in peace, and to achieve
  The silver livery of advised age,

And in thy reverence, and thy chair-days, thus
To die in ruffian battle? Even at this sight,
My heart is turn'd to stone: and while 'tis mine,
It shall be stony. York, not our old men spares:
No more will I their babes, tears virginal,
Shall be to me, even as the dew to fire,
And Beauty, that the Tyrant oft reclaims,
Shall to my flaming wrath, be oil and flax:
Henceforth, I will not have to do with pity.
Meet I an infant of the house of York,
Into as many gobbets will I cut it
As wild Medea young Absyrtus did.
In cruelty, will I seek out my fame.
Come thou new ruin of old Clifford's house:
As did Aeneas old Anchises bear,
So bear I thee upon my manly shoulders:
But then, Aeneas bare a living load;
Nothing so heavy as these woes of mine.

Exit, bearing off his father.
Enter Richard, and Somerset to fight. Somerset
is killed.

RICHARD: So lie thou there:
For underneath an ale-house' paltry sign,
The Castle in S. Alban's, Somerset
Hath made the Wizard famous in his death:
Sword, hold thy temper; Heart, be wrathful still:
Priests pray for enemies, but Princes kill.

Exit.
Fight. Excursions.
Enter King, Queen, and others.

QUEEN: Away my Lord, you are slow, for shame away.
KING: Can we outrun the Heavens? Good Margaret stay.
QUEEN: What are you made of? You'll not fight nor fly:
Now is it manhood, wisdom, and defence,

To give the enemy way, and to secure us
By what we can, which can no more but fly.
Alarum afar off.
If you be ta'en, we then should see the bottom
Of all our fortunes: but if we haply scape,
(As well we may, if not through your neglect)
We shall to London get, where you are lov'd,
And where this breach now in our fortunes made
May readily be stopp'd.
Enter young Clifford.
CLIFFORD: But that my heart's on future mischief set,
 I would speak blasphemy ere bid you fly:
 But fly you must: Uncurable discomfit
 Reigns in the hearts of all our present parts.
 Away for your relief, and we will live
 To see their day, and them our fortune give.
 Away my Lord, away.
Exeunt.

V. 3

Alarum. Retreat. Enter York, Richard, Warwick,
and Soldiers, with drum and colours.
YORK: Of Salisbury, who can report of him,
 That Winter Lion, who in rage forgets
 Aged contusions, and all brush of Time:
 And like a Gallant, in the brow of youth,
 Repairs him with occasion. This happy day
 Is not itself, nor have we won one foot,
 If Salisbury be lost.
RICHARD: My noble Father:
 Three times today I holp him to his horse,
 Three times bestrid him: Thrice I led him off,
 Persuaded him from any further act:

But still where danger was, still there I met him,
And like rich hangings in a homely house,
So was his will, in his old feeble body.
But noble as he is, look where he comes.

Enter Salisbury.

SALISBURY: Now by my sword, well hast thou fought today:
  By th' Mass so did we all. I thank you Richard.
  God knows how long it is I have to live:
  And it hath pleas'd him that three times today
  You have defended me from imminent death.
  Well Lords, we have not got that which we have,
  'Tis not enough our foes are this time fled,
  Being opposites of such repairing nature.
YORK: I know our safety is to follow them,
  For (as I hear) the King is fled to London,
  To call a present Court of Parliament:
  Let us pursue him ere the writs go forth.
  What says Lord Warwick, shall we after them?
WARWICK: After them: nay before them if we can:
  Now by my hand (Lords) 'twas a glorious day.
  Saint Alban's battle won by famous York,
  Shall be eterniz'd in all Age to come.
  Sound drum and trumpets, and to London all,
  And more such days as these, to us befall.

Exeunt.

The Third Part of
Henry the Sixth

WITH THE DEATH OF THE
DUKE OF YORK

THE ACTORS' NAMES

KING HENRY THE SIXTH
EDWARD, Prince of Wales, his son
LOUIS XI, King of France
DUKE OF SOMERSET
DUKE OF EXETER
EARL OF OXFORD
EARL OF NORTHUMBERLAND
EARL OF WESTMORLAND
LORD CLIFFORD
RICHARD PLANTAGENET, Duke of York
EDWARD, Earl of March, afterwards King Edward IV ⎫
EDMUND, Earl of Rutland   ⎪ his
GEORGE, afterwards Duke of Clarence   ⎬ sons
RICHARD, afterwards Duke of Gloucester   ⎭
DUKE OF NORFOLK
MARQUESS OF MONTAGUE
EARL OF WARWICK
EARL OF PEMBROKE
LORD HASTINGS
LORD STAFFORD
SIR JOHN MORTIMER,   ⎱ uncles to the Duke of York
SIR HUGH MORTIMER   ⎰
HENRY, Earl of Richmond, a youth
LORD RIVERS, brother to Lady Grey
SIR WILLIAM STANLEY
SIR JOHN MONTGOMERY
SIR JOHN SOMERVILLE
Tutor to Rutland   Mayor of York
Lieutenant of the Tower   A Nobleman
Two Keepers   A Huntsman
A Son that has killed his father
A Father that has killed his son
QUEEN MARGARET
LADY GREY, afterwards Queen to Edward IV
BONA, sister to the French Queen
Soldiers, Attendants, Messengers, Watchmen, &c.

I. 1

Alarum.
Enter Plantagenet (*Duke of York*), *Edward,*
Richard, Norfolk, Montague, Warwick, and
Soldiers.

WARWICK: I wonder how the King escap'd our hands?
YORK: While we pursu'd the horsemen of the North,
    He slily stole away, and left his men:
    Whereat the great Lord of Northumberland,
    Whose warlike ears could never brook retreat,
    Cheer'd up the drooping Army, and himself.
    Lord Clifford and Lord Stafford all a-breast
    Charg'd our main Battle's front: and breaking in,
    Were by the swords of common soldiers slain.
EDWARD: Lord Stafford's Father, Duke of Buckingham,
    Is either slain or wounded dangerous.
    I cleft his beaver with a down-right blow:
    That this is true (Father) behold his blood.
MONTAGUE: And Brother, here's the Earl of Wiltshire's
        blood,
    Whom I encounter'd as the battles join'd.
RICHARD: Speak thou for me, and tell them what I did.
YORK: Richard hath best deserv'd of all my sons:
    But is your Grace dead, my Lord of Somerset?
NORFOLK: Such hope have all the line of John of Gaunt.
RICHARD: Thus do I hope to shake King Henry's head.
WARWICK: And so do I, victorious Prince of York.
    Before I see thee seated in that Throne,
    Which now the House of Lancaster usurps,
    I vow by Heaven, these eyes shall never close.
    This is the Palace of the fearful King,

And this the Regal Seat: possess it York,
For this is thine, and not King Henry's Heirs'.

YORK: Assist me then, sweet Warwick, and I will,
For hither we have broken in by force.

NORFOLK: We'll all assist you: he that flies, shall die.

YORK: Thanks gentle Norfolk, stay by me my Lords,
And soldiers stay and lodge by me this night.

They go up.

WARWICK: And when the King comes, offer him no violence,
Unless he seek to thrust you out perforce.

YORK: The Queen this day here holds her Parliament,
But little thinks we shall be of her Council,
By words or blows here let us win our right.

RICHARD: Arm'd as we are, let's stay within this House.

WARWICK: The bloody Parliament shall this be call'd,
Unless Plantagenet, Duke of York, be King.
And bashful Henry depos'd, whose cowardice
Hath made us by-words to our enemies.

YORK: Then leave me not, my Lords be resolute,
I mean to take possession of my Right.

WARWICK: Neither the King, nor he that loves him best,
The proudest he that holds up Lancaster,
Dares stir a wing, if Warwick shake his bells.
I'll plant Plantagenet, root him up who dares:
Resolve thee Richard, claim the English Crown.

Flourish. Enter King Henry, Clifford, North-
umberland, Westmorland, Exeter, and the rest.

HENRY: My Lords, look where the sturdy rebel sits,
Even in the Chair of State: belike he means,
Back'd by the power of Warwick, that false Peer,
To aspire unto the Crown, and reign as King.
Earl of Northumberland, he slew thy Father,

And thine, Lord Clifford, and you both have vow'd revenge

On him, his sons, his favourites, and his friends.

NORTHUMBERLAND: If I be not, Heavens be reveng'd on me.

CLIFFORD: The hope thereof, makes Clifford mourn in steel.

WESTMORLAND: What, shall we suffer this? let's pluck him down,

My heart for anger burns, I cannot brook it.

HENRY: Be patient, gentle Earl of Westmorland.

CLIFFORD: Patience is for poltroons, such as he:

He durst not sit there, had your Father liv'd.

My gracious Lord, here in the Parliament

Let us assail the Family of York.

NORTHUMBERLAND: Well hast thou spoken, Cousin be it so.

HENRY: Ah, know you not the City favours them,

And they have troops of soldiers at their beck?

EXETER: But when the Duke is slain, they'll quickly fly.

HENRY: Far be the thought of this from Henry's heart,

To make a shambles of the Parliament House.

Cousin of Exeter, frowns, words, and threats,

Shall be the war that Henry means to use.

Thou factious Duke of York descend my Throne,

And kneel for grace and mercy at my feet,

I am thy Sovereign.

YORK: I am thine.

EXETER: For shame come down, he made thee Duke of York.

YORK: It was my inheritance, as the Earldom was.

EXETER: Thy Father was a Traitor to the Crown.

WARWICK: Exeter thou art a Traitor to the Crown,

In following this usurping Henry.

CLIFFORD: Whom should he follow, but his natural King?

WARWICK: True Clifford, and that's Richard Duke of York.

HENRY: And shall I stand, and thou sit in my Throne?

YORK: It must and shall be so, content thyself.

WARWICK: Be Duke of Lancaster, let him be King.

WESTMORLAND: He is both King, and Duke of Lancaster,

And that the Lord of Westmorland shall maintain.

WARWICK: And Warwick shall disprove it. You forget,

That we are those which chas'd you from the field,

And slew your Fathers, and with colours spread

March'd through the City to the Palace Gates.

NORTHUMBERLAND: Yes Warwick, I remember it to my grief,

And by his soul, thou and thy House shall rue it.

WESTMORLAND: Plantagenet, of thee and these thy Sons,

Thy kinsmen, and thy friends, I'll have more lives

Than drops of blood were in my Father's veins.

CLIFFORD: Urge it no more, lest that instead of words,

I send thee, Warwick, such a messenger,

As shall revenge his death, before I stir.

WARWICK: Poor Clifford, how I scorn his worthless threats.

YORK: Will you we show our Title to the Crown?

If not, our swords shall plead it in the field.

HENRY: What Title hast thou traitor to the Crown?

Thy Father was as thou art, Duke of York,

Thy Grandfather Roger Mortimer, Earl of March.

I am the son of Henry the Fifth,

Who made the Dolphin and the French to stoop,

And seiz'd upon their Towns and Provinces.

WARWICK: Talk not of France, sith thou hast lost it all.

HENRY: The Lord Protector lost it, and not I:
　When I was crown'd, I was but nine months old.
RICHARD: You are old enough now,
　And yet methinks you lose:
　Father tear the Crown from the Usurper's head.
EDWARD: Sweet Father do so, set it on your head.
MONTAGUE: Good Brother,
　As thou lov'st and honourest arms,
　Let 's fight it out, and not stand cavilling thus.
RICHARD: Sound drums and trumpets, and the King will
　　fly.
YORK: Sons peace.
HENRY: Peace thou, and give King Henry leave to speak.
WARWICK: Plantagenet shall speak first: Hear him Lords,
　And be you silent and attentive too,
　For he that interrupts him, shall not live.
HENRY: Think'st thou, that I will leave my Kingly
　　Throne,
　Wherein my Grandsire and my Father sat?
　No: first shall War unpeople this my Realm;
　Ay, and their colours often borne in France,
　And now in England, to our heart's great sorrow,
　Shall be my winding-sheet. Why faint you Lords?
　My Title 's good, and better far than his.
WARWICK: Prove it Henry, and thou shalt be King.
HENRY: Henry the Fourth by conquest got the Crown.
YORK: 'Twas by rebellion against his King.
HENRY: I know not what to say, my Title 's weak:
　Tell me, may not a King adopt an Heir?
YORK: What then?
HENRY: And if he may, then am I lawful King:
　For Richard, in the view of many Lords,
　Resign'd the Crown to Henry the Fourth,
　Whose Heir my Father was, and I am his.

YORK: He rose against him, being his Sovereign,
  And made him to resign his Crown perforce.
WARWICK: Suppose, my Lords, he did it unconstrain'd,
  Think you 'twere prejudicial to his Crown?
EXETER: No: for he could not so resign his Crown,
  But that the next Heir should succeed and reign.
HENRY: Art thou against us, Duke of Exeter?
EXETER: His is the right, and therefore pardon me.
YORK: Why whisper you, my Lords, and answer not?
EXETER: My conscience tells me he is lawful King.
HENRY: All will revolt from me, and turn to him.
NORTHUMBERLAND: Plantagenet, for all the claim thou
    lay'st,
  Think not, that Henry shall be so depos'd.
WARWICK: Depos'd he shall be, in despite of all.
NORTHUMBERLAND: Thou art deceiv'd:
  'Tis not thy Southern power
  Of Essex, Norfolk, Suffolk, nor of Kent,
  Which makes thee thus presumptuous and proud,
  Can set the Duke up in despite of me.
CLIFFORD: King Henry, be thy Title right or wrong,
  Lord Clifford vows to fight in thy defence:
  May that ground gape, and swallow me alive,
  Where I shall kneel to him that slew my Father.
HENRY: Oh Clifford, how thy words revive my heart.
YORK: Henry of Lancaster, resign thy Crown:
  What mutter you, or what conspire you Lords?
WARWICK: Do right unto this Princely Duke of York,
  Or I will fill the House with armed men,
  And over the Chair of State, where now he sits,
  Write up his Title with usurping blood.
      He stamps with his foot, and the Soldiers show
            themselves.
HENRY: My Lord of Warwick, hear but one word,

Let me for this my life-time reign as King.

YORK: Confirm the Crown to me and to mine Heirs,
  And thou shalt reign in quiet while thou liv'st.

HENRY: I am content: Richard Plantagenet,
  Enjoy the Kingdom after my decease.

CLIFFORD: What wrong is this unto the Prince, your Son?

WARWICK: What good is this to England, and himself?

WESTMORLAND: Base, fearful, and despairing Henry.

CLIFFORD: How hast thou injur'd both thyself and us?

WESTMORLAND: I cannot stay to hear these Articles.

NORTHUMBERLAND: Nor I.

CLIFFORD: Come Cousin, let us tell the Queen these
  news.

WESTMORLAND: Farewell faint-hearted and degenerate
  King,
  In whose cold blood no spark of Honour bides.

NORTHUMBERLAND: Be thou a prey unto the House of
  York,
  And die in bands, for this unmanly deed.

CLIFFORD: In dreadful war mayst thou be overcome,
  Or live in peace abandon'd and despis'd.
    Exit Northumberland, Clifford, and Westmorland.

WARWICK: Turn this way Henry, and regard them not.

EXETER: They seek revenge, and therefore will not yield.

HENRY: Ah Exeter.

WARWICK: Why should you sigh, my Lord?

HENRY: Not for myself Lord Warwick, but my Son,
  Whom I unnaturally shall disinherit.
  But be it as it may: I here entail
  The Crown to thee and to thine Heirs for ever,
  Conditionally, that here thou take an Oath,
  To cease this Civil War: and whilst I live,
  To honour me as thy King and Sovereign:
  And neither by treason nor hostility,

To seek to put me down, and reign thyself.

YORK: This Oath I willingly take, and will perform.

WARWICK: Long live King Henry: Plantagenet embrace him.

HENRY: And long live thou, and these thy forward sons.

YORK: Now York and Lancaster are reconcil'd.

EXETER: Accurs'd be he that seeks to make them foes.

Sennet. Here they come down.

YORK: Farewell my gracious Lord, I'll to my Castle.

WARWICK: And I'll keep London with my soldiers.

NORFOLK: And I to Norfolk with my followers.

MONTAGUE: And I unto the sea, from whence I came.

Exeunt York and his Sons, Warwick, Norfolk,
Montague, their Soldiers, and Attendants.

HENRY: And I with grief and sorrow to the Court.

Enter the Queen Margaret and the Prince of Wales.

EXETER: Here comes the Queen,
  Whose looks bewray her anger:
  I'll steal away.

HENRY: Exeter so will I.

QUEEN: Nay, go not from me, I will follow thee.

HENRY: Be patient gentle Queen, and I will stay.

QUEEN: Who can be patient in such extremes?
  Ah wretched man, would I had died a maid!
  And never seen thee, never borne thee Son,
  Seeing thou hast prov'd so unnatural a Father.
  Hath he deserv'd to lose his birth-right thus?
  Hadst thou but lov'd him half so well as I,
  Or felt that pain which I did for him once,
  Or nourish'd him, as I did with my blood;
  Thou wouldst have left thy dearest heart-blood there,
  Rather than have made that savage Duke thine Heir,
  And disinherited thine only Son.

PRINCE: Father, you cannot disinherit me:

If you be King, why should not I succeed?

HENRY: Pardon me Margaret, pardon me sweet Son,
The Earl of Warwick and the Duke enforc'd me.

QUEEN: Enforc'd thee? Art thou King, and wilt be
forc'd?
I shame to hear thee speak: ah timorous wretch,
Thou hast undone thyself, thy Son, and me,
And giv'n unto the House of York such head,
As thou shalt reign but by their sufferance.
To entail him and his Heirs unto the Crown,
What is it, but to make thy sepulchre,
And creep into it far before thy time?
Warwick is Chancellor, and the Lord of Callice,
Stern Falconbridge commands the Narrow Seas,
The Duke is made Protector of the Realm,
And yet shalt thou be safe? Such safety finds
The trembling lamb, environed with wolves.
Had I been there, which am a silly woman,
The soldiers should have toss'd me on their pikes,
Before I would have granted to that act.
But thou preferr'st thy life, before thine honour.
And seeing thou dost, I here divorce myself,
Both from thy table Henry, and thy bed,
Until that Act of Parliament be repeal'd,
Whereby my Son is disinherited.
The Northern Lords, that have forsworn thy colours,
Will follow mine, if once they see them spread:
And spread they shall be, to thy foul disgrace,
And utter ruin of the House of York.
Thus do I leave thee: Come Son, let's away,
Our Army is ready; come, we 'll after them.

HENRY: Stay gentle Margaret, and hear me speak.

QUEEN: Thou hast spoke too much already: get thee
gone.

HENRY: Gentle Son Edward, thou wilt stay with me?
QUEEN: Ay, to be murther'd by his enemies.
PRINCE: When I return with victory from the field,
    I'll see your Grace: till then, I'll follow her.
QUEEN: Come Son away, we may not linger thus.
                    Exeunt Queen Margaret and the Prince.
HENRY: Poor Queen,
    How love to me, and to her Son,
    Hath made her break out into terms of rage.
    Reveng'd may she be on that hateful Duke,
    Whose haughty spirit, winged with desire,
    Will cost my Crown, and like an empty eagle,
    Tire on the flesh of me, and of my Son.
    The loss of those three Lords torments my heart:
    I'll write unto them, and entreat them fair;
    Come Cousin, you shall be the messenger.
EXETER: And I, I hope, shall reconcile them all.
                    Exeunt.

I. 2

Flourish.
Enter Richard, Edward, and Montague.

RICHARD: Brother, though I be youngest, give me leave.
EDWARD: No, I can better play the Orator.
MONTAGUE: But I have reasons strong and forcible.
                    Enter the Duke of York.
YORK: Why how now Sons, and Brother, at a strife?
    What is your quarrel? how began it first?
EDWARD: No quarrel, but a slight contention.
YORK: About what?
RICHARD: About that which concerns your Grace and us.
    The Crown of England, Father, which is yours.
YORK: Mine boy? not till King Henry be dead.

RICHARD: Your right depends not on his life, or death.

EDWARD: Now you are Heir, therefore enjoy it now:
By giving the House of Lancaster leave to breathe,
It will outrun you, Father, in the end.

YORK: I took an Oath, that he should quietly reign.

EDWARD: But for a Kingdom any oath may be broken:
I would break a thousand oaths, to reign one year.

RICHARD: No: God forbid your Grace should be forsworn.

YORK: I shall be, if I claim by open war.

RICHARD: I'll prove the contrary, if you'll hear me speak.

YORK: Thou canst not, Son; it is impossible.

RICHARD: An Oath is of no moment, being not took
Before a true and lawful Magistrate,
That hath authority over him that swears.
Henry had none, but did usurp the place.
Then seeing 'twas he that made you to depose,
Your Oath, my Lord, is vain and frivolous.
Therefore to arms: and Father do but think,
How sweet a thing it is to wear a Crown,
Within whose circuit is Elysium,
And all that Poets feign of bliss and joy.
Why do we linger thus? I cannot rest,
Until the White Rose that I wear, be dyed
Even in the luke-warm blood of Henry's heart.

YORK: Richard enough: I will be King, or die.
Brother, thou shalt to London presently,
And whet on Warwick to this enterprise.
Thou Richard shalt to the Duke of Norfolk,
And tell him privily of our intent.
You Edward shall unto my Lord Cobham,
With whom the Kentishmen will willingly rise.
In them I trust: for they are soldiers,
Witty, courteous, liberal, full of spirit.

While you are thus employ'd, what resteth more?
But that I seek occasion how to rise,
And yet the King not privy to my drift,
Nor any of the House of Lancaster.

Enter Gabriel.

But stay, what news? Why com'st thou in such post?

GABRIEL: The Queen,
With all the Northern Earls and Lords,
Intend here to besiege you in your Castle.
She is hard by, with twenty thousand men:
And therefore fortify your hold, my Lord.

YORK: Ay, with my sword.
What? think'st thou, that we fear them?
Edward and Richard, you shall stay with me,
My Brother Montague shall post to London.
Let noble Warwick, Cobham, and the rest,
Whom we have left Protectors of the King,
With powerful policy strengthen themselves,
And trust not simple Henry, nor his oaths.

MONTAGUE: Brother, I go: I'll win them, fear it not.
And thus most humbly I do take my leave.

Exit.

Enter Mortimer, and his Brother.

YORK: Sir John, and Sir Hugh Mortimer, mine Uncles,
You are come to Sandal in a happy hour.
The Army of the Queen mean to besiege us.

MORTIMER: She shall not need, we'll meet her in the field.

YORK: What, with five thousand men?

RICHARD: Ay, with five hundred, Father, for a need.
A Woman's general: what should we fear?

A march afar off.

EDWARD: I hear their drums:
Let's set our men in order,
And issue forth, and bid them battle straight.

YORK: Five men to twenty: though the odds be great,
 I doubt not, Uncle, of our victory.
 Many a battle have I won in France,
 Whenas the enemy hath been ten to one:
 Why should I not now have the like success?
     Alarum. Exeunt.

I. 3

Enter Rutland, and his Tutor.

RUTLAND: Ah, whither shall I fly, to 'scape their hands?
 Ah Tutor, look where bloody Clifford comes.
    Enter Clifford and Soldiers.
CLIFFORD: Chaplain, away, thy Priesthood saves thy life.
 As for the Brat of this accursed Duke,
 Whose Father slew my Father, he shall die.
TUTOR: And I, my Lord, will bear him company.
CLIFFORD: Soldiers, away with him.
TUTOR: Ah Clifford, murther not this innocent child,
 Lest thou be hated both of God and Man.
     Exit.
CLIFFORD: How now? is he dead already?
 Or is it fear, that makes him close his eyes?
 I'll open them.
RUTLAND: So looks the pent-up lion o'er the wretch,
 That trembles under his devouring paws:
 And so he walks, insulting o'er his prey,
 And so he comes, to rend his limbs asunder.
 Ah gentle Clifford, kill me with thy sword,
 And not with such a cruel threat'ning look.
 Sweet Clifford hear me speak, before I die:
 I am too mean a subject for thy wrath,
 Be thou reveng'd on men, and let me live.
CLIFFORD: In vain thou speak'st, poor boy:

My Father's blood hath stopp'd the passage
Where thy words should enter.

RUTLAND: Then let my Father's blood open it again,
He is a man, and Clifford cope with him.

CLIFFORD: Had I thy Brethren here, their lives and thine
Were not revenge sufficient for me:
No, if I digg'd up thy fore-fathers' graves,
And hung their rotten coffins up in chains,
It could not slake mine ire, nor ease my heart.
The sight of any of the House of York,
Is as a fury to torment my soul:
And till I root out their accursed Line,
And leave not one alive, I live in Hell.
Therefore –

RUTLAND: Oh let me pray, before I take my death.
To thee I pray; sweet Clifford pity me.

CLIFFORD: Such pity as my rapier's point affords.

RUTLAND: I never did thee harm: why wilt thou slay
me?

CLIFFORD: Thy Father hath.

RUTLAND: But 'twas ere I was born.
Thou hast one Son, for his sake pity me,
Lest in revenge thereof, sith God is just,
He be as miserably slain as I.
Ah, let me live in prison all my days,
And when I give occasion of offence,
Then let me die, for now thou hast no cause.

CLIFFORD: No cause? thy Father slew my Father: therefore die.

Stabs him.

RUTLAND: *Di faciant laudis summa sit ista tuae.*

Dies.

CLIFFORD: Plantagenet, I come Plantagenet:
And thus thy Son's blood cleaving to my blade,

Shall rust upon my weapon, till thy blood
Congeal'd with this, do make me wipe off both.
Exit.

I. 4

Alarum. Enter Richard, Duke of York.

YORK: The Army of the Queen hath got the field:
My Uncles both are slain, in rescuing me;
And all my followers, to the eager foe
Turn back, and fly, like ships before the wind,
Or lambs pursu'd by hunger-starved wolves.
My Sons, God knows what hath bechanced them:
But this I know, they have demean'd themselves
Like men born to renown, by life or death.
Three times did Richard make a lane to me,
And thrice cried, Courage Father, fight it out:
And full as oft came Edward to my side,
With purple falchion, painted to the hilt,
In blood of those that had encounter'd him:
And when the hardiest warriors did retire,
Richard cried, Charge, and give no foot of ground,
And cried, A Crown, or else a glorious Tomb,
A Sceptre, or an earthly Sepulchre.
With this we charg'd again: but out alas,
We bodg'd again, as I have seen a swan
With bootless labour swim against the tide,
And spend her strength with over-matching waves.
                    A short alarum within.
Ah hark, the fatal followers do pursue,
And I am faint, and cannot fly their fury:
And were I strong, I would not shun their fury.
The sands are number'd, that makes up my life,
Here must I stay, and here my life must end.

Enter the Queen, Clifford, Northumberland,
the young Prince, and Soldiers.

Come bloody Clifford, rough Northumberland,
I dare your quenchless fury to more rage:
I am your butt, and I abide your shot.

NORTHUMBERLAND: Yield to our mercy, proud Plantagenet.

CLIFFORD: Ay, to such mercy, as his ruthless arm
With downright payment, show'd unto my Father.
Now Phaeton hath tumbled from his car,
And made an evening at the noontide prick.

YORK: My ashes, as the Phoenix, may bring forth
A Bird, that will revenge upon you all:
And in that hope, I throw mine eyes to Heaven,
Scorning whate'er you can afflict me with.
Why come you not? what, multitudes, and fear?

CLIFFORD: So cowards fight, when they can fly no further,
So doves do peck the falcon's piercing talons,
So desperate thieves, all hopeless of their lives,
Breathe out invectives 'gainst the Officers.

YORK: Oh Clifford, but bethink thee once again,
And in thy thought o'er-run my former time:
And if thou canst, for blushing, view this face,
And bite thy tongue, that slanders him with cowardice,
Whose frown hath made thee faint and fly ere this.

CLIFFORD: I will not bandy with thee word for word,
But buckler with thee blows twice two for one.

QUEEN: Hold valiant Clifford, for a thousand causes
I would prolong a while the Traitor's life:
Wrath makes him deaf; speak thou Northumberland.

NORTHUMBERLAND: Hold Clifford, do not honour him
so much,
To prick thy finger, though to wound his heart.
What valour were it, when a cur doth grin,

For one to thrust his hand between his teeth,
When he might spurn him with his foot away?
It is War's prize, to take all vantages,
And ten to one, is no impeach of valour.

CLIFFORD: Ay, ay, so strives the woodcock with the gin.

NORTHUMBERLAND: So doth the cony struggle in the
net.

YORK: So triumph thieves upon their conquer'd booty,
So true men yield with robbers, so o'er-match'd.

NORTHUMBERLAND: What would your Grace have
done unto him now?

QUEEN: Brave warriors, Clifford and Northumberland,
Come make him stand upon this mole-hill here,
That raught at mountains with outstretched arms,
Yet parted but the shadow with his hand.
What, was it you that would be England's King?
Was 't you that revell'd in our Parliament,
And made a preachment of your high descent?
Where are your mess of Sons, to back you now?
The wanton Edward, and the lusty George?
And where 's that valiant Crook-back Prodigy,
Dicky, your Boy, that with his grumbling voice
Was wont to cheer his Dad in mutinies?
Or with the rest, where is your Darling, Rutland?
Look York, I stain'd this napkin with the blood
That valiant Clifford, with his rapier's point.
Made issue from the bosom of the Boy:
And if thine eyes can water for his death,
I give thee this to dry thy cheeks withal.
Alas poor York, but that I hate thee deadly,
I should lament thy miserable state.
I prithee grieve, to make me merry, York.
What, hath thy fiery heart so parch'd thine entrails,
That not a tear can fall, for Rutland's death?

I

Why art thou patient, man? thou shouldst be mad:
And I, to make thee mad, do mock thee thus.
Stamp, rave, and fret, that I may sing and dance.
Thou would'st be fee'd, I see, to make me sport:
York cannot speak, unless he wear a Crown.
A Crown for York; and Lords, bow low to him:
Hold you his hands, whilst I do set it on.
Ay marry Sir, now looks he like a King:
Ay, this is he that took King Henry's Chair,
And this is he was his adopted Heir.
But how is it, that great Plantagenet
Is crown'd so soon, and broke his solemn Oath?
As I bethink me you should not be King,
Till our King Henry had shook hands with Death.
And will you pale your head in Henry's glory,
And rob his temples of the Diadem,
Now in his life, against your holy Oath?
Oh 'tis a fault too too unpardonable.
Off with the Crown; and with the Crown, his head,
And whilst we breathe, take time to do him dead.

CLIFFORD: That is my office, for my Father's sake.

QUEEN: Nay stay, let's hear the orisons he makes.

YORK: She-Wolf of France,
But worse than wolves of France,
Whose tongue more poisons than the adder's tooth:
How ill-beseeming is it in thy Sex,
To triumph like an Amazonian trull,
Upon their woes, whom Fortune captivates?
But that thy face is vizard-like, unchanging,
Made impudent with use of evil deeds,
I would assay, proud Queen, to make thee blush.
To tell thee whence thou cam'st, of whom deriv'd,
Were shame enough, to shame thee,
Wert thou not shameless.

Thy Father bears the type of King of Naples,
Of both the Sicils, and Jerusalem,
Yet not so wealthy as an English Yeoman.
Hath that poor Monarch taught thee to insult?
It needs not, nor it boots thee not, proud Queen,
Unless the Adage must be verifi'd,
That beggars mounted, run their horse to death.
'Tis Beauty that doth oft make women proud,
But God he knows, thy share thereof is small.
'Tis Virtue, that doth make them most admir'd,
The contrary, doth make thee wonder'd at.
'Tis Government that makes them seem divine,
The want thereof, makes thee abominable.
Thou art as opposite to every good,
As the Antipodes are unto us,
Or as the South to the Septentrion.
Oh Tiger's heart, wrapp'd in a Woman's hide,
How couldst thou drain the life-blood of the Child,
To bid the Father wipe his eyes withal,
And yet be seen to bear a Woman's face?
Women are soft, mild, pitiful, and flexible;
Thou stern, obdurate, flinty, rough, remorseless.
Bid'st thou me rage? why now thou hast thy wish.
Wouldst have me weep? why now thou hast thy will.
For raging wind blows up incessant showers,
And when the rage allays, the rain begins.
These tears are my sweet Rutland's obsequies,
And every drop cries vengeance for his death,
'Gainst thee fell Clifford, and thee false Frenchwoman.

NORTHUMBERLAND: Beshrew me, but his passions
    moves me so,
That hardly can I check my eyes from tears.

YORK: That face of his,
The hungry Cannibals would not have touch'd,

Would not have stain'd with blood:
But you are more inhuman, more inexorable,
Oh, ten times more than tigers of Hyrcania.
See, ruthless Queen, a hapless Father's tears:
This cloth thou dip'dst in blood of my sweet Boy,
And I with tears do wash the blood away.
Keep thou the napkin, and go boast of this,
And if thou tell'st the heavy story right,
Upon my soul, the hearers will shed tears:
Yea, even my foes will shed fast-falling tears,
And say, Alas, it was a piteous deed.
There, take the Crown, and with the Crown, my curse,
And in thy need, such comfort come to thee,
As now I reap at thy too cruel hand.
Hard-hearted Clifford, take me from the World,
My soul to Heaven, my blood upon your heads.

NORTHUMBERLAND: Had he been slaughter-man to all
     my kin,
I should not for my life but weep with him,
To see how inly sorrow gripes his soul.

QUEEN: What, weeping ripe, my Lord Northumberland?
Think but upon the wrong he did us all,
And that will quickly dry thy melting tears.

CLIFFORD: Here's for my Oath, here's for my Father's
     death.

QUEEN: And here's to right our gentle-hearted King.
                    They stab him.

YORK: Open thy Gate of Mercy, gracious God,
My soul flies through these wounds, to seek out Thee.
                    Dies.

QUEEN: Off with his head, and set it on York Gates,
So York may over-look the Town of York.
                    Flourish. Exeunt.

· II. 1

A march. Enter Edward, Richard, and their power.

EDWARD: I wonder how our Princely Father 'scap'd:
Or whether he be 'scap'd away, or no,
From Clifford's and Northumberland's pursuit?
Had he been ta'en, we should have heard the news;
Had he been slain, we should have heard the news:
Or had he 'scap'd, methinks we should have heard
The happy tidings of his good escape.
How fares my Brother? why is he so sad?

RICHARD: I cannot joy, until I be resolv'd
Where our right valiant Father is become.
I saw him in the battle range about,
And watch'd him how he singled Clifford forth.
Methought he bore him in the thickest troop,
As doth a lion in a herd of neat,
Or as a bear encompass'd round with dogs:
Who having pinch'd a few, and made them cry,
The rest stand all aloof, and bark at him.
So far'd our Father with his enemies,
So fled his enemies my Warlike Father:
Methinks 'tis prize enough to be his Son.
See how the morning opes her golden gates,
And takes her farewell of the glorious Sun.
How well resembles it the prime of youth,
Trimm'd like a younker, prancing to his love!

EDWARD: Dazzle mine eyes, or do I see three Suns?

RICHARD: Three glorious Suns, each one a perfect Sun,
Not separated with the racking clouds,
But sever'd in a pale clear-shing sky.
See, see, they join, embrace, and seem to kiss,
As if they vow'd some League inviolable.

Now are they but one lamp, one light, one sun:
In this, the Heaven figures some event.
EDWARD: 'Tis wondrous strange,
  The like yet never heard of.
  I think it cites us (Brother) to the field,
  That we, the Sons of brave Plantagenet,
  Each one already blazing by our meeds,
  Should notwithstanding join our lights together,
  And over-shine the Earth, as this the World.
  Whate'er it bodes, henceforward will I bear
  Upon my target three fair-shining suns.
RICHARD: Nay, bear three daughters:
  By your leave, I speak it,
  You love the breeder better than the male.

Enter one blowing.

  But what art thou, whose heavy looks foretell
  Some dreadful story hanging on thy tongue?
MESSENGER: Ah, one that was a woeful looker on,
  Whenas the Noble Duke of York was slain,
  Your Princely Father, and my loving Lord.
EDWARD: Oh speak no more, for I have heard too much.
RICHARD: Say how he died, for I will hear it all.
MESSENGER: Environed he was with many foes,
  And stood against them, as the hope of Troy
  Against the Greeks, that would have enter'd Troy.
  But Hercules himself must yield to odds:
  And many strokes, though with a little axe,
  Hews down and fells the hardest-timber'd oak.
  By many hands your Father was subdu'd,
  But only slaughter'd by the ireful arm
  Of unrelenting Clifford, and the Queen:
  Who crown'd the gracious Duke in high despite,
  Laugh'd in his face: and when with grief he wept,
  The ruthless Queen gave him, to dry his cheeks,

A napkin, steeped in the harmless blood
Of sweet young Rutland, by rough Clifford slain:
And after many scorns, many foul taunts,
They took his head, and on the Gates of York
They set the same, and there it doth remain,
The saddest spectacle that e'er I view'd.

EDWARD: Sweet Duke of York, our prop to lean upon,
Now thou art gone, we have no staff, no stay.
Oh Clifford, boist'rous Clifford, thou hast slain
The flower of Europe, for his Chivalry,
And treacherously hast thou vanquish'd him,
For hand to hand he would have vanquish'd thee.
Now my soul's palace is become a prison:
Ah, would she break from hence, that this my body
Might in the ground be closed up in rest:
For never henceforth shall I joy again:
Never, oh never shall I see more joy.

RICHARD: I cannot weep: for all my body's moisture
Scarce serves to quench my furnace-burning heart:
Nor can my tongue unload my heart's great burthen,
For self-same wind that I should speak withal,
Is kindling coals that fires all my breast,
And burns me up with flames, that tears would quench.
To weep, is to make less the depth of grief:
Tears then for babes; blows, and revenge for me.
Richard, I bear thy name, I'll venge thy death,
Or die renowned by attempting it.

EDWARD: His name that valiant Duke hath left with
thee:
His Dukedom, and his Chair with me is left.

RICHARD: Nay, if thou be that Princely Eagle's Bird,
Show thy descent by gazing 'gainst the Sun:
For Chair and Dukedom, Throne and Kingdom say,
Either that is thine, or else thou wert not his.

March. Enter Warwick, Marquess Montague,
and their Army.

WARWICK: How now fair Lords? What fare? What news
    abroad?

RICHARD: Great Lord of Warwick, if we should recompt
    Our baleful news, and at each word's deliverance
    Stab poniards in our flesh, till all were told,
    The words would add more anguish than the wounds.
    O valiant Lord, the Duke of York is slain.

EDWARD: O Warwick, Warwick, that Plantagenet
    Which held thee dearly, as his soul's redemption,
    Is by the stern Lord Clifford done to death.

WARWICK: Ten days ago, I drown'd these news in tears.
    And now to add more measure to your woes,
    I come to tell you things sith then befall'n.
    After the bloody fray at Wakefield fought,
    Where your brave Father breath'd his latest gasp,
    Tidings, as swiftly as the posts could run,
    Were brought me of your loss, and his depart.
    I then in London, keeper of the King,
    Muster'd my soldiers, gather'd flocks of friends,
    March'd toward S. Alban's, to intercept the Queen,
    Bearing the King in my behalf along:
    For by my scouts, I was advertised
    That she was coming with a full intent
    To dash our late Decree in Parliament,
    Touching King Henry's Oath, and your Succession:
    Short tale to make, we at S. Alban's met,
    Our battles join'd, and both sides fiercely fought:
    But whether 'twas the coldness of the King,
    Who look'd full gently on his warlike Queen,
    That robb'd my soldiers of their heated spleen.
    Or whether 'twas report of her success,
    Or more than common fear of Clifford's rigour,

Who thunders to his captives, blood and death,
I cannot judge: but to conclude with truth,
Their weapons like to lightning, came and went:
Our soldiers like the night-owl's lazy flight,
Or like a lazy thresher with a flail,
Fell gently down, as if they struck their friends.
I cheer'd them up with justice of our cause,
With promise of high pay, and great rewards:
But all in vain, they had no heart to fight,
And we (in them) no hope to win the day,
So that we fled: the King unto the Queen,
Lord George, your Brother, Norfolk, and myself,
In haste, post haste, are come to join with you:
For in the Marches here we heard you were,
Making another head, to fight again.

EDWARD: Where is the Duke of Norfolk, gentle Warwick?
And when came George from Burgundy to England?

WARWICK: Some six miles off the Duke is with the soldiers,
And for your Brother he was lately sent
From your kind Aunt Duchess of Burgundy,
With aid of soldiers to this needful war.

RICHARD: 'Twas odds belike, when valiant Warwick fled;
Oft have I heard his praises in pursuit,
But ne'er till now, his scandal of retire.

WARWICK: Nor now my scandal Richard, dost thou hear:
For thou shalt know this strong right hand of mine,
Can pluck the Diadem from faint Henry's head,
And wring the aweful Sceptre from his fist,
Were he as famous, and as bold in War,
As he is fam'd for mildness, peace, and prayer.

RICHARD: I know it well Lord Warwick, blame me not,

'Tis love I bear thy glories makes me speak:
But in this troublous time, what's to be done.
Shall we go throw away our coats of steel,
And wrap our bodies in black mourning gowns,
Numb'ring our Ave-Maries with our beads?
Or shall we on the helmets of our foes
Tell our devotion with revengeful arms?
If for the last, say ay, and to it Lords.

WARWICK: Why therefore Warwick came to seek you
    out,
And therefore comes my Brother Montague:
Attend me Lords, the proud insulting Queen,
With Clifford, and the haught Northumberland,
And of their feather, many moe proud birds,
Have wrought the easy-melting King, like wax.
He swore consent to your Succession,
His Oath enrolled in the Parliament.
And now to London all the crew are gone,
To frustrate both his Oath, and what beside
May make against the house of Lancaster.
Their power (I think) is thirty thousand strong:
Now, if the help of Norfolk, and myself,
With all the friends that thou brave Earl of March,
Amongst the loving Welshmen canst procure,
Will but amount to five and twenty thousand,
Why Via, to London will we march,
And once again, bestride our foaming steeds,
And once again cry Charge upon our Foes,
But never once again turn back and fly.

RICHARD: Ay, now methinks I hear great Warwick
    speak;
Ne'er may he live to see a sunshine day,
That cries Retire, if Warwick bid him stay.

EDWARD: Lord Warwick, on thy shoulder will I lean,

And when thou fail'st (as God forbid the hour)
Must Edward fall, which peril heaven forfend.

WARWICK: No longer Earl of March, but Duke of York:
The next degree, is England's Royal Throne:
For King of England shalt thou be proclaim'd
In every Borough as we pass along,
And he that throws not up his cap for joy,
Shall for the fault make forfeit of his head.
King Edward, valiant Richard Montague:
Stay we no longer, dreaming of renown,
But sound the trumpets, and about our task.

RICHARD: Then Clifford, were thy heart as hard as steel,
As thou hast shown in flinty by thy deeds,
I come to pierce it, or to give thee mine.

EDWARD: Then strike up drums, God and S. George for
us.

Enter a Messenger.

WARWICK: How now? what news?

MESSENGER: The Duke of Norfolk sends you word by me,
The Queen is coming with a puissant host,
And craves your company, for speedy counsel.

WARWICK: Why then it sorts, brave Warriors, let 's
away.

Exeunt omnes.

II. 2

*Flourish. Enter the King, the Queen, Clifford,
Northumberland, and Young Prince, with drum and
trumpets.*

QUEEN: Welcome my Lord, to this brave town of York,
Yonder's the head of that Arch-enemy,
That sought to be encompass'd with your Crown.
Doth not the object cheer your heart, my Lord?

KING: Ay, as the rocks cheer them that fear their wrack,
  To see this sight, it irks my very soul:
  Withhold revenge (dear God) 'tis not my fault,
  Nor wittingly have I infring'd my vow.
CLIFFORD: My gracious Liege, this too much lenity
  And harmful pity must be laid aside:
  To whom do lions cast their gentle looks?
  Not to the beast, that would usurp their den.
  Whose hand is that the forest bear doth lick?
  Not his that spoils her young before her face.
  Who 'scapes the lurking serpent's mortal sting?
  Not he that sets his foot upon her back.
  The smallest worm will turn, being trodden on,
  And doves will peck in safeguard of their brood.
  Ambitious York, did level at thy Crown,
  Thou smiling, while he knit his angry brows.
  He but a Duke, would have his Son a King,
  And raise his issue like a loving Sire.
  Thou being a King, blest with a goodly son,
  Didst yield consent to disinherit him:
  Which argued thee a most unloving Father.
  Unreasonable creatures feed their young,
  And though man's face be fearful to their eyes,
  Yet in protection of their tender ones,
  Who hath not seen them even with those wings,
  Which sometime they have us'd with fearful flight,
  Make war with him that climb'd unto their nest,
  Offering their own lives in their young's defence?
  For shame, my Liege, make them your precedent:
  Were it not pity that this goodly Boy
  Should lose his birth-right by his Father's fault,
  And long hereafter say unto his child,
  What my great Grandfather, and Grandsire got,
  My careless Father fondly gave away.

Ah, what a shame were this? Look on the Boy,
And let his manly face, which promiseth
Successful fortune steel thy melting heart,
To hold thine own, and leave thine own with him.

KING: Full well hath Clifford play'd the orator,
Inferring arguments of mighty force:
But Clifford tell me, didst thou never hear,
That things ill got, had ever bad success.
And happy always was it for that Son,
Whose Father for his hoarding went to hell:
I'll leave my Son my virtuous deeds behind,
And would my Father had left me no more:
For all the rest is held at such a rate,
As brings a thousand-fold more care to keep,
Than in possession any jot of pleasure.
Ah Cousin York, would thy best friends did know,
How it doth grieve me that thy head is here.

QUEEN: My Lord cheer up your spirits, our foes are nigh,
And this soft courage makes your followers faint:
You promised Knighthood to our forward son,
Unsheathe your sword, and dub him presently.
Edward, kneel down.

KING: Edward Plantagenet, arise a Knight,
And learn this lesson; Draw thy sword in right.

PRINCE: My gracious Father, by your kingly leave,
I'll draw it as Apparent to the Crown,
And in that quarrel, use it to the death.

CLIFFORD: Why, that is spoken like a toward Prince.

Enter a Messenger.

MESSENGER: Royal Commanders, be in readiness,
For with a band of thirty thousand men,
Comes Warwick backing of the Duke of York,
And in the Towns as they do march along,
Proclaims him King, and many fly to him,

Darraign your battle, for they are at hand.

CLIFFORD: I would your Highness would depart the field,
The Queen hath best success when you are absent.

QUEEN: Ay good my Lord, and leave us to our fortune.

KING: Why, that 's my fortune too, therefore I 'll stay.

NORTHUMBERLAND: Be it with resolution then to fight.

PRINCE: My Royal Father, cheer these Noble Lords,
And hearten those that fight in your defence:
Unsheathe your sword, good Father: Cry S. George.

March. Enter Edward, Warwick, Richard,
Clarence, Norfolk, Montague, and Soldiers.

EDWARD: Now perjur'd Henry, wilt thou kneel for grace?
And set thy diadem upon my head?
Or bide the mortal fortune of the field.

QUEEN: Go rate thy minions, proud insulting Boy,
Becomes it thee to be thus bold in terms,
Before thy Sovereign, and thy lawful King?

EDWARD: I am his King, and he should bow his knee:
I was adopted Heir by his consent.
Since when, his Oath is broke: for as I hear,
You that are King, though he do wear the Crown,
Have caus'd him by new Act of Parliament,
To blot out me, and put his own son in.

CLIFFORD: And reason too,
Who should succeed the Father, but the Son?

RICHARD: Are you there Butcher? O, I cannot speak.

CLIFFORD: Ay Crook-back, here I stand to answer thee,
Or any he, the proudest of thy sort.

RICHARD: 'Twas you that kill'd young Rutland, was it
not?

CLIFFORD: Ay, and old York, and yet not satisfied.

RICHARD: For God's sake Lords give signal to the fight.

WARWICK: What say'st thou Henry,
Wilt thou yield the Crown?

QUEEN: Why how now long-tongu'd Warwick, dare
  you speak?
  When you and I, met at S. Alban's last,
  Your legs did better service than your hands.
WARWICK: Then 'twas my turn to fly, and now 'tis thine.
CLIFFORD: You said so much before, and yet you fled.
WARWICK: 'Twas not your valour Clifford drove me
  thence.
NORTHUMBERLAND: No, nor your manhood that durst
  make you stay.
RICHARD: Northumberland, I hold thee reverently,
  Break off the parley, for scarce I can refrain
  The execution of my big-swoln heart
  Upon that Clifford, that cruel Child-killer.
CLIFFORD: I slew thy Father, call'st thou him a Child?
RICHARD: Ay like a dastard, and a treacherous coward,
  As thou didst kill our tender Brother Rutland,
  But ere sunset, I'll make thee curse the deed.
KING: Have done with words (my Lords) and hear me
  speak.
QUEEN: Defy them then, or else hold close thy lips.
KING: I prithee give no limits to my tongue,
  I am a King, and privileg'd to speak.
CLIFFORD: My Liege, the wound that bred this meeting
  here,
  Cannot be cur'd by words, therefore be still.
RICHARD: Then Executioner unsheathe thy sword:
  By him that made us all, I am resolv'd,
  That Clifford's manhood, lies upon his tongue.
EDWARD: Say Henry, shall I have my right, or no:
  A thousand men have broke their fasts today,
  That ne'er shall dine, unless thou yield the Crown.
WARWICK: If thou deny, their blood upon thy head,
  For York in justice puts his armour on.

PRINCE: If that be right, which Warwick says is right,
　　There is no wrong, but every thing is right.

RICHARD: Whoever got thee, there thy Mother stands,
　　For well I wot, thou hast thy Mother's tongue.

QUEEN: But thou art neither like thy Sire nor Dam,
　　But like a foul mishapen stigmatic,
　　Mark'd by the Destinies to be avoided,
　　As venom toads, or lizards' dreadful stings.

RICHARD: Iron of Naples, hid with English gilt,
　　Whose Father bears the Title of a King,
　　(As if a Channel should be call'd the Sea)
　　Sham'st thou not, knowing whence thou art extraught,
　　To let thy tongue detect thy base-born heart.

EDWARD: A wisp of straw were worth a thousand crowns,
　　To make this shameless callet know herself:
　　Helen of Greece was fairer far than thou,
　　Although thy Husband may be Menelaus;
　　And ne'er was Agamemnon's Brother wrong'd
　　By that false Woman, as this King by thee.
　　His Father revell'd in the heart of France,
　　And tam'd the King, and made the Dolphin stoop:
　　And had he match'd according to his State,
　　He might have kept that glory to this day.
　　But when he took a beggar to his bed,
　　And grac'd thy poor Sire with his bridal day,
　　Even then that sunshine brew'd a shower for him,
　　That wash'd his Father's fortunes forth of France,
　　And heap'd sedition on his Crown at home:
　　For what hath broach'd this tumult but thy pride?
　　Hadst thou been meek, our Title still had slept,
　　And we in pity of the Gentle King,
　　Had slipp'd our claim, until another age.

CLARENCE: But when we saw, our sunshine made thy
　　spring,

And that thy summer bred us no increase,
We set the axe to thy usurping root:
And though the edge hath something hit ourselves,
Yet know thou, since we have begun to strike,
We 'll never leave, till we have hewn thee down,
Or bath'd thy growing, with our heated bloods.
EDWARD: And in this resolution, I defy thee,
Not willing any longer conference,
Since thou denied'st the gentle King to speak.
Sound trumpets, let our bloody colours wave,
And either victory, or else a grave.
QUEEN: Stay, Edward.
EDWARD: No wrangling woman, we 'll no longer stay,
These words will cost ten thousand lives this day.
Exeunt Omnes.

II. 3

Alarum. Excursions. Enter Warwick.

WARWICK: Forspent with toil, as runners with a race,
I lay me down a little while to breathe:
For strokes receiv'd, and many blows repaid,
Have robb'd my strong knit sinews of their strength,
And spite of spite, needs must I rest awhile.
Enter Edward running.

EDWARD: Smile gentle heaven, or strike ungentle death,
For this world frowns, and Edward's sun is clouded.
WARWICK: How now my Lord, what hap? what hope of
good?
Enter Clarence.

CLARENCE: Our hap is loss, our hope but sad despair,
Our ranks are broke, and ruin follows us.
What counsel give you? whither shall we fly?
EDWARD: Bootless is flight, they follow us with wings,

And weak we are, and cannot shun pursuit.

Enter Richard.

RICHARD: Ah Warwick, why hast thou withdrawn thyself?

Thy Brother's blood the thirsty earth hath drunk,
Broach'd with the steely point of Clifford's lance:
And in the very pangs of death, he cried,
Like a dismal clangor heard from far,
Warwick, revenge; Brother, revenge my death.
So underneath the belly of their steeds,
That stain'd their fetlocks in his smoking blood,
The noble Gentleman gave up the ghost.

WARWICK: Then let the earth be drunken with our blood:
I'll kill my horse, because I will not fly:
Why stand we like soft-hearted women here,
Wailing our losses, whiles the foe doth rage,
And look upon, as if the Tragedy
Were play'd in jest, by counterfeiting actors.
Here on my knee, I vow to God above,
I'll never pause again, never stand still,
Till either death hath clos'd these eyes of mine,
Or Fortune given me measure of revenge.

EDWARD: Oh Warwick, I do bend my knee with thine,
And in this vow do chain my soul to thine:
And ere my knee rise from the Earth's cold face,
I throw my hands, mine eyes, my heart to thee,
Thou setter up, and plucker down of Kings:
Beseeching thee (if with thy will it stands)
That to my foes this body must be prey,
Yet that thy brazen gates of heaven may ope,
And give sweet passage to my sinful soul.
Now Lords, take leave until we meet again,
Where'er it be, in heaven, or in earth.

RICHARD: Brother,

Give me thy hand, and gentle Warwick,
Let me embrace thee in my weary arms:
I that did never weep, now melt with woe,
That winter should cut off our spring-time so.

WARWICK: Away, away:
Once more, sweet Lords farewell.

CLARENCE: Yet let us all together to our troops,
And give them leave to fly, that will not stay:
And call them pillars that will stand to us:
And if we thrive, promise them such rewards
As victors wear at the Olympian Games.
This may plant courage in their quailing breasts,
For yet is hope of life and victory:
Forslow no longer, make we hence amain.

Exeunt.

II. 4

Excursions. Enter Richard and Clifford.

RICHARD: Now Clifford, I have singled thee alone,
Suppose this arm is for the Duke of York,
And this for Rutland, both bound to revenge,
Wert thou environ'd with a brazen wall.

CLIFFORD: Now Richard, I am with thee here alone,
This is the hand that stabb'd thy Father York,
And this the hand, that slew thy Brother Rutland,
And here 's the heart, that triumphs in their death,
And cheers these hands, that slew thy Sire and Brother,
To execute the like upon thyself,
And so have at thee.

They fight. Warwick comes, Clifford flies.

RICHARD: Nay Warwick, single out some other chase,
For I myself will hunt this Wolf to death.

Exeunt.

II. 5

Alarum. Enter King Henry alone.

HENRY: This battle fares like to the morning's war,
    When dying clouds contend, with growing light,
    What time the shepherd blowing of his nails,
    Can neither call it perfect day, nor night.
    Now sways it this way, like a mighty sea,
    Forc'd by the tide, to combat with the wind:
    Now sways it that way, like the self-same sea,
    Forc'd to retire by fury of the wind.
    Sometime, the flood prevails; and then the wind:
    Now, one the better: then, another best;
    Both tugging to be victors, breast to breast:
    Yet neither conqueror, nor conquered.
    So is the equal poise of this fell war.
    Here on this mole-hill will I sit me down,
    To whom God will, there be the victory:
    For Margaret my Queen, and Clifford too
    Have chid me from the battle: Swearing both,
    They prosper best of all when I am thence.
    Would I were dead, if God's good will were so;
    For what is in this world, but grief and woe.
    Oh God! methinks it were a happy life,
    To be no better than a homely swain,
    To sit upon a hill, as I do now,
    To carve out dials quaintly, point by point,
    Thereby to see the minutes how they run:
    How many makes the hour full complete,
    How many hours brings about the day,
    How many days will finish up the year,
    How many years, a mortal man may live.
    When this is known, then to divide the times:

So many hours, must I tend my flock;
So many hours, must I take my rest:
So many hours, must I contemplate:
So many hours, must I sport myself:
So many days, my ewes have been with young:
So many weeks, ere the poor fools will ean:
So many years, ere I shall shear the fleece:
So minutes, hours, days, months, and years,
Pass'd over to the end they were created,
Would bring white hairs, unto a quiet grave.
Ah! what a life were this? How sweet? how lovely?
Gives not the hawthorn bush a sweeter shade
To shepherds looking on their silly sheep,
Than doth a rich embroider'd canopy
To Kings, that fear their Subjects' treachery?
Oh yes, it doth; a thousand-fold it doth.
And to conclude, the shepherd's homely curds,
His cold thin drink out of his leather bottle,
His wonted sleep, under a fresh tree's shade,
All which secure, and sweetly he enjoys,
Is far beyond a Prince's delicates:
His viands sparkling in a golden cup,
His body couched in a curious bed,
When Care, Mistrust, and Treason waits on him.
> *Alarum. Enter a Son that hath killed his Father,*
> *at one door: and a Father that hath kill'd his*
> *Son at another door.*

SON: Ill blows the wind that profits nobody.
This man whom hand to hand I slew in fight,
May be possessed with some store of crowns,
And I that (haply) take them from him now,
May yet (ere night) yield both my life and them
To some man else, as this dead man doth me.
Who's this? Oh God! It is my Father's face,

Whom in this conflict, I (unwares) have kill'd:
Oh heavy times! begetting such events.
From London, by the King was I press'd forth,
My Father being the Earl of Warwick's man,
Came on the part of York, press'd by his Master:
And I, who at his hands receiv'd my life,
Have by my hands, of life bereaved him.
Pardon me God, I knew not what I did:
And pardon Father, for I knew not thee.
My tears shall wipe away these bloody marks:
And no more words, till they have flow'd their fill.

KING: O piteous spectacle! O bloody times!
Whiles lions war, and battle for their dens,
Poor harmless lambs abide their enmity.
Weep wretched man: I'll aid thee tear for tear,
And let our hearts and eyes, like Civil War,
Be blind with tears, and break o'ercharg'd with grief.

Enter Father, bearing of his Son.

FATHER: Thou that so stoutly hast resisted me,
Give me thy gold, if thou hast any gold:
For I have bought it with an hundred blows.
But let me see: Is this our foeman's face?
Ah, no, no, no, it is mine only Son.
Ah Boy, if any life be left in thee,
Throw up thine eye: see, see what showers arise,
Blown with the windy tempest of my heart,
Upon thy wounds, that kills mine eye, and heart.
O pity God, this miserable Age!
What stratagems? how fell? how butcherly?
Erroneous, mutinous, and unnatural,
This deadly quarrel daily doth beget?
O Boy! thy Father gave thee life too soon,
And hath bereft thee of thy life too late.

KING: Woe above woe: grief, more than common grief.

O that my death would stay these ruthful deeds:
O pity, pity, gentle heaven pity:
The Red Rose and the White are on his face,
The fatal Colours of our striving Houses:
The one, his purple blood right well resembles,
The other his pale cheeks (methinks) presenteth:
Wither one Rose, and let the other flourish:
If you contend, a thousand lives must wither.

SON: How will my Mother, for a Father's death
Take on with me, and ne'er be satisfied?

FATHER: How will my Wife, for slaughter of my Son,
Shed seas of tears, and ne'er be satisfied?

KING: How will the Country, for these woeful chances,
Misthink the King, and not be satisfied?

SON: Was ever Son, so rued a Father's death?

FATHER: Was ever Father so bemoan'd his son?

KING: Was ever King so griev'd for Subjects' woe?
Much is your sorrow; Mine, ten times so much.

SON: I'll bear thee hence, where I may weep my fill.

Exit with body.

FATHER: These arms of mine shall be thy winding sheet:
My heart (sweet Boy) shall be thy sepulchre,
For from my heart, thine image ne'er shall go.
My sighing breast, shall be thy funeral bell;
And so obsequious will thy Father be,
Even for the loss of thee, having no more,
As Priam was for all his valiant sons.
I'll bear thee hence, and let them fight that will,
For I have murthered where I should not kill.

Exit with the body.

KING: Sad-hearted men, much overgone with care;
Here sits a King, more woeful than you are.

*Alarums. Excursions. Enter the Queen, the
Prince, and Exeter.*

PRINCE: Fly Father, fly: for all your friends are fled.
  And Warwick rages like a chafed bull:
  Away, for death doth hold us in pursuit.
QUEEN: Mount you my Lord, towards Berwick post
    amain:
  Edward and Richard like a brace of greyhounds,
  Having the fearful flying hare in sight,
  With fiery eyes, sparkling for very wrath,
  And bloody steel grasp'd in their ireful hands
  Are at our backs, and therefore hence amain.
EXETER: Away: for vengeance comes along with them.
  Nay, stay not to expostulate, make speed,
  Or else come after, I 'll away before.
HENRY: Nay take me with thee, good sweet Exeter:
  Not that I fear to stay, but love to go
  Whether the Queen intends. Forward, away.

Exeunt.

II. 6

A loud alarum. Enter Clifford wounded.

CLIFFORD: Here burns my candle out; ay, here it dies,
  Which whiles it lasted, gave King Henry light.
  O Lancaster! I fear thy overthrow,
  More than my body's parting with my soul:
  My love and fear, glued many friends to thee,
  And now I fall. Thy tough commixtures melts,
  Impairing Henry, strength'ning misproud York;
  And whether fly the gnats, but to the Sun?
  And who shines now, but Henry's enemies?
  O Phoebus! hadst thou never given consent,
  That Phaethon should check thy fiery steeds,
  Thy burning car never had scorch'd the earth.
  And Henry, hadst thou sway'd as Kings should do,

Or as thy Father, and his Father did,
Giving no ground unto the house of York,
They never then had sprung like summer flies:
I, and ten thousand in this luckless Realm,
Had left no mourning widows for our death,
And thou this day, hadst kept thy Chair in peace.
For what doth cherish weeds, but gentle air?
And what makes robbers bold, but too much lenity?
Bootless are plaints, and cureless are my wounds:
No way to fly, nor strength to hold out flight:
The foe is merciless, and will not pity:
For at their hands I have deserv'd no pity.
The air hath got into my deadly wounds,
And much effuse of blood, doth make me faint:
Come York, and Richard, Warwick, and the rest;
I stabb'd your Father's bosoms; Split my breast.

Alarum and retreat. Enter Edward, Warwick,
Richard, and Soldiers, Montague and Clarence.

EDWARD: Now breathe we Lords, good fortune bids us
    pause,
And smooth the frowns of War, with peaceful looks:
Some troops pursue the bloody-minded Queen,
That led calm Henry, though he were a King,
As doth a sail, fill'd with a fretting gust
Command an Argosy to stem the waves.
But think you (Lords) that Clifford fled with them?

WARWICK: No, 'tis impossible he should escape:
(For though before his face I speak the words)
Your Brother Richard mark'd him for the grave.
And wheresoe'er he is, he's surely dead.

Clifford groans.

RICHARD: Whose soul is that which takes her heavy leave?
A deadly groan, like life and death's departing.
See who it is.

EDWARD: And now the battle's ended,
  If friend or foe, let him be gently used.
RICHARD: Revoke that doom of mercy, for 'tis Clifford,
  Who not contented that he lopp'd the Branch
  In hewing Rutland, when his leaves put forth,
  But set his murth'ring knife unto the root,
  From whence that tender spray did sweetly spring,
  I mean our Princely Father, Duke of York.
WARWICK: From off the gates of York, fetch down the
    head,
  Your Father's head, which Clifford placed there:
  Instead whereof, let this supply the room,
  Measure for measure, must be answered.
EDWARD: Bring forth that fatal screech owl to our house,
  That nothing sung but death, to us and ours:
  Now death shall stop his dismal threat'ning sound,
  And his ill-boding tongue, no more shall speak.
WARWICK: I think his understanding is bereft:
  Speak Clifford, dost thou know who speaks to thee?
  Dark cloudy death o'ershades his beams of life,
  And he nor sees, nor hears us, what we say.
RICHARD: O would he did, and so (perhaps) he doth,
  'Tis but his policy to counterfet,
  Because he would avoid such bitter taunts
  Which in the time of death he gave our Father.
CLARENCE: If so thou think'st,
  Vex him with eager words.
RICHARD: Clifford, ask mercy, and obtain no grace.
EDWARD: Clifford, repent in bootless penitence.
WARWICK: Clifford, devise excuses for thy faults.
CLARENCE: While we devise fell tortures for thy faults.
RICHARD: Thou didst love York, and I am son to York.
EDWARD: Thou pitied'st Rutland, I will pity thee.
CLARENCE: Where's Captain Margaret, to fence you now?

WARWICK: They mock thee Clifford,
  Swear as thou wast wont.
RICHARD: What, not an oath? Nay then the world goes hard
  When Clifford cannot spare his friends an oath:
  I know by that he's dead, and by my soul,
  If this right hand would buy two hours' life,
  That I (in all despite) might rail at him,
  This hand should chop it off: and with the issuing blood
  Stifle the villain, whose unstaunched thirst
  York, and young Rutland could not satisfy.
WARWICK: Ay, but he's dead. Off with the Traitor's head,
  And rear it in the place your Father's stands.
  And now to London with triumphant march,
  There to be crowned England's Royal King:
  From whence, shall Warwick cut the sea to France,
  And ask the Lady Bona for thy Queen:
  So shalt thou sinew both these lands together,
  And having France thy friend, thou shalt not dread
  The scatter'd foe, that hopes to rise again:
  For though they cannot greatly sting to hurt,
  Yet look to have them buzz to offend thine ears:
  First, will I see the Coronation,
  And then to Brittany I'll cross the sea,
  To effect this marriage, so it please my Lord.
EDWARD: Even as thou wilt sweet Warwick, let it be:
  For in thy shoulder do I build my seat;
  And never will I undertake the thing
  Wherein thy counsel and consent is wanting:
  Richard, I will create thee Duke of Gloucester,
  And George of Clarence; Warwick as our Self,
  Shall do, and undo as him pleaseth best.
RICHARD: Let me be Duke of Clarence, George of Gloucester,

For Gloucester's Dukedom is too ominous.

WARWICK: Tut, that's a foolish observation:

Richard, be Duke of Gloucester: Now to London,

To see these honours in possession.

Exeunt.

III. 1

*Enter Sinklo, and Humphrey, with cross-bows
in their hands.*

SINKLO: Under this thick grown brake, we'll shroud our-

selves:

For through this laund anon the deer will come,

And in this covert will we make our stand,

Culling the principal of all the deer.

HUMPHREY: I'll stay above the hill, so both may shoot.

SINKLO: That cannot be, the noise of thy cross-bow

Will scarre the herd, and so my shoot is lost:

Here stand we both, and aim we at the best:

And for the time shall not seem tedious,

I'll tell thee what befel me on a day,

In this self-place, where now we mean to stand.

HUMPHREY: Here comes a man, let's stay till he be past.

Enter the King with a prayer book.

HENRY: From Scotland am I stol'n even of pure love,

To greet mine own Land with my wishful sight:

No Harry, Harry, 'tis no Land of thine,

Thy place is fill'd, thy sceptre wrung from thee,

Thy balm wash'd off, wherewith thou wast anointed:

No bending knee will call thee Caesar now,

No humble suitors prease to speak for right:

No, not a man comes for redress of thee:

For how can I help them, and not myself?

SINKLO: Ay, here's a deer, whose skin's a keeper's fee:

This is the quondam King; Let 's seize upon him.

HENRY: Let me embrace thee sour Adversity,
    For wise men say, it is the wisest course.

HUMPHREY: Why linger we? Let us lay hands upon him.

SINKLO: Forbear awhile, we 'll hear a little more.

HENRY: My Queen and Son are gone to France for aid:
    And (as I hear) the great commanding Warwick
    Is thither gone, to crave the French King's Sister
    To wife for Edward. If this news be true,
    Poor Queen, and Son, your labour is but lost:
    For Warwick is a subtle Orator:
    And Lewis a Prince soon won with moving words:
    By this account then, Margaret may win him,
    For she 's a woman to be pitied much:
    Her sighs will make a batt'ry in his breast,
    Her tears will pierce into a marble heart:
    The tiger will be mild, whiles she doth mourn;
    And Nero will be tainted with remorse,
    To hear and see her plaints, her brinish tears.
    Ay, but she 's come to beg, Warwick to give:
    She on his left side, craving aid for Henry;
    He on his right, asking a wife for Edward.
    She weeps, and says, her Henry is depos'd:
    He smiles, and says, his Edward is install'd;
    That she (poor wretch) for grief can speak no more:
    Whiles Warwick tells his title, smooths the wrong,
    Inferreth arguments of mighty strength,
    And in conclusion wins the King from her,
    With promise of his Sister, and what else,
    To strengthen and support King Edward's place.
    O Margaret, thus 'twill be, and thou (poor soul)
    Art then forsaken, as thou went'st forlorn.

HUMPHREY: Say, what art thou talk'st of Kings and
    Queens?

HENRY: More than I seem, and less than I was born to:
  A man at least, for less I should not be:
  And men may talk of Kings, and why not I?

HUMPHREY: Ay, but thou talk'st, as if thou wert a King.

HENRY: Why so I am (in mind) and that's enough.

HUMPHREY: But if thou be a King, where is thy Crown?

HENRY: My Crown is in my heart, not on my head:
  Not deck'd with diamonds, and Indian stones:
  Nor to be seen: my Crown, is call'd content,
  A Crown it is, that seldom Kings enjoy.

HUMPHREY: Well, if you be a King crown'd with content,
  Your Crown content, and you, must be contented
  To go along with us. For (as we think)
  You are the king King Edward hath depos'd:
  And we his subjects, sworn in all allegiance,
  Will apprehend you, as his enemy.

HENRY: But did you never swear, and break an oath.

HUMPHREY: No, never such an oath, nor will not now.

HENRY: Where did you dwell when I was King of England?

HUMPHREY: Here in this country, where we now remain.

HENRY: I was anointed King at nine months old,
  My Father, and my Grandfather were Kings:
  And you were sworn true subjects unto me:
  And tell me then, have you not broke your oaths?

SINKLO: No, for we were subjects, but while you were King.

HENRY: Why? Am I dead? Do I not breathe a man?
  Ah simple men, you know not what you swear:
  Look, as I blow this feather from my face,
  And as the air blows it to me again,
  Obeying with my wind when I do blow,
  And yielding to another, when it blows,

Commanded always by the greater gust:
Such is the lightness of you, common men.
But do not break your oaths, for of that sin,
My mild entreaty shall not make you guilty.
Go where you will, the king shall be commanded,
And be you kings, command, and I'll obey.

SINKLO: We are true subjects to the king,
King Edward.

HENRY: So would you be again to Henry,
If he were seated as King Edward is.

SINKLO: We charge you in God's name and the King's,
To go with us unto the Officers.

HENRY: In God's name lead, your King's name be obey'd,
And what God will, that let your King perform,
And what he will, I humbly yield unto.

Exeunt.

III. 2

*Enter King Edward, Richard, Gloucester,
Clarence, Lady Grey.*

KING EDWARD: Brother of Gloucester, at S. Alban's
field
This Lady's Husband, Sir Richard Grey, was slain,
His land then seiz'd on by the conqueror;
Her suit is now, to repossess those Lands,
Which we in justice cannot well deny,
Because in quarrel of the House of York,
The worthy Gentleman did lose his life.

RICHARD: Your Highness shall do well to grant her suit:
It were dishonour to deny it her.

KING EDWARD: It were no less, but yet I'll make a pause.

RICHARD: Yea, is it so.
I see the Lady hath a thing to grant,

Before the King will grant her humble suit.

CLARENCE: He knows the game, how true he keeps the
wind!

RICHARD: Silence.

KING EDWARD: Widow, we will consider of your suit,
And come some other time to know our mind.

WIDOW: Right gracious Lord, I cannot brook delay:
May it please your Highness to resolve me now,
And what your pleasure is, shall satisfy me.

RICHARD: Ay Widow? then I'll warrant you all your
Lands,
And if what pleases him, shall pleasure you:
Fight closer, or good faith you'll catch a blow.

CLARENCE: I fear her not, unless she chance to fall.

RICHARD: God forbid that, for he'll take vantages.

KING EDWARD: How many children hast thou, Widow?
tell me.

CLARENCE: I think he means to beg a child of her.

RICHARD: Nay then whip me: he'll rather give her two.

WIDOW: Three, my most gracious Lord.

RICHARD: You shall have four, if you'll be rul'd by him.

KING EDWARD: 'Twere pity they should lose their
Father's Lands.

WIDOW: Be pitiful, dread Lord, and grant it then.

KING EDWARD: Lords give us leave, I'll try this Widow's
wit.

RICHARD: Ay, good leave have you, for you will have
leave,
Till youth take leave, and leave you to the crutch.

KING EDWARD: Now tell me, Madame, do you love your
children?

WIDOW: Ay, full as dearly as I love myself.

KING EDWARD: And would you not do much to do them
good?

WIDOW: To do them good, I would sustain some harm.

KING EDWARD: Then get your Husband's Lands, to do them good.

WIDOW: Therefore I came unto your Majesty.

KING EDWARD: I 'll tell you how these Lands are to be got.

WIDOW: So shall you bind me to your Highness' service.

KING EDWARD: What service wilt thou do me, if I give them?

WIDOW: What you command, that rests in me to do.

KING EDWARD: But you will take exceptions to my boon.

WIDOW: No, gracious Lord, except I cannot do it.

KING EDWARD: Ay, but thou canst do what I mean to ask.

WIDOW: Why then I will do what your Grace commands.

RICHARD: He plies her hard, and much rain wears the marble.

CLARENCE: As red as fire? nay then, her wax must melt.

WIDOW: Why stops my Lord? shall I not hear my task?

KING EDWARD: An easy task, 'tis but to love a King.

WIDOW: That 's soon perform'd, because I am a subject.

KING EDWARD: Why then, thy Husband's Lands I freely give thee.

WIDOW: I take my leave with many thousand thanks.

RICHARD: The match is made, she seals it with a cursy.

KING EDWARD: But stay thee, 'tis the fruits of love I mean.

WIDOW: The fruits of love, I mean, my loving Liege.

KING EDWARD: Ay, but I fear me in another sense.
   What love, think'st thou, I sue so much to get?

WIDOW: My love till death, my humble thanks, my prayers,
   That love which Virtue begs, and Virtue grants.

K

KING EDWARD: No by my troth, I did not mean such
   love.

WIDOW: Why then you mean not, as I thought you did.

KING EDWARD: But now you partly may perceive my
   mind.

WIDOW: My mind will never grant what I perceive
   Your Highness aims at, if I aim aright.

KING EDWARD: To tell thee plain, I aim to lie with thee.

WIDOW: To tell you plain, I had rather lie in prison.

KING EDWARD: Why then thou shalt not have thy
   Husband's lands.

WIDOW: Why then mine honesty shall be my dower,
   For by that loss, I will not purchase them.

KING EDWARD: Therein thou wrong'st thy Children
   mightily.

WIDOW: Herein your Highness wrongs both them and
   me:
   But mighty Lord, this merry inclination
   Accords not with the sadness of my suit:
   Please you dismiss me, either with ay, or no.

KING EDWARD: Ay, if thou wilt say Ay to my request:
   No, if thou dost say No to my demand.

WIDOW: Then No, my Lord: my suit is at an end.

RICHARD: The Widow likes him not, she knits her
   brows.

CLARENCE: He is the bluntest wooer in Christendom.

KING EDWARD: Her looks doth argue her replete with
   modesty,
   Her words do show her wit incomparable,
   All her perfections challenge sovereignty,
   One way, or other, she is for a King,
   And she shall be my love, or else my Queen.
   Say, that King Edward take thee for his Queen?

WIDOW: 'Tis better said than done, my gracious Lord:

I am a subject fit to jest withal,
But far unfit to be a Sovereign.

KING EDWARD: Sweet Widow, by my State I swear to thee,
I speak no more than what my soul intends,
And that is, to enjoy thee for my love.

WIDOW: And that is more than I will yield unto:
I know, I am too mean to be your Queen,
And yet too good to be your Concubine.

KING EDWARD: You cavil, Widow, I did mean my Queen.

WIDOW: 'Twill grieve your Grace, my Sons should call you Father.

KING EDWARD: No more, than when my Daughters
Call thee Mother.
Thou art a widow, and thou hast some children,
And by God's Mother, I being but a bachelor,
Have other-some. Why, 'tis a happy thing,
To be the Father unto many Sons:
Answer no more, for thou shalt be my Queen.

RICHARD: The Ghostly Father now hath done his shrift.

CLARENCE: When he was made a shriver, 'twas for shift.

KING EDWARD: Brothers, you muse what chat we two have had.

RICHARD: The Widow likes it not, for she looks very sad.

KING EDWARD: You 'ld think it strange, if I should marry her.

CLARENCE: To who, my Lord?

KING EDWARD: Why Clarence, to myself.

RICHARD: That would be ten days' wonder at the least.

CLARENCE: That's a day longer than a Wonder lasts.

RICHARD: By so much is the Wonder in extremes.

KING EDWARD: Well, jest on Brothers: I can tell you both,

Her suit is granted for her Husband's Lands.

Enter a Nobleman.

NOBLEMAN: My gracious Lord, Henry your foe is taken,
And brought your prisoner to your Palace Gate.

KING EDWARD: See that he be convey'd unto the Tower:
And go we Brothers to the man that took him,
To question of his apprehension.
Widow go you along: Lords, use her honourable.

Exeunt.

Manet Richard.

RICHARD: Ay, Edward will use women honourably:
Would he were wasted, marrow, bones, and all,
That from his loins no hopeful branch may spring,
To cross me from the golden time I look for:
And yet, between my soul's desire, and me,
The lustful Edward's Title buried,
Is Clarence, Henry, and his son young Edward,
And all the unlook'd-for issue of their bodies,
To take their rooms, ere I can place myself:
A cold premeditation for my purpose.
Why then I do but dream on Sovereignty,
Like one that stands upon a promontory,
And spies a far-off shore, where he would tread,
Wishing his foot were equal with his eye,
And chides the sea, that sunders him from thence,
Saying, he 'll lade it dry, to have his way:
So do I wish the Crown, being so far off,
And so I chide the means that keeps me from it,
And so (I say) I 'll cut the causes off,
Flattering me with impossibilities:
My eye 's too quick, my heart o'erweens too much,
Unless my hand and strength could equal them.
Well, say there is no Kingdom then for Richard:
What other pleasure can the World afford?

I 'll make my heaven in a Lady's lap,
And deck my body in gay ornaments,
And witch sweet Ladies with my words and looks.
Oh miserable thought! and more unlikely,
Than to accomplish twenty Golden Crowns.
Why Love forswore me in my Mother's womb:
And for I should not deal in her soft laws,
She did corrupt frail Nature with some bribe,
To shrink mine arm up like a wither'd shrub,
To make an envious mountain on my back,
Where sits Deformity to mock my body;
To shape my legs of an unequal size,
To disproportion me in every part:
Like to a chaos, or an unlick'd bear-whelp,
That carries no impression like the dam.
And am I then a man to be belov'd?
Oh monstrous fault, to harbour such a thought.
Then since this Earth affords no joy to me,
But to command, to check, to o'erbear such,
As are of better person than myself:
I 'll make my Heaven, to dream upon the Crown,
And whiles I live, t' account this World but Hell,
Until my mis-shap'd trunk, that bears this head,
Be round impaled with a glorious Crown.
And yet I know not how to get the Crown,
For many lives stand between me and home:
And I, like one lost in a thorny wood,
That rents the thorns, and is rent with the thorns,
Seeking a way, and straying from the way,
Not knowing how to find the open air,
But toiling desperately to find it out,
Torment myself, to catch the English Crown:
And from that torment I will free myself,
Or hew my way out with a bloody axe.

Why I can smile, and murther whiles I smile,
And cry, Content, to that which grieves my heart,
And wet my cheeks with artificial tears,
And frame my face to all occasions.
I'll drown more sailors than the mermaid shall,
I'll slay more gazers than the basilisk,
I'll play the orator as well as Nestor,
Deceive more slily than Ulysses could,
And like a Sinon, take another Troy.
I can add colours to the chameleon,
Change shapes with Proteus, for advantages,
And set the murtherous Machiavel to school.
Can I do this, and cannot get a Crown?
Tut, were it further off, I'll pluck it down.

Exit.

III. 3

Flourish.
*Enter Lewis the French King, his Sister Bona,
his Admiral, call'd Bourbon: Prince Edward,
Queen Margaret, and the Earl of Oxford. Lewis
sits, and riseth up again.*

LEWIS: Fair Queen of England, worthy Margaret,
Sit down with us: it ill befits thy State,
And Birth, that thou shouldst stand, while Lewis doth
sit.

MARGARET: No, mighty King of France: now Margaret
Must strike her sail, and learn a while to serve,
Where Kings command. I was (I must confess)
Great Albion's Queen, in former golden days:
But now mischance hath trod my Title down,
And with dishonour laid me on the ground,
Where I must take like seat unto my fortune,

And to my humble seat conform myself.

LEWIS: Why say, fair Queen, whence springs this deep
despair?

MARGARET: From such a cause, as fills mine eyes with
tears,
And stops my tongue, while heart is drown'd in cares.

LEWIS: Whate'er it be, be thou still like thyself,
And sit thee by our side. *Seats her by him.*
Yield not thy neck to Fortune's yoke,
But let thy dauntless mind still ride in triumph,
Over all mischance.
Be plain, Queen Margaret, and tell thy grief,
It shall be eas'd, if France can yield relief.

MARGARET: Those gracious words
Revive my drooping thoughts,
And give my tongue-tied sorrows leave to speak.
Now therefore be it known to Noble Lewis,
That Henry, sole possessor of my love,
Is, of a King, become a banish'd man,
And forc'd to live in Scotland a forlorn;
While proud ambitious Edward, Duke of York,
Usurps the Regal Title, and the Seat
Of England's true anointed lawful King.
This is the cause that I, poor Margaret,
With this my Son, Prince Edward, Henry's Heir,
Am come to crave thy just and lawful aid:
And if thou fail us, all our hopes is done.
Scotland hath will to help, but cannot help:
Our People, and our Peers, are both misled,
Our Treasure seiz'd, our Soldiers put to flight,
And (as thou seest) ourselves in heavy plight.

LEWIS: Renowned Queen,
With patience calm the storm,
While we bethink a means to break it off.

MARGARET: The more we stay, the stronger grows our
    foe.

LEWIS: The more I stay, the more I 'll succour thee.

MARGARET: O, but impatience waiteth on true sorrow.
  And see where comes the breeder of my sorrow.

Enter Warwick.

LEWIS: What 's he approacheth boldly to our presence?

MARGARET: Our Earl of Warwick, Edward's greatest
    friend.

LEWIS: Welcome brave Warwick, what brings thee to
    France? *He descends. She ariseth.*

MARGARET: Ay now begins a second storm to rise,
  For this is he that moves both wind and tide.

WARWICK: From worthy Edward, King of Albion,
  My Lord and Sovereign, and thy vowed friend,
  I come (in kindness, and unfeigned love)
  First, to do greetings to thy Royal Person,
  And then to crave a League of Amity:
  And lastly, to confirm that Amity
  With nuptial knot, if thou vouchsafe to grant
  That virtuous Lady Bona, thy fair Sister,
  To England's King, in lawful marriage.

MARGARET: If that go forward, Henry's hope is done.

WARWICK: And gracious Madam, *Speaking to Bona.*
  In our King's behalf,
  I am commanded, with your leave and favour,
  Humbly to kiss your hand, and with my tongue
  To tell the passion of my Sovereign's heart;
  Where Fame, late ent'ring at his heedful ears,
  Hath plac'd thy Beauty's image, and thy Virtue.

MARGARET: King Lewis, and Lady Bona, hear me speak,
  Before you answer Warwick. His demand
  Springs not from Edward's well-meant honest love,
  But from deceit, bred by necessity:

For how can Tyrants safely govern home,
Unless abroad they purchase great alliance?
To prove him Tyrant, this reason may suffice,
That Henry liveth still: but were he dead,
Yet here Prince Edward stands, King Henry's Son.
Look therefore Lewis, that by this League and Marriage
Thou draw not on thy danger, and dishonour:
For though Usurpers sway the rule a while,
Yet Heav'ns are just, and Time suppresseth wrongs.

WARWICK: Injurious Margaret.

PRINCE: And why not Queen?

WARWICK: Because thy father Henry did usurp,
And thou no more art Prince, than she is Queen.

OXFORD: Then Warwick disannuls great John of Gaunt,
Which did subdue the greatest part of Spain;
And, after John of Gaunt, Henry the Fourth,
Whose wisdom was a mirror to the wisest:
And after that wise Prince, Henry the Fifth,
Who by his prowess conquered all France:
From these, our Henry lineally descends.

WARWICK: Oxford, how haps it in this smooth discourse,
You told not, how Henry the Sixth hath lost
All that, which Henry the Fifth had gotten:
Methinks these Peers of France should smile at that.
But for the rest: you tell a pedigree
Of threescore and two years, a silly time
To make prescription for a Kingdom's worth.

OXFORD: Why Warwick, canst thou speak against thy
    Liege,
Whom thou obeyed'st thirty and six years,
And not bewray thy treason with a blush?

WARWICK: Can Oxford, that did ever fence the right,
Now buckler falsehood with a pedigree?
For shame leave Henry, and call Edward King.

OXFORD: Call him my King, by whose injurious doom
  My elder Brother, the Lord Aubrey Vere
  Was done to death? and more than so, my Father,
  Even in the downfall of his mellow'd years,
  When Nature brought him to the door of Death?
  No Warwick, no; while life upholds this arm,
  This arm upholds the House of Lancaster.

WARWICK: And I the House of York.

LEWIS: Queen Margaret, Prince Edward, and Oxford,
  Vouchsafe at our request, to stand aside,
  While I use further conference with Warwick.

They stand aloof.

MARGARET: Heavens grant, that Warwick's words bewitch him not.

LEWIS: Now Warwick, tell me even upon thy conscience
  Is Edward your true King? for I were loath
  To link with him, that were not lawful chosen.

WARWICK: Thereon I pawn my credit, and mine honour.

LEWIS: But is he gracious in the People's eye?

WARWICK: The more, that Henry was unfortunate.

LEWIS: Then further: all dissembling set aside,
  Tell me for truth, the measure of his love
  Unto our Sister Bona.

WARWICK: Such it seems,
  As may beseem a Monarch like himself.
  Myself have often heard him say, and swear,
  That this his love was an eternal plant,
  Whereof the root was fix'd in Virtue's ground,
  The leaves and fruit maintain'd with Beauty's Sun,
  Exempt from envy, but not from disdain,
  Unless the Lady Bona quit his pain.

LEWIS: Now Sister, let us hear your firm resolve.

BONA: Your grant, or your denial, shall be mine.
  Yet I confess, that often ere this day, *Speaks to Warwick.*

When I have heard your King's desert recounted,
Mine ear hath tempted judgement to desire.

LEWIS: Then Warwick, thus:
Our Sister shall be Edward's.
And now forthwith shall Articles be drawn,
Touching the jointure that your King must make,
Which with her dowry shall be counter-pois'd:
Draw near, Queen Margaret, and be a witness,
That Bona shall be Wife to the English King.

PRINCE: To Edward, but not to the English King.

MARGARET: Deceitful Warwick, it was thy device,
By this alliance to make void my suit:
Before thy coming, Lewis was Henry's friend.

LEWIS: And still is friend to him, and Margaret.
But if your Title to the Crown be weak,
As may appear by Edward's good success:
Then 'tis but reason, that I be releas'd
From giving aid, which late I promised.
Yet shall you have all kindness at my hand,
That your estate requires, and mine can yield.

WARWICK: Henry now lives in Scotland, at his ease;
Where having nothing, nothing can he lose.
And as for you yourself (our quondam Queen)
You have a Father able to maintain you,
And better 'twere, you troubled him, than France.

MARGARET: Peace impudent, and shameless Warwick,
Proud setter up, and puller down of Kings,
I will not hence, till with my talk and tears
(Both full of truth) I make King Lewis behold
Thy sly conveyance, and thy Lord's false love,
                    Post blowing a horn within.
For both of you are birds of self-same feather.

LEWIS: Warwick, this is some post to us, or thee.
                    Enter the Post.

POST: My Lord Ambassador,
  These letters are for you. *Speaks to Warwick.*
  Sent from your Brother Marquess Montague.
  These from our King, unto your Majesty. *To Lewis.*
  And Madam, these for you: *To Margaret.*
  From whom, I know not.
                    They all read their letters.

OXFORD: I like it well, that our fair Queen and Mistress
  Smiles at her news, while Warwick frowns at his.

PRINCE: Nay mark how Lewis stamps as he were nettled.
  I hope, all 's for the best.

LEWIS: Warwick, what are thy news?
  And yours, fair Queen.

MARGARET: Mine such, as fill my heart with unhop'd
  joys.

WARWICK: Mine full of sorrow, and heart's discontent.

LEWIS: What? has your King married the Lady Grey?
  And now to soothe your forgery, and his,
  Sends me a paper to persuade me patience?
  Is this th' Alliance that he seeks with France?
  Dare he presume to scorn us in this manner?

MARGARET: I told your Majesty as much before:
  This proveth Edward's love, and Warwick's honesty.

WARWICK: King Lewis, I here protest in sight of heaven,
  And by the hope I have of heavenly bliss,
  That I am clear from this misdeed of Edward's;
  No more my King, for he dishonours me,
  But most himself, if he could see his shame.
  Did I forget, that by the House of York
  My Father came untimely to his death?
  Did I let pass th' abuse done to my Niece?
  Did I impale him with the Regal Crown?
  Did I put Henry from his Native Right?
  And am I guerdon'd at the last, with shame?

Shame on himself, for my desert is honour.
And to repair my honour lost for him,
I here renounce him, and return to Henry.
My Noble Queen, let former grudges pass,
And henceforth, I am thy true Servitor:
I will revenge his wrong to Lady Bona,
And replant Henry in his former state.

MARGARET: Warwick,
These words have turn'd my hate, to love,
And I forgive, and quite forget old faults,
And joy that thou becom'st King Henry's Friend.

WARWICK: So much his friend, ay, his unfeigned Friend,
That if King Lewis vouchsafe to furnish us
With some few bands of chosen soldiers,
I 'll undertake to land them on our coast,
And force the Tyrant from his seat by war.
'Tis not his new-made Bride shall succour him,
And as for Clarence, as my letters tell me,
He 's very likely now to fall from him,
For matching more for wanton lust, than honour,
Or than for strength and safety of our Country.

BONA: Dear Brother, how shall Bona be reveng'd,
But by thy help to this distressed Queen?

MARGARET: Renowned Prince, how shall poor Henry
live,
Unless thou rescue him from foul despair?

BONA: My quarrel, and this English Queen's, are one.

WARWICK: And mine fair Lady Bona, joins with yours.

LEWIS: And mine, with hers, and thine, and Margaret's.
Therefore, at last, I firmly am resolv'd
You shall have aid.

MARGARET: Let me give humble thanks for all, at once.

LEWIS: Then England's messenger, return in post,
And tell false Edward, thy supposed King,

That Lewis of France, is sending over Maskers
To revel it with him, and his new Bride.
Thou seest what 's past, go fear thy King withal.

BONA: Tell him, in hope he 'll prove a widower shortly,
I 'll wear the willow garland for his sake.

MARGARET: Tell him, my mourning weeds are laid aside,
And I am ready to put armour on.

WARWICK: Tell him from me, that he hath done me wrong,
And therefore I 'll uncrown him, ere 't be long.
There 's thy reward, be gone.
                              Exit Post.

LEWIS: But Warwick,
Thou and Oxford, with five thousand men
Shall cross the seas, and bid false Edward battle:
And as occasion serves, this noble Queen
And Prince, shall follow with a fresh supply.
Yet ere thou go, but answer me one doubt:
What pledge have we of thy firm loyalty?

WARWICK: This shall assure my constant loyalty,
That if our Queen, and this young Prince agree,
I 'll join mine eldest daughter, and my joy,
To him forthwith, in holy wedlock bands.

MARGARET: Yes, I agree, and thank you for your motion.
Son Edward, she is fair and virtuous,
Therefore delay not, give thy hand to Warwick,
And, with thy hand, thy faith irrevocable,
That only Warwick's daughter shall be thine.

PRINCE: Yes, I accept her, for she well deserves it,
And here to pledge my vow, I give my hand.
                    He gives his hand to Warwick.

LEWIS: Why stay we now? These soldiers shall be levied,
And thou Lord Bourbon, our High Admiral
Shalt waft them over with our Royal Fleet.

I long till Edward fall by War's mischance,
For mocking marriage with a Dame of France.
Exeunt. Manet Warwick.

WARWICK: I came from Edward as Ambassador,
But I return his sworn and mortal Foe:
Matter of marriage was the charge he gave me,
But dreadful war shall answer his demand.
Had he none else to make a stale but me?
Then none but I, shall turn his jest to sorrow.
I was the Chief that rais'd him to the Crown,
And I'll be Chief to bring him down again:
Not that I pity Henry's misery,
But seek revenge on Edward's mockery.
Exit.

IV. I

*Enter Richard, Clarence, Somerset, and
Montague.*

RICHARD: Now tell me Brother Clarence, what think
you
Of this new marriage with the Lady Grey?
Hath not our Brother made a worthy choice?
CLARENCE: Alas, you know, 'tis far from hence to France,
How could he stay till Warwick made return?
SOMERSET: My Lords, forbear this talk: here comes the
King.

Flourish.
*Enter King Edward, Lady Grey, Pembroke,
Stafford, Hastings: four stand on one side,
and four on the other.*

RICHARD: And his well-chosen Bride.
CLARENCE: I mind to tell him plainly what I think.
KING EDWARD: Now Brother of Clarence,

How like you our choice,
That you stand pensive, as half malcontent?

CLARENCE: As well as Lewis of France,
Or the Earl of Warwick,
Which are so weak of courage, and in judgement,
That they 'll take no offence at our abuse.

KING EDWARD: Suppose they take offence without a
cause:
They are but Lewis and Warwick, I am Edward,
Your King and Warwick's, and must have my will.

RICHARD: And shall have your will, because our King:
Yet hasty marriage seldom proveth well.

KING EDWARD: Yea, Brother Richard, are you offended
too?

RICHARD: Not I: no:
God forbid, that I should wish them sever'd,
Whom God hath join'd together:
Ay, and 'twere pity, to sunder them,
That yoke so well together.

KING EDWARD: Setting your scorns, and your mislike
aside,
Tell me some reason, why the Lady Grey
Should not become my Wife, and England's Queen?
And you too, Somerset, and Montague,
Speak freely what you think.

CLARENCE: Then this is mine opinion:
That King Lewis becomes your enemy,
For mocking him about the marriage
Of the Lady Bona.

RICHARD: And Warwick, doing what you gave in charge,
Is now dishonoured by this new marriage.

KING EDWARD: What, if both Lewis and Warwick be
appeas'd,
By such invention as I can devise?

MONTAGUE: Yet, to have join'd with France in such
    alliance,
    Would more have strengthen'd this our Commonwealth
    'Gainst foreign storms, than any home-bred marriage.
HASTINGS: Why, knows not Montague, that of itself,
    England is safe, if true within itself?
MONTAGUE: But the safer, when 'tis back'd with France.
HASTINGS: 'Tis better using France, than trusting France:
    Let us be back'd with God, and with the seas,
    Which he hath given for fence impregnable,
    And with their helps, only defend ourselves:
    In them, and in ourselves, our safety lies.
CLARENCE: For this one speech, Lord Hastings well de-
    serves
    To have the Heir of the Lord Hungerford.
KING EDWARD: Ay, what of that? it was my will, and
    grant,
    And for this once, my Will shall stand for Law.
RICHARD: And yet methinks, your Grace hath not done
    well,
    To give the Heir and Daughter of Lord Scales
    Unto the Brother of your loving Bride;
    She better would have fitted me, or Clarence:
    But in your Bride you bury brotherhood.
CLARENCE: Or else you would not have bestow'd the Heir
    Of the Lord Bonville on your new Wife's Son,
    And leave your Brothers to go speed elsewhere.
KING EDWARD: Alas, poor Clarence: is it for a Wife
    That thou art malcontent? I will provide thee.
CLARENCE: In choosing for yourself,
    You show'd your judgement:
    Which being shallow, you shall give me leave
    To play the broker in mine own behalf;
    And to that end, I shortly mind to leave you.

KING EDWARD: Leave me, or tarry, Edward will be King,
  And not be tied unto his Brother's will.

QUEEN: My Lords, before it pleas'd his Majesty
  To raise my state to Title of a Queen,
  Do me but right, and you must all confess,
  That I was not ignoble of descent,
  And meaner than myself have had like fortune.
  But as this Title honours me and mine,
  So your dislikes, to whom I would be pleasing,
  Doth cloud my joys with danger, and with sorrow.

KING EDWARD: My Love, forbear to fawn upon their
    frowns:
  What danger, or what sorrow can befall thee,
  So long as Edward is thy constant friend,
  And their true Sovereign, whom they must obey?
  Nay, whom they shall obey, and love thee too,
  Unless they seek for hatred at my hands:
  Which if they do, yet will I keep thee safe,
  And they shall feel the vengeance of my wrath.

RICHARD: I hear, yet say not much, but think the more.

Enter a Post.

KING EDWARD: Now Messenger, what letters, or what
    news from France?

POST: My Sovereign Liege, no letters, and few words,
  But such, as I (without your special pardon)
  Dare not relate.

KING EDWARD: Go to, we pardon thee:
  Therefore, in brief, tell me their words,
  As near as thou canst guess them.
  What answer makes King Lewis unto our letters?

POST: At my depart, these were his very words:
  Go tell false Edward, the supposed King,
  That Lewis of France is sending over Maskers,
  To revel it with him, and his new Bride.

KING EDWARD: Is Lewis so brave? belike he thinks me
    Henry.
  But what said Lady Bona to my marriage?
POST: These were her words, utter'd with mild disdain:
  Tell him, in hope he 'll prove a widower shortly,
  I 'll wear the willow garland for his sake.
KING EDWARD: I blame not her; she could say little less:
  She had the wrong. But what said Henry's Queen?
  For I have heard, that she was there in place.
POST: Tell him (quoth she)
  My mourning weeds are done,
  And I am ready to put armour on.
KING EDWARD: Belike she minds to play the Amazon.
  But what said Warwick to these injuries?
POST: He, more incens'd against your Majesty,
  Than all the rest, discharg'd me with these words:
  Tell him from me, that he hath done me wrong,
  And therefore I 'll uncrown him ere 't be long.
KING EDWARD: Ha? durst the Traitor breathe out so
    proud words?
  Well, I will arm me, being thus forewarn'd:
  They shall have wars, and pay for their presumption.
  But say, is Warwick friends with Margaret?
POST: Ay, gracious sovereign,
  They are so link'd in friendship,
  That young Prince Edward marries Warwick's Daughter.
CLARENCE: Belike, the elder;
  Clarence will have the younger.
  Now Brother King farewell, and sit you fast,
  For I will hence to Warwick's other Daughter,
  That though I want a Kingdom, yet in marriage
  I may not prove inferior to yourself.
  You that love me, and Warwick, follow me.
      Exit Clarence, and Somerset follows.

RICHARD: Not I:

  My thoughts aim at a further matter:

  I stay not for the love of England, but the Crown.

KING EDWARD: Clarence and Somerset both gone to
    Warwick?

  Yet am I arm'd against the worst can happen:

  And haste is needful in this desp'rate case.

  Pembroke and Stafford, you in our behalf

  Go levy men, and make prepare for war;

  They are already, or quickly will be landed:

  Myself in person will straight follow you.

           Exeunt Pembroke and Stafford.

  But ere I go, Hastings and Montague

  Resolve my doubt: you twain, of all the rest,

  Are near to Warwick, by blood, and by alliance:

  Tell me, if you love Warwick more than me;

  If it be so, then both depart to him:

  I rather wish you foes, than hollow friends.

  But if you mind to hold your true obedience,

  Give me assurance with some friendly vow,

  That I may never have you in suspect.

MONTAGUE: So God help Montague, as he proves true.

HASTINGS: And Hastings, as he favours Edward's cause.

KING EDWARD: Now, Brother Richard, will you stand
    by us?

GLOUCESTER: Ay, in despite of all that shall withstand
    you.

KING EDWARD: Why so: then am I sure of victory.

  Now therefore let us hence, and lose no hour,

  Till we meet Warwick, with his foreign power.

           Exeunt.

IV. 2

*Enter Warwick and Oxford in England, with
French soldiers.*

WARWICK: Trust me, my Lord, all hitherto goes well,
  The common people by numbers swarm to us.
Enter Clarence and Somerset.
  But see where Somerset and Clarence comes:
  Speak suddenly, my Lords, are we all friends?
CLARENCE: Fear not that, my Lord.
WARWICK: Then gentle Clarence, welcome unto Warwick,
  And welcome Somerset: I hold it cowardize,
  To rest mistrustful, where a noble heart
  Hath pawn'd an open hand, in sign of love;
  Else might I think, that Clarence, Edward's Brother,
  Were but a feigned friend to our proceedings:
  But welcome sweet Clarence, my Daughter shall be thine.
  And now, what rests? but in Night's coverture,
  Thy Brother being carelessly encamp'd,
  His soldiers lurking in the Town about,
  And but attended by a simple Guard,
  We may surprise and take him at our pleasure,
  Our scouts have found the adventure very easy:
  That as Ulysses, and stout Diomede,
  With sleight and manhood stole to Rhesus' tents,
  And brought from thence the Thracian fatal steeds;
  So we, well cover'd with the Night's black mantle,
  At unawares may beat down Edward's Guard,
  And seize himself: I say not, slaughter him,
  For I intend but only to surprise him.
  You that will follow me to this attempt,

Applaud the name of Henry, with your Leader.
> *They all cry, Henry.*
Why then, let's on our way in silent sort,
For Warwick and his friends, God and Saint George.
> *Exeunt.*

IV. 3

Enter three Watchmen to guard the King's tent.

1 WATCHMAN: Come on my Masters, each man take his stand,
The King by this, is set him down to sleep.

2 WATCHMAN: What, will he not to bed?

1 WATCHMAN: Why, no: for he hath made a solemn vow,
. Never to lie and take his natural rest,
Till Warwick, or himself, be quite suppress'd.

2 WATCHMAN: Tomorrow then belike shall be the day,
If Warwick be so near as men report.

3 WATCHMAN: But say, I pray, what Nobleman is that,
That with the King here resteth in his tent?

1 WATCHMAN: 'Tis the Lord Hastings, the King's chiefest friend.

3 WATCHMAN: O, is it so? but why commands the King,
That his chief followers lodge in Towns about him,
While he himself keeps in the cold field?

2 WATCHMAN: 'Tis the more honour, because more dangerous.

3 WATCHMAN: Ay, but give me worship, and quietness,
I like it better than a dangerous honour.
If Warwick knew in what estate he stands,
'Tis to be doubted he would waken him.

1 WATCHMAN: Unless our halberds did shut up his passage.

2 WATCHMAN: Ay: wherefore else guard we his Royal Tent,

But to defend his person from night-foes?
Enter Warwick, Clarence, Oxford, Somerset,
and French soldiers, silent all.

WARWICK: This is his tent, and see where stand his
Guard:

Courage my Masters: Honour now, or never:

But follow me, and Edward shall be ours.

1 WATCHMAN: Who goes there?

2 WATCHMAN: Stay, or thou diest.

Warwick and the rest cry all, Warwick, Warwick, and set
upon the Guard, who fly, crying, Arm, Arm, Warwick
and the rest following them.

The drum playing, and trumpet sounding.
Enter Warwick, Somerset, and the rest, bringing
the King out in his gown, sitting in a chair:
Richard and Hastings flies over the stage.

SOMERSET: What are they that fly there?

WARWICK: Richard and Hastings: let them go, here is
the Duke.

KING EDWARD: The Duke?

Why Warwick, when we parted,

Thou call'dst me King.

WARWICK: Ay, but the case is alter'd.

When you disgrac'd me in my Embassade,

Then I degraded you from being King,

And come now to create you Duke of York.

Alas, how should you govern any Kingdom,

That know not how to use Ambassadors,

Nor how to be contented with one Wife,

Nor how to use your Brothers brotherly,

Nor how to study for the People's welfare,

Nor how to shroud yourself from Enemies?

KING EDWARD: Yea, brother of Clarence,

Art thou here too?

Nay then I see, that Edward needs must down.
Yet Warwick, in despite of all mischance,
Of thee thyself, and all thy complices,
Edward will always bear himself as King:
Though Fortune's malice overthrow my State,
My mind exceeds the compass of her wheel.

WARWICK: Then for his mind, be Edward England's
 King:

    Takes off his crown.

But Henry now shall wear the English Crown,
And be true King indeed: thou but the shadow.
My Lord of Somerset, at my request,
See that forthwith Duke Edward be convey'd
Unto my Brother Archbishop of York:
When I have fought with Pembroke, and his fellows,
I'll follow you, and tell what answer
Lewis and the Lady Bona send to him.
Now for a while farewell good Duke of York.

    They lead him out forcibly.

KING EDWARD: What Fates impose, that men must needs
 abide;
It boots not to resist both wind and tide.

    Exeunt.

OXFORD: What now remains my Lords for us to do,
But march to London with our soldiers?

WARWICK: Ay, that's the first thing that we have to do,
To free King Henry from imprisonment,
And see him seated in the Regal Throne.

    Exeunt.

IV. 4

Enter Queen Elizabeth and Rivers.

RIVERS: Madam, what makes you in this sudden change?

QUEEN: Why Brother Rivers, are you yet to learn
What late misfortune is befall'n King Edward?

RIVERS: What loss of some pitch'd battle
Against Warwick?

QUEEN: No, but the loss of his own royal person.

RIVERS: Then is my Sovereign slain?

QUEEN: Ay almost slain, for he is taken prisoner,
Either betray'd by falsehood of his Guard,
Or by his foe surpris'd at unawares:
And as I further have to understand,
Is new committed to the Bishop of York,
Fell Warwick's Brother, and by that our foe.

RIVERS: These news I must confess are full of grief,
Yet gracious Madam, bear it as you may,
Warwick may lose, that now hath won the day.

QUEEN: Till then, fair hope must hinder life's decay:
And I the rather wean me from despair
For love of Edward's offspring in my womb:
This is it that makes me bridle passion,
And bear with mildness my misfortune's cross:
Ay, ay, for this I draw in many a tear,
And stop the rising of blood-sucking sighs,
Lest with my sighs or tears, I blast or drown
King Edward's fruit, true Heir to th' English Crown.

RIVERS: But Madam,
Where is Warwick then become?

QUEEN: I am inform'd that he comes towards London,
To set the Crown once more on Henry's head,
Guess thou the rest, King Edward's friends must down.

But, to prevent the Tyrant's violence,
(For trust not him that hath once broken faith)
I 'll hence forthwith unto the Sanctuary,
To save (at least) the heir of Edward's right:
There shall I rest secure from force and fraud:
Come therefore let us fly, while we may fly,
If Warwick take us, we are sure to die.

Exeunt.

IV. 5

Enter Richard, Lord Hastings, and Sir William
Stanley.

RICHARD: Now my Lord Hastings, and Sir William
 Stanley,
Leave off to wonder why I drew you hither,
Into this chiefest thicket of the Park.
Thus stands the case: you know our King, my Brother,
Is prisoner to the Bishop here, at whose hands
He hath good usage, and great liberty,
And often but attended with weak guard,
Comes hunting this way to disport himself.
I have advertis'd him by secret means,
That if about this hour he make this way
Under the colour of his usual game,
He shall here find his friends with horse and men,
To set him free from his captivity.

Enter King Edward, and a Huntsman with him.

HUNTSMAN: This way my Lord,
For this way lies the game.

KING EDWARD: Nay this way man,
See where the huntsmen stand.
Now Brother of Gloucester, Lord Hastings, and the rest,
Stand you thus close to steal the Bishop's deer?

RICHARD: Brother, the time and case, requireth haste,
  Your horse stands ready at the Park-corner.
KING EDWARD: But whether shall we then?
HASTINGS: To Lynn my Lord,
  And ship 't from thence to Flanders.
RICHARD: Well guess'd believe me, for that was my
    meaning.
KING EDWARD: Stanley, I will requite thy forwardness.
RICHARD: But wherefore stay we? 'tis no time to talk.
KING EDWARD: Huntsman, what say'st thou?
  Wilt thou go along?
HUNTSMAN: Better do so, than tarry and be hang'd.
RICHARD: Come then away, let 's ha' no more ado.
KING EDWARD: Bishop farewell,
  Shield thee from Warwick's frown,
  And pray that I may repossess the Crown.
                    Exeunt.

IV. 6

*Flourish. Enter King Henry the Sixth, Clarence,
Warwick, Somerset, young Henry, Oxford,
Montague, and Lieutenant.*

KING HENRY: M. Lieutenant, now that God and friends
  Have shaken Edward from the regal seat,
  And turn'd my captive state to liberty,
  My fear to hope, my sorrows unto joys,
  At our enlargement what are thy due fees?
LIEUTENANT: Subjects may challenge nothing of their
    Sov'reigns;
  But, if an humble prayer may prevail,
  I then crave pardon of your Majesty.
KING HENRY: For what, Lieutenant? For well using me?
  Nay, be thou sure, I 'll well requite thy kindness,

For that it made my imprisonment, a pleasure:
Ay, such a pleasure, as incaged birds
Conceive; when after many moody thoughts,
At last, by notes of household harmony,
They quite forget their loss of liberty.
But Warwick, after God, thou set'st me free,
And chiefly therefore, I thank God, and thee,
He was the Author, thou the Instrument.
Therefore that I may conquer Fortune's spite,
By living low, where Fortune cannot hurt me,
And that the people of this blessed Land
May not be punish'd with my thwarting stars,
Warwick, although my head still wear the Crown,
I here resign my government to thee,
For thou art fortunate in all thy deeds.

WARWICK: Your Grace hath still been fam'd for virtuous,
And now may seem as wise as virtuous,
By spying and avoiding Fortune's malice,
For few men rightly temper with the stars:
Yet in this one thing let me blame your Grace,
For choosing me, when Clarence is in place.

CLARENCE: No Warwick, thou art worthy of the sway,
To whom the Heav'ns in thy nativity,
Adjudg'd an olive branch, and laurel crown,
As likely to be blest in Peace and War:
And therefore I yield thee my free consent.

WARWICK: And I choose Clarence only for Protector.

KING HENRY: Warwick and Clarence, give me both your
      hands:
Now join your hands, and with your hands your hearts,
That no dissension hinder government:
I make you both Protectors of this Land,
While I myself will lead a private life,
And in devotion spend my latter days,

To sin's rebuke, and my Creator's praise.

WARWICK: What answers Clarence to his Sovereign's will?

CLARENCE: That he consents, if Warwick yield consent,
For on thy fortune I repose myself.

WARWICK: Why then, though loath, yet must I be content:
We 'll yoke together, like a double shadow
To Henry's body, and supply his place;
I mean, in bearing weight of government,
While he enjoys the honour, and his ease.
And Clarence, now then it is more than needful,
Forthwith that Edward be pronounc'd a Traitor,
And all his lands and goods be confiscate.

CLARENCE: What else? and that Succession be determin'd.

WARWICK: Ay, therein Clarence shall not want his part.

KING HENRY: But with the first, of all your chief affairs,
Let me entreat (for I command no more)
That Margaret your Queen, and my Son Edward,
Be sent for, to return from France with speed:
For till I see them here, by doubtful fear,
My joy of liberty is half eclips'd.

CLARENCE: It shall be done, my Sovereign, with all speed.

KING HENRY: My Lord of Somerset, what youth is that,
Of whom you seem to have so tender care?

SOMERSET; My Liege, it is young Henry, Earl of Richmond.

KING HENRY: Come hither, England's Hope:
                    Lays his hand on his head.
If secret Powers suggest but truth
To my divining thoughts,
This pretty Lad will prove our Country's bliss.
His looks are full of peaceful majesty,

His head by nature framed to wear a Crown,
His hand to wield a Sceptre, and himself
Likely in time to bless a Regal Throne:
Make much of him, my Lords; for this is he
Must help you more, than you are hurt by me.

Enter a Post.

WARWICK: What news, my friend?

POST: That Edward is escaped from your Brother,
And fled (as he hears since) to Burgundy.

WARWICK: Unsavoury news: but how made he escape?

POST: He was convey'd by Richard, Duke of Gloucester,
And the Lord Hastings, who attended him
In secret ambush, on the Forest side,
And from the Bishop's Huntsmen rescued him:
For hunting was his daily exercise.

WARWICK: My Brother was too careless of his charge.
But let us hence, my Sovereign, to provide
A salve for any sore, that may betide.   *Exeunt.*

Manet Somerset, Richmond, and Oxford.

SOMERSET: My Lord, I like not of this flight of Edward's:
For doubtless, Burgundy will yield him help,
And we shall have more wars before 't be long.
As Henry's late presaging prophecy
Did glad my heart, with hope of this young Richmond:
So doth my heart misgive me, in these conflicts,
What may befall him, to his harm and ours.
Therefore, Lord Oxford, to prevent the worst,
Forthwith we 'll send him hence to Brittany,
Till storms be past of civil enmity.

OXFORD: Ay: for if Edward repossess the Crown,
'Tis like that Richmond, with the rest, shall down.

SOMERSET: It shall be so: he shall to Brittany.
Come therefore, let 's about it speedily.

Exeunt.

IV. 7

Flourish. Enter Edward, Richard, Hastings,
and Soldiers.

EDWARD: Now Brother Richard, Lord Hastings, and the
   rest,
   Yet thus far Fortune maketh us amends,
   And says, that once more I shall interchange
   My waned state, for Henry's Regal Crown.
   Well have we pass'd, and now re-pass'd the Seas,
   And brought desired help from Burgundy.
   What then remains, we being thus arriv'd
   From Ravenspurgh Haven, before the Gates of York,
   But that we enter, as into our Dukedom?

RICHARD: The gates made fast?
   Brother, I like not this.
   For many men that stumble at the threshold,
   Are well foretold, that danger lurks within.

EDWARD: Tush man, abodements must not now affright
   us:
   By fair or foul means we must enter in,
   For hither will our friends repair to us.

HASTINGS: My Liege, I'll knock once more, to summon
   them.

   Enter on the Walls, the Mayor of York, and his
   Brethren.

MAYOR: My Lords,
   We were forewarned of your coming,
   And shut the Gates, for safety of ourselves;
   For now we owe allegiance unto Henry.

EDWARD: But, Master Mayor, if Henry be your King,
   Yet Edward, at the least, is Duke of York.

MAYOR: True, my good Lord, I know you for no less.

EDWARD: Why, and I challenge nothing but my Dukedom,

As being well content with that alone.

RICHARD: But when the Fox hath once got in his nose,

He'll soon find means to make the body follow.

HASTINGS: Why, Master Mayor, why stand you in a
doubt?

Open the Gates, we are King Henry's friends.

MAYOR: Ay, say you so? the gates shall then be open'd.

He descends.

RICHARD: A wise stout Captain, and soon persuaded.

HASTINGS: The good old man would fain that all were
well,

So 'twere not long of him: but being enter'd,

I doubt not I, but we shall soon persuade

Both him, and all his Brothers, unto reason.

Enter the Mayor, and two Aldermen.

EDWARD: So, Master Mayor: these Gates must not be
shut,

But in the night, or in the time of war.

What, fear not man, but yield me up the keys,

Takes his keys.

For Edward will defend the Town, and thee,

And all those friends, that deign to follow me.

March. Enter Montgomery, with drum and soldiers.

RICHARD: Brother, this is Sir John Montgomery,

Our trusty friend, unless I be deceiv'd.

EDWARD: Welcome Sir John: but why come you in
arms?

MONTGOMERY: To help King Edward in his time of
storm,

As every loyal subject ought to do.

EDWARD: Thanks good Montgomery:

But we now forget our title to the Crown,

And only claim our Dukedom,
Till God please to send the rest.

MONTGOMERY: Then fare you well, for I will hence again,
I came to serve a King, and not a Duke:
Drummer strike up, and let us march away.

The drum begins to march.

EDWARD: Nay stay, Sir John, a while, and we 'll debate
By what safe means the Crown may be recover'd.

MONTGOMERY: What talk you of debating? in few words,
If you 'll not here proclaim yourself our King,
I 'll leave you to your fortune, and be gone,
To keep them back, that come to succour you.
Why shall we fight, if you pretend no Title?

RICHARD: Why Brother, wherefore stand you on nice
points?

EDWARD: When we grow stronger,
Then we 'll make our claim:
Till then, 'tis wisdom to conceal our meaning.

HASTINGS: Away with scrupulous wit, now arms must
rule.

RICHARD: And fearless minds climb soonest unto Crowns.
Brother, we will proclaim you out of hand,
The bruit thereof will bring you many friends.

EDWARD: Then be it as you will: for 'tis my right,
And Henry but usurps the Diadem.

MONTGOMERY: Ay, now my Sovereign speaketh like
himself,
And now will I be Edward's Champion.

HASTINGS: Sound trumpet, Edward shall be here proclaim'd:
Come, fellow soldier, make thou proclamation.

Flourish. Sound.

SOLDIER: *Edward the Fourth, by the Grace of God, King of
England and France, and Lord of Ireland, &c.*

L

MONTGOMERY: And whosoe'er gainsays King Edward's
  right,
  By this I challenge him to single fight.
                    Throws down his gauntlet.
ALL: Long live Edward the Fourth.
EDWARD: Thanks brave Montgomery,
  And thanks unto you all:
  If fortune serve me, I'll requite this kindness.
  Now for this night, let's harbour here in York:
  And when the morning sun shall raise his car
  Above the border of this horizon,
  We'll forward towards Warwick, and his mates;
  For well I wot, that Henry is no soldier.
  Ah froward Clarence, how evil it beseems thee,
  To flatter Henry, and forsake thy Brother?
  Yet as we may, we'll meet both thee and Warwick.
  Come on brave soldiers: doubt not of the day,
  And that once gotten, doubt not of large pay.
                    Exeunt.

IV. 8

Flourish. Enter King Henry, Warwick, Montague,
Clarence, Exeter, and Oxford.

WARWICK: What counsel, Lords? Edward from Belgia,
  With hasty Germans, and blunt Hollanders,
  Hath pass'd in safety through the Narrow Seas,
  And with his troops doth march amain to London,
  And many giddy people flock to him.
KING HENRY: Let's levy men, and beat him back again.
CLARENCE: A little fire is quickly trodden out,
  Which being suffer'd, rivers cannot quench.
WARWICK: In Warwickshire I have true-hearted friends,
  Not mutinous in peace, yet bold in war,

Those will I muster up: and thou Son Clarence
Shalt stir up in Suffolk, Norfolk, and in Kent,
The Knights and Gentlemen, to come with thee.
Thou Brother Montague, in Buckingham,
Northampton, and in Leicestershire, shalt find
Men well inclin'd to hear what thou command'st.
And thou, brave Oxford, wondrous well belov'd,
In Oxfordshire shalt muster up thy friends.
My Sovereign, with the loving Citizens,
Like to his Island, girt in with the Ocean,
Or modest Dian, circled with her Nymphs,
Shall rest in London, till we come to him:
Fair Lords take leave, and stand not to reply.
Farewell my Sovereign.

KING HENRY: Farewell my Hector, and my Troy's true
    hope.

CLARENCE: In sign of truth, I kiss your Highness' hand.

KING HENRY: Well-minded Clarence, be thou fortunate.

MONTAGUE: Comfort, my Lord, and so I take my leave.

OXFORD: And thus I seal my truth, and bid adieu.

KING HENRY: Sweet Oxford, and my loving Montague,
    And all at once, once more a happy farewell.

WARWICK: Farewell, sweet Lords, let's meet at Coventry.
    Exeunt. Manent King Henry and Exeter.

KING HENRY: Here at the Palace will I rest a while.
    Cousin of Exeter, what thinks your Lordship?
    Methinks, the power that Edward hath in field,
    Should not be able to encounter mine.

EXETER: The doubt is, that he will seduce the rest.

KING HENRY: That's not my fear, my meed hath got me
    fame:
    I have not stopp'd mine ears to their demands,
    Nor posted off their suits with slow delays,
    My pity hath been balm to heal their wounds,

My mildness hath allay'd their swelling griefs,
My mercy dried their water-flowing tears.
I have not been desirous of their wealth,
Nor much oppress'd them with great Subsidies,
Nor forward of revenge, though they much err'd.
Then why should they love Edward more than me?
No Exeter, these graces challenge grace:
And when the lion fawns upon the lamb,
The lamb will never cease to follow him.

Shout within, A Lancaster, A Lancaster.

EXETER: Hark hark, my Lord, what shouts are these?

Enter Edward, Richard, and his Soldiers.

EDWARD: Seize on the shame-fac'd Henry, bear him hence,
And once again proclaim us King of England.
You are the fount, that makes small brooks to flow,
Now stops thy spring, my sea shall suck them dry,
And swell so much the higher, by their ebb.
Hence with him to the Tower, let him not speak.

Exit with King Henry.

And Lords, towards Coventry bend we our course.
Where peremptory Warwick now remains:
The sun shines hot, and if we use delay,
Cold biting winter mars our hop'd-for hay.

GLOUCESTER: Away betimes, before his forces join,
And take the great-grown Traitor unawares:
Brave warriors, march amain towards Coventry.

Exeunt.

V. 1

*Enter Warwick, the Mayor of Coventry, two
Messengers, and others upon the walls.*

WARWICK: Where is the post that came from valiant
Oxford?

How far hence is thy Lord, mine honest fellow?

1 MESSENGER: By this at Dunsmore, marching hither-
    ward.

WARWICK: How far off is our Brother Montague?
    Where is the post that came from Montague?

2 MESSENGER: By this at Daintry, with a puissant troop.

        Enter Somerville.

WARWICK: Say Somerville, what says my loving Son?
    And by thy guess, how nigh is Clarence now?

SOMERVILLE: At Southam I did leave him with his forces,
    And do expect him here some two hours hence.

WARWICK: Then Clarence is at hand, I hear his drum.

SOMERVILLE: It is not his, my Lord, here Southam lies:
    The drum your Honour hears, marcheth from Warwick.

WARWICK: Who should that be? belike unlook'd-for
    friends.

SOMERVILLE: They are at hand, and you shall quickly
    know.

    March. Flourish. Enter Edward, Richard, and
        Soldiers.

EDWARD: Go, Trumpet, to the walls, and sound a parle.

RICHARD: See how the surly Warwick mans the wall.

WARWICK: Oh unbid spite, is sportful Edward come?
    Where slept our scouts, or how are they seduc'd,
    That we could hear no news of his repair?

EDWARD: Now Warwick, wilt thou ope the City Gates,
    Speak gentle words, and humbly bend thy knee,
    Call Edward King, and at his hands beg mercy,
    And he shall pardon thee these outrages?

WARWICK: Nay rather, wilt thou draw thy forces hence,
    Confess who set thee up and pluck'd thee down,
    Call Warwick Patron, and be penitent,
    And thou shalt still remain the Duke of York.

RICHARD: I thought at least he would have said the King,

Or did he make the jest against his will?

WARWICK: Is not a Dukedom, Sir, a goodly gift?

RICHARD: Ay, by my faith, for a poor Earl to give,
I'll do thee service for so good a gift.

WARWICK: 'Twas I that gave the Kingdom to thy Brother.

EDWARD: Why then 'tis mine, if but by Warwick's gift.

WARWICK: Thou art no Atlas for so great a weight:
And weakling, Warwick takes his gift again,
And Henry is my King, Warwick his Subject.

EDWARD: But Warwick's King is Edward's prisoner:
And gallant Warwick, do but answer this,
What is the body, when the head is off?

RICHARD: Alas, that Warwick had no more fore-cast,
But whiles he thought to steal the single ten,
The King was slily finger'd from the deck:
You left poor Henry at the Bishop's Palace,
And ten to one you'll meet him in the Tower.

EDWARD: 'Tis even so, yet you are Warwick still.

RICHARD: Come Warwick,
Take the time, kneel down, kneel down:
Nay when? strike now, or else the iron cools.

WARWICK: I had rather chop this hand off at a blow,
And with the other, fling it at thy face,
Than bear so low a sail, to strike to thee.

EDWARD: Sail how thou canst,
Have wind and tide thy friend,
This hand, fast wound about thy coal-black hair,
Shall, whiles thy head is warm, and new cut off,
Write in the dust this sentence with thy blood,
Wind-changing Warwick now can change no more.

Enter Oxford, with drum and colours.

WARWICK: Oh cheerful colours, see where Oxford comes.

OXFORD: Oxford, Oxford, for Lancaster.

Exit.

RICHARD: The gates are open, let us enter too.

EDWARD: So other foes may set upon our backs.
   Stand we in good array: for they no doubt
   Will issue out again, and bid us battle;
   If not, the City being but of small defence,
   We 'll quickly rouse the Traitors in the same.

WARWICK: Oh welcome Oxford, for we want thy help.

Enter Montague, with drum and colours.

MONTAGUE: Montague, Montague, for Lancaster.

Exit.

RICHARD: Thou and thy Brother both shall buy this
      treason
   Even with the dearest blood your bodies bear.

EDWARD: The harder match'd, the greater victory,
   My mind presageth happy gain, and conquest.

Enter Somerset, with drum and colours.

SOMERSET: Somerset, Somerset, for Lancaster.

Exit.

RICHARD: Two of thy Name, both Dukes of Somerset,
   Have sold their lives unto the House of York,
   And thou shalt be the third, if this sword hold.

Enter Clarence, with drum and colours.

WARWICK: And lo, where George of Clarence sweeps
      along,
   Of force enough to bid his Brother battle:
   With whom, in upright zeal to right, prevails
   More than the nature of a Brother's love.
   Come Clarence, come; thou wilt, if Warwick call.

CLARENCE: Father of Warwick, know you what this
      means?
   Look here, I throw my infamy at thee:
   I will not ruinate my Father's House,
   Who gave his blood to lime the stones together,
   And set up Lancaster. Why, trow'st thou, Warwick,

That Clarence is so harsh, so blunt, unnatural,
To bend the fatal instruments of war
Against his Brother, and his lawful King.
Perhaps thou wilt object my holy Oath:
To keep that Oath, were more impiety,
Than Jephthah's, when he sacrific'd his Daughter.
I am so sorry for my trespass made,
That to deserve well at my Brother's hands,
I here proclaim myself thy mortal foe:
With resolution, wheresoe'er I meet thee,
(As I will meet thee, if thou stir abroad)
To plague thee, for thy foul misleading me.
And so, proud-hearted Warwick, I defy thee,
And to my Brother turn my blushing cheeks.
Pardon me Edward, I will make amends:
And Richard, do not frown upon my faults,
For I will henceforth be no more unconstant.

EDWARD: Now welcome more, and ten times more belov'd,
Than if thou never hadst deserv'd our hate.

RICHARD: Welcome good Clarence, this is brother-like.

WARWICK: Oh passing Traitor, perjur'd and unjust.

EDWARD: What Warwick,
Wilt thou leave the Town, and fight?
Or shall we beat the stones about thine ears?

WARWICK: Alas, I am not coop'd here for defence:
I will away towards Barnet presently,
And bid thee battle, Edward, if thou dar'st.

EDWARD: Yes Warwick, Edward dares, and leads the
way:
Lords to the field: Saint George, and victory.

Exeunt. March. Warwick and his company
follows.

V. 2

*Alarum, and Excursions. Enter Edward, bringing
forth Warwick wounded.*

EDWARD: So, lie thou there: die thou, and die our fear,
For Warwick was a bug that fear'd us all.
Now Montague sit fast, I seek for thee,
That Warwick's bones may keep thine company.

Exit.

WARWICK: Ah, who is nigh? come to me, friend, or foe,
And tell me who is victor, York, or Warwick?
Why ask I that? my mangled body shows,
My blood, my want of strength, my sick heart shows,
That I must yield my body to the earth,
And by my fall, the conquest to my foe.
Thus yields the cedar to the axe's edge,
Whose arms gave shelter to the Princely Eagle,
Under whose shade the ramping Lion slept,
Whose top-branch overpeer'd Jove's spreading tree,
And kept low shrubs from Winter's powerful wind.
These eyes, that now are dimm'd with Death's black
    veil,
Have been as piercing as the mid-day Sun,
To search the secret treasons of the World:
The wrinkles in my brows, now fill'd with blood,
Were liken'd oft to kingly sepulchres:
For who liv'd King, but I could dig his grave?
And who durst smile, when Warwick bent his brow?
Lo, now my glory smear'd in dust and blood.
My parks, my walks, my manors that I had,
Even now forsake me; and of all my lands,
Is nothing left me, but my body's length.
Why, what is Pomp, Rule, Reign, but earth and dust?

And live we how we can, yet die we must.

Enter Oxford and Somerset.

SOMERSET: Ah Warwick, Warwick! wert thou as we are,
We might recover all our loss again:
The Queen from France hath brought a puissant power.
Even now we heard the news: ah, couldst thou fly.

WARWICK: Why then I would not fly. Ah Montague,
If thou be there, sweet Brother, take my hand,
And with thy lips keep in my soul a while.
Thou lov'st me not: for, Brother, if thou didst,
Thy tears would wash this cold congealed blood,
That glues my lips, and will not let me speak.
Come quickly Montague, or I am dead.

SOMERSET: Ah Warwick, Montague hath breath'd his last,
And to the latest gasp, cri'd out for Warwick:
And said, Commend me to my valiant Brother.
And more he would have said, and more he spoke,
Which sounded like a cannon in a vault,
That mought not be distinguish'd: but at last,
I well might hear, delivered with a groan,
Oh farewell Warwick.

WARWICK: Sweet rest his soul:
Fly Lords, and save yourselves,
For Warwick bids you all farewell, to meet in heaven.

OXFORD: Away, away, to meet the Queen's great power.

Here they bear away his body. Exeunt.

V. 3

*Flourish. Enter King Edward in triumph, with
Richard, Clarence, and the rest.*

KING EDWARD: Thus far our fortune keeps an upward
course,

And we are grac'd with wreaths of Victory:
But in the midst of this bright-shining day,
I spy a black suspicious threat'ning cloud,
That will encounter with our glorious Sun,
Ere he attain his easeful western bed:
I mean, my Lords, those powers that the Queen
Hath rais'd in Gallia, have arriv'd our coast,
And, as we hear, march on to fight with us.

CLARENCE: A little gale will soon disperse that cloud,
And blow it to the source from whence it came,
Thy very beams will dry those vapours up,
For every cloud engenders not a storm.

RICHARD: The Queen is valued thirty thousand strong,
And Somerset, with Oxford, fled to her:
If she have time to breathe, be well assur'd
Her faction will be full as strong as ours.

KING EDWARD: We are advertis'd by our loving friends,
That they do hold their course toward Tewkesbury.
We having now the best at Barnet field,
Will thither straight, for willingness rids way,
And as we march, our strength will be augmented:
In every county as we go along,
Strike up the drum, cry courage, and away.

Exeunt.

V. 4

Flourish. March. Enter the Queen, young Ed-
ward, Somerset, Oxford, and Soldiers.

QUEEN: Great Lords, wise men ne'er sit and wail their loss,
But cheerly seek how to redress their harms.
What though the mast be now blown over-board,
The cable broke, the holding-anchor lost,
And half our sailors swallow'd in the flood?

Yet lives our Pilot still. Is 't meet, that he
Should leave the helm, and like a fearful lad,
With tearful eyes add water to the sea,
And give more strength to that which hath too much,
Whiles in his moan, the ship splits on the rock,
Which industry and courage might have sav'd?
Ah what a shame, ah what a fault were this.
Say Warwick was our anchor: what of that?
And Montague our topmast: what of him?
Our slaughter'd friends, the tackles: what of these?
Why is not Oxford here, another anchor?
And Somerset, another goodly mast?
The friends of France our shrouds and tacklings?
And though unskilful, why not Ned and I,
For once allow'd the skilful Pilot's charge?
We will not from the helm, to sit and weep,
But keep our course (though the rough wind say no)
From shelves and rocks, that threaten us with wrack.
As good to chide the waves, as speak them fair.
And what is Edward, but a ruthless sea?
What Clarence, but a quick-sand of deceit?
And Richard, but a ragged fatal rock?
All these, the enemies to our poor bark.
Say you can swim, alas 'tis but a while:
Tread on the sand, why there you quickly sink,
Bestride the rock, the tide will wash you off,
Or else you famish, that 's a threefold death.
This speak I (Lords) to let you understand,
If case some one of you would fly from us,
That there 's no hop'd-for mercy with the Brothers,
More than with ruthless waves, with sands and rocks.
Why courage then, what cannot be avoided,
'Twere childish weakness to lament, or fear.
PRINCE: Methinks a Woman of this valiant spirit,

Should, if a coward heard her speak these words,
Infuse his breast with magnanimity,
And make him, naked, foil a man at arms.
I speak not this, as doubting any here:
For did I but suspect a fearful man,
He should have leave to go away betimes,
Lest in our need he might infect another,
And make him of like spirit to himself.
If any such be here, as God forbid,
Let him depart, before we need his help.

OXFORD: Women and children of so high a courage,
And warriors faint, why 'twere perpetual shame.
Oh brave young Prince: thy famous Grandfather
Doth live again in thee; long mayst thou live,
To bear his image, and renew his glories.

SOMERSET: And he that will not fight for such a hope,
Go home to bed, and like the owl by day,
If he arise, be mock'd and wonder'd at.

QUEEN: Thanks gentle Somerset, sweet Oxford thanks.

PRINCE: And take his thanks, that yet hath nothing else.

Enter a Messenger.

MESSENGER: Prepare you Lords, for Edward is at hand,
Ready to fight: therefore be resolute.

OXFORD: I thought no less: it is his policy,
To haste thus fast, to find us unprovided.

SOMERSET: But he 's deceiv'd, we are in readiness.

QUEEN: This cheers my heart, to see your forwardness.

OXFORD: Here pitch our battle, hence we will not budge.

Flourish, and March. Enter Edward, Richard,
Clarence, and Soldiers.

EDWARD: Brave followers, yonder stands the thorny wood,
Which by the Heavens' assistance, and your strength,
Must by the roots be hew'n up yet ere night.
I need not add more fuel to your fire,

For well I wot, ye blaze, to burn them out:
Give signal to the fight, and to it Lords.
QUEEN: Lords, Knights, and Gentlemen, what I should say
My tears gainsay: for every word I speak,
Ye see I drink the water of mine eye.
Therefore no more but this: Henry your Sovereign
Is prisoner to the Foe, his State usurp'd,
His Realm a slaughter-house, his subjects slain,
His Statutes cancell'd, and his Treasure spent:
And yonder is the Wolf, that makes this spoil.
You fight in justice: then in God's Name, Lords,
Be valiant, and give signal to the fight.
  Alarum, Retreat, Excursions. Exeunt.

V. 5

Flourish. Enter Edward, Richard, Queen,
Clarence, Oxford, Somerset.

EDWARD: Now here a period of tumultuous broils.
Away with Oxford to Hames Castle straight:
For Somerset, off with his guilty head.
Go bear them hence, I will not hear them speak.
OXFORD: For my part, I 'll not trouble thee with words.
SOMERSET: Nor I, but stoop with patience to my fortune.
                Exeunt.
QUEEN: So part we sadly in this troublous World,
To meet with joy in sweet Jerusalem.
EDWARD: Is Proclamation made, That who finds Edward,
Shall have a high reward, and he his life?
RICHARD: It is, and lo where youthful Edward comes.
           Enter Soldiers, with the Prince.
EDWARD: Bring forth the Gallant, let us hear him speak.
What? can so young a thorn begin to prick?
Edward, what satisfaction canst thou make,

For bearing arms, for stirring up my subjects,
And all the trouble thou hast turn'd me to?

PRINCE: Speak like a subject, proud ambitious York.
Suppose that I am now my Father's mouth,
Resign thy Chair, and where I stand, kneel thou,
Whilst I propose the self-same words to thee,
Which (Traitor) thou wouldst have me answer to.

QUEEN: Ah, that thy Father had been so resolv'd.

RICHARD: That you might still have worn the petticoat,
And ne'er have stol'n the breech from Lancaster.

PRINCE: Let Aesop fable in a winter's night,
His currish riddles sorts not with this place.

RICHARD: By Heaven, Brat, I'll plague ye for that word.

QUEEN: Ay, thou wast born to be a plague to men.

RICHARD: For God's sake, take away this captive scold.

PRINCE: Nay, take away this scolding Crook-back, rather.

EDWARD: Peace wilful Boy, or I will charm your tongue.

CLARENCE: Untutor'd lad, thou art too malapert.

PRINCE: I know my duty, you are all undutiful:
Lascivious Edward, and thou perjur'd George,
And thou mis-shapen Dick, I tell ye all,
I am your better, Traitors as ye are,
And thou usurp'st my Father's right and mine.

EDWARD: Take that, thou likeness of this railer here.
Stabs him.

RICHARD: Sprawl'st thou? take that, to end thy agony.
Richard stabs him.

CLARENCE: And there's for twitting me with perjury.
Clarence stabs him.

QUEEN: Oh, kill me too.

RICHARD: Marry, and shall.
Offers to kill her.

EDWARD: Hold, Richard, hold, for we have done too
much.

RICHARD: Why should she live, to fill the World with
    words.

EDWARD: What? doth she swoun? use means for her
    recovery.

RICHARD: Clarence excuse me to the King my Brother:
  I'll hence to London on a serious matter,
  Ere ye come there, be sure to hear some news.

CLARENCE: What? what?

RICHARD: Tower, the Tower.

Exit.

QUEEN: Oh Ned, sweet Ned, speak to thy Mother Boy.
  Canst thou not speak? O Traitors, Murtherers!
  They that stabb'd Caesar, shed no blood at all:
  Did not offend, nor were not worthy blame,
  If this foul deed were by, to equal it.
  He was a man; this (in respect) a child,
  And men, ne'er spend their fury on a child.
  What's worse than Murtherer, that I may name it?
  No, no, my heart will burst, and if I speak,
  And I will speak, that so my heart may burst.
  Butchers and villains, bloody cannibals,
  How sweet a plant have you untimely cropp'd:
  You have no children (butchers) if you had,
  The thought of them would have stirr'd up remorse,
  But if you ever chance to have a child,
  Look in his youth to have him so cut off,
  As deathsmen you have rid this sweet young Prince.

EDWARD: Away with her, go bear her hence perforce.

QUEEN: Nay, never bear me hence, dispatch me here:
  Here sheathe thy sword, I'll pardon thee my death:
  What? wilt thou not? Then Clarence do it thou.

CLARENCE: By heaven, I will not do thee so much ease.

QUEEN: Good Clarence do: sweet Clarence do thou do
    it.

CLARENCE: Didst thou not hear me swear I would not do
    it?

QUEEN: Ay, but thou usest to forswear thyself.
  'Twas sin before, but now 'tis charity.
  What wilt thou not? Where is that devil's butcher
    Richard?
  Hard-favour'd Richard? Richard, where art thou?
  Thou art not here; Murther is thy alms-deed:
  Petitioners for blood, thou ne'er put'st back.

EDWARD: Away I say, I charge ye bear her hence.

QUEEN: So come to you, and yours, as to this Prince.

Exit Queen.

EDWARD: Where 's Richard gone?

CLARENCE: To London all in post, and as I guess,
  To make a bloody supper in the Tower.

EDWARD: He 's sudden if a thing comes in his head.
  Now march we hence, discharge the common sort
  With pay and thanks, and let 's away to London,
  And see our gentle Queen how well she fares,
  By this (I hope) she hath a son for me.

Exeunt.

V. 6

*Enter Henry the Sixth, and Richard, with the
Lieutenant, on the walls.*

RICHARD: Good day, my Lord, what at your book so
    hard?

HENRY: Ay my good Lord: my Lord I should say rather,
  'Tis sin to flatter, Good was little better:
  Good Gloucester, and good Devil, were alike,
  And both preposterous: therefore, not Good Lord.

RICHARD: Sirrah, leave us to ourselves, we must confer.

Exit Lieutenant.

HENRY: So flies the wreakless shepherd from the wolf:
    So first the harmless sheep doth yield his fleece,
    And next his throat, unto the butcher's knife.
    What scene of death hath Roscius now to act?
RICHARD: Suspicion always haunts the guilty mind,
    The thief doth fear each bush an officer.
HENRY: The bird that hath been limed in a bush,
    With trembling wings misdoubteth every bush;
    And I, the hapless male to one sweet bird,
    Have now the fatal object in my eye,
    Where my poor young was lim'd, was caught, and
        kill'd.
RICHARD: Why what a peevish fool was that of Crete,
    That taught his son the office of a fowl,
    And yet for all his wings, the fool was drown'd.
HENRY: I Daedalus, my poor Boy Icarus,
    Thy Father Minos, that denied our course,
    The Sun that sear'd the wings of my sweet Boy.
    Thy Brother Edward, and thyself, the sea
    Whose envious gulf did swallow up his life:
    Ah, kill me with thy weapon, not with words.
    My breast can better brook thy dagger's point,
    Than can my ears that Tragic History.
    But wherefore dost thou come? Is 't for my life?
RICHARD: Think'st thou I am an executioner?
HENRY: A persecutor I am sure thou art,
    If murthering innocents be executing,
    Why then thou art an executioner.
RICHARD: Thy Son I kill'd for his presumption.
HENRY: Hadst thou been kill'd, when first thou didst
        presume,
    Thou hadst not liv'd to kill a Son of mine:
    And thus I prophesy, that many a thousand,
    Which now mistrust no parcel of my fear,

And many an old man's sigh, and many a widow's,
And many an orphan's water-standing eye,
Men for their sons, wives for their husbands,
Orphans, for their parents' timeless death,
Shall rue the hour that ever thou wast born.
The owl shriek'd at thy birth, an evil sign,
The night-crow cried, aboding luckless time,
Dogs howl'd, and hideous tempest shook down trees:
The raven rook'd her on the chimney top,
And chattering pies in dismal discords sung:
Thy Mother felt more than a Mother's pain,
And yet brought forth less than a Mother's hope,
To wit, an indigested and deformed lump,
Not like the fruit of such a goodly tree.
Teeth hadst thou in thy head, when thou wast born,
To signify, thou cam'st to bite the world:
And if the rest be true, which I have heard,
Thou cam'st –

RICHARD: I 'll hear no more:
Die Prophet, in thy speech,
> *Stabs him.*
For this (amongst the rest) was I ordain'd.

HENRY: Ay, and for much more slaughter after this,
O God forgive my sins, and pardon thee.
> *Dies.*

RICHARD: What? will the aspiring blood of Lancaster
Sink in the ground? I thought it would have mounted.
See how my sword weeps for the poor King's death.
O may such purple tears be always shed
From those that wish the downfall of our house.
If any spark of life be yet remaining,
Down, down to hell, and say I sent thee thither.
> *Stabs him again.*
I that have neither pity, love, nor fear,

Indeed 'tis true that Henry told me of:
For I have often heard my Mother say,
I came into the world with my legs forward.
Had I not reason (think ye) to make haste,
And seek their ruin, that usurp'd our right?
The midwife wonder'd, and the women cried
O Jesus bless us, he is born with teeth,
And so I was, which plainly signified,
That I should snarl, and bite, and play the dog:
Then since the Heavens have shap'd my body so,
Let Hell make crook'd my mind to answer it.
I have no Brother, I am like no Brother:
And this word (Love) which greybeards call divine,
Be resident in men like one another,
And not in me: I am myself alone.
Clarence beware, thou keep'st me from the light,
But I will sort a pitchy day for thee:
For I will buzz abroad such prophecies,
That Edward shall be fearful of his life,
And then to purge his fear, I 'll be thy death.
King Henry, and the Prince his Son are gone,
Clarence thy turn is next, and then the rest,
Counting myself but bad, till I be best.
I 'll throw thy body in another room,
And triumph Henry, in thy day of doom.

Exit.

V. 7

Flourish. Enter King, Queen, Clarence,
Richard, Hastings, Nurse with infant, and
Attendants.

KING: Once more we sit in England's Royal Throne,
Re-purchas'd with the blood of enemies:

What valiant foemen, like an autumn's corn,
Have we mow'd down in tops of all their pride?
Three Dukes of Somerset, threefold renown'd,
For hardy and undoubted champions:
Two Cliffords, as the Father and the Son,
And two Northumberlands: two braver men,
Ne'er spurr'd their coursers at the trumpet's sound.
With them, the two brave Bears, Warwick and Monta-
gue,
That in their chains fetter'd the Kingly Lion,
And made the forest tremble when they roar'd.
Thus have we swept suspicion from our seat,
And made our footstool of security.
Come hither Bess, and let me kiss my Boy:
Young Ned, for thee, thine Uncles, and myself,
Have in our armours watch'd the winter's night,
Went all afoot in summer's scalding heat,
That thou mightst repossess the Crown in peace,
And of our labours thou shalt reap the gain.

RICHARD: I 'll blast his harvest, if your head were laid,
For yet I am not look'd on in the world.
This shoulder was ordain'd so thick, to heave,
And heave it shall some weight, or break my back,
Work thou the way, and that shalt execute.

KING: Clarence and Gloucester, love my lovely Queen,
And kiss your Princely Nephew, Brothers both.

CLARENCE: The duty that I owe unto your Majesty,
I seal upon the lips of this sweet babe.

QUEEN: Thanks noble Clarence, worthy brother thanks.

RICHARD: And that I love the tree from whence thou
sprang'st:
Witness the loving kiss I give the fruit,
To say the truth, so Judas kiss'd his master,
And cried all hail, when as he meant all harm.

KING: Now am I seated as my soul delights,
   Having my Country's peace, and Brothers' loves.
CLARENCE: What will your grace have done with Margaret?
   Reignier her Father, to the King of France
   Hath pawn'd the Sicils and Jerusalem,
   And hither have they sent it for her ransom.
KING: Away with her, and waft her hence to France:
   And now what rests, but that we spend the time
   With stately triumphs, mirthful comic shows,
   Such as befits the pleasure of the Court.
   Sound drums and trumpets, farewell sour annoy,
   For here I hope begins our lasting joy.

                                   Exeunt omnes.

NOTES

References are to the page and line of this edition.
There are 34 lines to a full page.

PART ONE

The Actors' Names: Sir John Falstaffe: In the Folio he   P. 40 L. 15
is always called 'Falstaffe'; his real name was Fas-
tolf; but since the fat knight of *I* and *II Henry IV*
derives from this person it seems best to leave his
name as Shakespeare wrote it.

Charles the Dolphin: usually corrected to Dauphin,   P. 40 L. 21
but Dolphin is the normal word in Elizabethan
English. *Dauphin* was the title of the heir of the
French throne.

Duke of Alanson: the Elizabethan form of Alençon.   P. 40 L. 24

Joan of Arc: is variously called in the Folio text   P. 40 L. 31
'Joane Puzel', 'Joane de Puzel', 'Pucell', 'Jone',
'Jone de Pucell'. It seemed better to keep these forms
than to refine them into 'Jeanne La Pucelle'.

Hung ... black: Black curtains were used on the   P. 41 L. 7
stage when a tragedy was being played.

Comets ... sky: i.e., Henry's death is such a universal   P. 41
disaster that there should be such signs in the sky as   LL. 9–10
heralded the death of Julius Caesar.

crystal tresses: bright hairs. The 'tail' of a comet was   P. 41 L. 10
compared to hair.

wooden: i.e., useless.   P. 41 L. 27

effeminate Prince: Shakespeare has overlooked the   P. 42 L. 14
fact that the infant King was less than a year old at
his father's death.

Protector: acting for the King during his minority.   P. 42 L. 17

holdeth ... awe: keeps you afraid of her.   P. 42 L. 19

invocate: call upon, as if Henry was a canonized   P. 42 L. 34
Saint.

adverse planets: unlucky stars. It was a common be-   P. 43 L. 2
lief that the planets directly influenced men's lives.

burst his lead: The bodies of the illustrious dead were   P. 43 L. 14
enclosed in an inner coffin of lead.

P. 43 L. 15   *Roan:* the normal Elizabethan spelling and pronunciation of Rouen.

P. 43 L. 21   *maintain several factions:* back different parties.

P. 43 L. 30   *flower-de-luces:* fleur-de-lis, the heraldic emblem of France. Edward I first combined the fleur-de-lis in the English coat-of-arms, where it remained for nearly five hundred years.

P. 44 L. 2   *wailing robes:* mourning cloaks. It was the Elizabethan custom for mourners at funerals to wear long black hooded cloaks.

P. 44 L. 10   *Dolphin:* see note on the Actors' Names above.

P. 45 L. 19   *seal'd up:* completed.

P. 45 L. 20   *Falstaffe:* see note on the Actors' names above.

P. 45 L. 21   *vaward:* i.e., in support of the vanguard.

P. 45 L. 26   *Walloon:* an inhabitant of what is now Belgium.

P. 46 L. 9   *Saint George's feast:* 23rd April.

P. 46 L. 21   *preparation:* a 5-syllable word. It was usual to pronounce both syllables of words ending in -*ion*.

P. 46 L. 23   *Tower:* In earlier times the Tower of London was the main arsenal of the Kingdom.

P. 47 L. 1   *sit . . . stern:* i.e., be chief steersman.

P. 47 L. 7   *Mars his:* Mar's. Mars here is both the god of war and the planet whose course in the heavens had not yet been accurately traced.

P. 47
LL. 15–16   *bull beeves:* bull beef was regarded as the proper diet for full-blooded Englishmen.

P. 47 L. 23   *spend his gall:* wear out his anger.

P. 48 L. 8   *Froissart:* Jean Froissart (1338–1410), a famous French Chronicler, who recorded the wars of Edward III in France.

P. 48 L. 9   *Olivers and Rowlands:* Rowland and Oliver were the two most famous and doughty knights of Charlemagne, much celebrated in romantic legend.

P. 48 L. 12   *Samsons and Goliases:* The deeds of Samson are recorded in Judges 13–16; the story of Goliath the Philistine giant is told in I Samuel 17.

P. 48 L. 21   *gimmors:* 'gimcrack'; lit., a ring so made that it opens out into two rings.

P. 49 L. 14   *Puzell:* a version of *pucelle:* maid. See note on the Actors' Names above.

P. 49 L. 23   *takes . . . her:* plays her part.

God's Mother: the Blessed Virgin Mary.   P. 49 L. 30
Resolve on this: if you decide to do this.   P. 50 L. 9
high terms: lofty claims.   P. 50 L. 11
flower-de-luces: see note on P. 43 L. 30.   P. 50 L. 17
Amazon: The Amazons were a legendary race of P. 50 L. 23
female warriors who lived in South Russia.
Debora: a prophetess who 'judged' Israel in the P. 50 L. 24
early days: see Judges 4–5.
shrives ... smock: makes improper love to; lit., P. 51 LL. 5–6
hears her confession in her nightgown.
Saint Martin's summer: a patch of fine weather which P. 51 L. 19
often occurs in the autumn. St Martin's day is 11th
November.
halcyons' days: i.e., fine weather in winter. According P. 51 L. 19
to Pliny's *Natural History,* for a week before and after
midwinter's day the sea is calm so that the halcyon
(kingfisher) can hatch the eggs in her floating nest.
proud ... once: Plutarch, in his life of Julius Caesar, P. 51
records that when Caesar needed to cross over dan-   LL. 26–7
gerous seas in a small boat, he said to the reluctant
master of the ship: 'Good fellow ... fear not, for
thou hast Caesar and his fortunes with thee.'
Mahomet ... dove: The prophet Mahomet was said P. 51 L. 28
to have been divinely inspired by a dove or pigeon
which whispered in his ear.
Helen: St Helena, the Christian mother of the P. 51 L. 30
Emperor Constantine.
S. Philip's daughters: see Acts 21: 8–9, 'And we P. 51 L. 31
entered into the house of Philip the Evangelist ...
and the same man had four daughters, virgins,
which did prophesy.'
tawny coats: liveries of yellow-brown.   P. 53 L. 12
Proditor: betrayer, with a poor pun on *Protector.*   P. 53 L. 17
Damascus: by tradition the place where Cain killed P. 53 L. 26
his brother Abel.
bearing-cloth: the robe in which an infant is carried P. 53 L. 29
to its christening.
privileged place: The Tower, being a royal palace, P. 54 L. 1
was invested with certain 'privileges'; it was a
capital offence to draw a sword in anger within the
precincts of a palace.

P. 54 L. 3   *tug*: To pluck a man by the beard was a contemptuous and deadly insult.

P. 54 L. 9   *Winchester Goose*: The Bishops of Winchester owned property in the suburb of Southwark which was used for brothels. So a *Winchester goose* is a prostitute, or one suffering from venereal disease.

P. 54 L. 9   *a rope, a rope*: an abusive cry, meaning 'you should be hanged.'

P. 55 L. 10   *call for clubs*: 'Clubs!' was the cry raised in London streets to call on the apprentices to leave their shops and assist the city officers in quelling a riot.

P. 56 L. 16   *never trouble you*: i.e., I'll shoot without first sending for you.

P. 56 L. 30   *pill'd esteem'd*: regarded as so plucked. Sometimes amended to *vile esteemed*.

P. 57 L. 17   *chosen shot*: picked musketeers.

P. 58 L. 8   *Mirror . . . men*: perfect example of a soldier.

P. 58 L. 29   *Nero*: the name is missing in the text, but the context shows what was intended: the Roman Emperor who played on his lyre while Rome burned.

P. 59 L. 11   *Puzel or Pussel*: pucelle (maid) or slut. *Dogfish*: a term of contempt.

P. 59 L. 14   *me*: for me.

P. 60 L. 14   *Hannibal*: the Carthaginian general who so often defeated the Romans.

P. 60 L. 22   *lions*: the coat-of-arms of the English Kings bear three lions.

P. 60 L. 23   *sheep . . . stead*: i.e., sheep are a more appropriate emblem for you than lions.

P. 60 L. 26   *oft-subdued*: whom you have often beaten.

P. 61 L. 9   *Astraea*: daughter of the god Jupiter and a pattern of feminine beauty.

P. 61 L. 11   *Adonis*: a beautiful youth beloved by the goddess Venus (a story which Shakespeare told in his poem *Venus and Adonis*). There is a long description of the Garden of Adonis in Spenser's *Faerie Queen*. III. iv. 29.

P. 61 L. 28   *Rhodope's or Memphis'*: Rhodope was a courtesan who married the King of Memphis (the Egyptian city near the pyramids).

P. 61 L. 31   *Darius*: King of Persia, defeated by Alexander the Great.

Saint Denis: patron saint of France.   P. 62 L. 2

Joan . . . Saint: This prophecy was fulfilled when St   P. 62 L. 3
Joan of Arc was canonized on May 16, 1920.

Court of Guard: guard room.   P. 62 L. 12

Dead March: i.e., for Salisbury's funeral.   P. 62 L. 18

friend: lover.   P. 64 L. 8

Dolphin's Grace: his Grace the Dolphin.   P. 65 L. 27

more . . . will: i.e., you won't want our company in   P. 66 L. 33
this amorous adventure.

Scythian Tomyris: She was Queen of the Massagetae,   P. 67 L. 15
a Scythian (South Russian) tribe, against which
Cyrus King of Persia led an expedition. Cyrus was
killed in the battle. Tomyris had his head cut off and
enclosed in a bag full of blood so that he might have
his fill of it.

Hector: the doughty champion of Troy.   P. 67 L. 30

for the nonce: lit., for the occasion; it is one of those   P. 69 L. 6
somewhat meaningless expressions which are so use-
ful for filling up a line of verse. Chaucer often used it.

Temple: one of the Inns of Court in the City of   P. 70 L. 7
London.

mannerly forbearance: polite refusal to take sides.   P. 70 L. 25

colours: pretences. Puns on the various meanings of   P. 71 L. 9
colour are common.

Boy: youngster – a deadly insult.   P. 72 L. 20

grace the yeoman: honour one who is no gentleman.   P. 72 L. 25

crestless: without a crest, i.e., not recognized as a   P. 72 L. 30
gentleman.

bears . . . privilege: i.e., he knows that he is safe in   P. 72 L. 31
this privileged place; see note on P. 54 L. 1.

exempt: excluded. The children of a nobleman con-   P. 73 L. 5
demned for treason lost all the family privileges.

growing . . . will: if ever I get my chance.   P. 73 L. 11

whipp'd: (Folio reads *whip't*). Editors often amend   P. 73 L. 32
to *wiped*.

for the truce: to make peace between.   P. 73 L. 33

Mortimer: See Genealogical Table, p. 384. Mortimer   P. 74 L. 18
was descended on the female side from Lionel, Duke
of Clarence, second son of Edward III. Henry IV
who usurped the throne after the deposition of
Richard II was son of John of Gaunt, the third son of

	Edward III. Mortimer was thus the lineal heir to the Throne; he was also uncle of Richard Plantagenet.

P. 74 L. 24 *Nestor-like:* Nestor was the Grand Old Man of the Greek worthies who attacked Troy.

P. 75 L. 9 *Henry Monmouth:* Henry V, son of Henry IV.

P. 75 L. 14 *Arbitrator of Despairs:* Death, who by acting as umpire, brings to an end the conflict of despair.

P. 76 L. 16– *Henry the fourth ... suppressed:* the wrongs of Morti-
P. 77 L. 11 mer are in part the theme of Shakespeare's later play *Richard the Second.*

P. 77 L. 8 *install'd ... Diadem:* crowned as King.

P. 78 L. 15 *restored ... Blood:* see note on P. 73 L. 5.

P. 78 L. 30 *this place:* i.e., the presence of the King.

P. 80 L. 2 *Bastard:* Beaufort was born before his mother was married to John of Gaunt, his father.

P. 80 L. 25 *Must ... Lords:* you express an insolent opinion in the presence of your betters.

P. 80 L. 34 *viperous worm:* poisonous caterpillar.

P. 81 L. 13 *contrary parts:* opposing sides.

P. 81 L. 19 *on allegiance:* on your loyalty as a subject. This is the strongest command that could be laid on a subject by his King; to disobey involved the crime of high treason, with its penalties.

P. 82 L. 1 *ink-horn mate:* scribbling rascal.

P. 82 L. 5 *pitch a field:* fight a battle.

P. 83 L. 2 *kindly gird:* gentle rebuke.

P. 83 L. 32 *of force:* powerful, convincing.

P. 84 L. 28 *Sennet:* a trumpet call denoting the departure of a procession.

P. 85 L. 1 *fester'd members:* gangrened limbs.

P. 86 L. 23 *excursion:* (usually coupled with *alarum*) the rapid entrance and exit of soldiers to symbolize the fury of battle.

P. 87 L. 14 *run a tilt:* make a charge at.

P. 87 L. 16 *Hag of all despite:* most spiteful witch.

P. 87 L. 34 *foot-boys:* servants who walk beside their master, who is mounted.

P. 88 L. 15 *Cordelion:* Cœur-de-lion, Richard I, the fiercest of the English warrior Kings. He died of an arrow wound received in France in 1199; his heart was buried in Rouen.

Pendragon: Uther Pendragon, the father of King P. 88 L. 28
Arthur.

be but rul'd: accept advice. P. 90 L. 24

here: i.e., in France. Since the English Kings claimed P. 91 L. 10
the throne of France, English noblemen also claimed
privileges in that country.

French march: a slow march. P. 91 L. 19

Fortune in favour: good luck. P. 91 L. 21

parley: trumpet call summoning the other side to P. 91 L. 23
negotiate.

like a Frenchman: When this play was written there P. 93 L. 8
was an uneasy alliance between the English and the
French. Sneers at the French habit of changing sides
were common.

I do remember: see note on P. 42 L. 14. P. 94 L. 7

present death: see note on P. 54 L. 1. P. 94 L. 32

Calice: the normal Elizabethan spelling and pro- P. 95 L. 20
nouncing of Calais.

Patay: for the Folio reading *Poictiers*. P. 95 L. 30

trusty Squire: squire usually means a gentleman be- P. 96 L. 2
low the rank of knight, but is sometimes used as a
term of contempt – 'fellow'.

furnish'd . . . sort: of such a nature. P. 96 L. 18

style: manner of address. In addressing a Prince or P. 96 L. 31
King, it was customary to inscribe the letter with all
his titles. To neglect this courtesy was a sign of
deliberate contempt.

churlish superscription: ill-mannered form of address P. 96 L. 34
(on the outside of the letter.)

Grant . . . combat: give me leave to fight. P. 97 L. 28

Rose: the red rose of the Lancastrian party. P. 98 L. 8

forged . . . conceit: false, neat term of phrase. P. 98 L. 19

paleness . . . flower: i.e., the white rose of York. P. 98 L. 23

malice . . . left: will you never cease from your P. 98 L. 25
malice?

my pledge: Here he throws down a glove as token of P. 99 L. 4
challenge to mortal combat.

grudging stomachs: discontented resentment. P. 99 L. 26

And . . . : The sentence is unfinished. *Wish* is some- P. 100 L. 32
times emended to *wist*: thought.

'Tis much: it's a bad business. P. 101 L. 11

P. 102 L. 1   *Owl:* regarded as a bird of evil omen.

P. 102 L. 9   *thee:* of thee.

P. 102 L. 12   *apparent spoil:* clear destruction.

P. 102   *This ... withal:* this is the last time I, your enemy,
LL. 19–20   will bestow (*due thee*) praise upon your fame.

P. 102   *For ... hour:* before the sand in the hour glass has
LL. 21–2   run through.

P. 102 L. 26   *bell:* passing bell, which was tolled at the moment of
               death in order that the faithful might pray for a
               passing soul.

P. 102. L. 33 *park'd:* enclosed in a park. A *park* was originally so
               called because it was an enclosure for deer. The
               image of the hunted deer is kept up to P. 103 L. 6.

P. 102 L. 33   *bounded ... pale:* kept in by a fence.

P. 103 L. 2   *in blood:* in fine condition and therefore courageous.

P. 103 L. 3   *rascal-like:* A rascal is a deer in poor condition which
               showed no fight.

P. 103 L. 6   *stand aloof:* keep their distance.

P. 104 L. 17   *He dies:* if he dies.

P. 105 L. 4   *scarce-cold:* Actually Henry V died nearly thirty
               years before the death of Talbot !

P. 105 L. 31   *in ... ling'ring:* holding out because he has an ad-
               vantageous position.

P. 106 L. 17   *take ... scorn:* regard it as a foul disgrace.

P. 107 L. 24   *your regard ... be:* you should remember how serious
               it will be to lose you.

P. 107 L. 30   *vantage:* 'good strategic reasons.'

P. 109 L. 7   *determin'd time:* fated end.

P. 109 L. 12   *Quicken'd ... spleen:* i.e., in my wrath I am become
               a young man again.

P. 110 L. 14   *subject of Mischance:* one who is servant of (deserv-
               ing) misfortune.

P. 110   *sire of Crete ... Icarus:* Daedalus of Crete and his son
LL. 19–20   Icarus, hoping to escape from Minos their King,
               attempted to fly by fastening wings to their shoulders.
               Daedalus successfully returned to earth, but Icarus
               crashed and was killed when the sun melted the
               wax by which his wings were fastened.

P. 110 L. 28   *smear'd with captivity:* an obscure phrase. Presumably
               Talbot means that he welcomes death since neither he
               nor his son have disgraced themselves by surrendering.

guardant: a heraldic term. A lion guardant is pictured P. III L. 2
as standing on his hind legs brandishing a sword.

Tendring my ruin: caring for me in my overthrow.   P. III L. 3

Two ... mortality: i.e., we two Talbots will over- P. III
come death and fly straight to Heaven.   LL. 16–17

flesh: draw blood for the first time.   P. 112 L. I

puny: inexperienced. *A puny*, in Elizabethan lan- P. 112 L. I
guage, is a freshman student in the Law.

Hell ... is: i.e., we have sent our prisoners to Hell – P. 112 L. 25
killed them.

St Michael ... Fleece: two famous Orders of P. 113 L. 2
Knighthood. St Michael was a French order; the
Golden Fleece was founded in 1429 by Philip, Duke
of Burgundy.

style: the description of a man's titles read out by a P. 113 L. 5
herald at his funeral.

The Turk ... style: According to a pamphlet P. 113
printed in 1606, the Great Turk's style was 'by the LL. 6–7
Grace of the High God Most Well-Beloved in
Heaven, descended of the Line of the Great Prophet
Mahomet, Champion of Babylon, God on Earth,
Baron of Turkey, Lord of the Country of India,
even unto the Earthly Paradise, Conqueror of Con-
stantinople and of Greece, Governor of the High
and Lower Seas, Commander of Hungary, and
future Conqueror of Christendom.'

Phoenix: a mythical bird. According to the legend P. 113 L. 27
only one phoenix lived at a time. It lived for five
hundred years. Then it built itself a nest of spices
which it set alight by the rapid beating of its wings.
From the ashes a new phoenix arose.

affect their motion: like their proposal.   P. 114 L. 9

charming spells: incantations.   P. 117 L. 4

Lordly ... North: The Devil and his fiends were re- P. 117 L. 9
garded as dwellers in the dark regions of the North.

feed ... blood: Witches were supposed to feed the P. 117 L. 19
animals which were their familiar spirits with their
own blood. In contemporary witch trials it was
common for the accused to be searched for signs indicating that they had allowed their flesh to be sucked.

spelling charms: incantations.   P. 118 L. 10

P. 118 L. 12   *devil's grace:* his Grace the Devil.

P. 118 L. 14   *Circe:* Circe was an enchantress who lured men into her palace and then by magic turned them into animals. She was subdued by Ulysses. The story is told in the *Odyssey* (Book X).

P. 119   *She's beautiful ... won:* Shakespeare so liked this
LL. 28–9   turn of phrase that he used it also in *Richard the Third* (I. 2. 255–6) and *Titus Andronicus* (II. 1. 82–4).

P. 119 L. 34   *cooling card:* a common proverbial phrase, meaning 'damper'.

P. 120 L. 5   *wooden:* useless, senseless, not interested in women.

P. 122 L. 20   *traffic of:* i.e., acting as agent.

P. 123 L. 16   *Minotaurs:* The Minotaur was a creature – half man, half bull – who lived in Crete, and to whom maidens were offered in sacrifice. The Minotaur lived in the middle of a maze (*labyrinth*) and was finally slain by the hero Theseus.

P. 123 L. 19   *And:* Folio reads *Mad.*

P. 123 L. 19   *Art:* artificial beauty.

P. 123 L. 20   *Repeat ... semblance:* call up my recollection of her beauty to your imagination.

P. 125 L. 22   *warranteth ... privilege:* A woman condemned to death could declare that she was pregnant. If the plea was accepted, her life was spared until the child had been born.

P. 126 L. 1   *Machiavel:* Pietro Machiavelli, a Florentine, composed his famous treatise *The Prince* (*Il Principe*) in 1513. Machiavelli's cynical and realistic advice on statecraft was regarded by contemporaries (especially by those who had not read it) as so immoral and devilish that the word 'Machiavellian' was used to denote a man who utterly despised all religious, moral, and human laws. Richard, Duke of Gloucester, afterwards Richard III, was regarded as a typical example.

P. 127 L. 30   *coronet:* small crown worn by one of lesser rank than a King.

P. 128 L. 12   *stand'st ... comparison:* do you refuse to sign at the last moment? *comparison:* the final scrutiny of both copies of an agreement to ensure that there are no discrepancies.

P. 128 L. 31   *Towns of Garrison:* fortified cities.

poor Earl's daughter: According to Halle, it had al- P. 130 L. 10
ready been agreed that Henry should marry the
daughter of the 'Earl of Arminack'.

by attorneyship: as a business arrangement. P. 130 L. 33

you were: i.e., when you were young. P. 132 L. 6

Paris ... Greece: Paris, son of Priam King of Troy, P. 132 L. 15
ran away with Helen the beautiful wife of Menelaus
King of Sparta. This was the cause of the ten years'
siege of Troy.

PART TWO

As by ... receiv'd: The Second Part of the play re- P. 135
sumes the action where the First Part ended – with LL. 7–23
the proxy bethrothal of Henry and Margaret, at
which Suffolk represented the King.

Calaber: Calabre. This list of notables is taken from P. 135 L. 13
Holinshed.

Imprimis: firstly – the normal beginning of the first P. 136 L. 20
clause setting out the details of an agreement: sub-
sequent clauses begin with *Item:* also.

toil his wits: scheme. P. 137 L. 27

Racing the characters: erasing the inscriptions. P. 138 L. 11

peroration ... circumstance: elaborately prepared P. 138 L. 16
oration.

rules the roast: domineers over the feast. P. 138 L. 20

large style: pompous title. P. 138 L. 22

fifteenth: a tax of one fifteenth on the income from P. 139 L. 10
land.

What though: even if. P. 140 L. 3

unto the main: a term in hazard – a dice game, with P. 141 L. 25
the inevitable pun on Maine. In hazard, the caster
called a *main* (i.e., a throw of 5, 6, 7, 8 or 9). If the
opponent threw the main he won the stake.

stands ... point: is in a delicate state. *tickle:* delicately P. 142 L. 2
balanced.

pennyworths: pronounced 'pennoths'. P. 142 L. 8

Althaea ... Calydon: Althaea, at the birth of her son P. 142
Meleager, was told by the Fates, that he would die LL. 20–1
when a firebrand then burning was consumed. She

M

took the brand from the fire and guarded it. Meleager, having become Prince of Calydon, angered his mother by slaying her brethren; whereupon in rage she cast the brand on the fire and Meleager died.

P. 142 L. 21　*Unto ... heart:* i.e., with fatal results.

P. 142 L. 26　*Nevils:* Neville was the family name of the Earl of Warwick, the most powerful nobleman in England, known in history as 'Warwick the King-maker'.

P. 142 L. 28　*spy advantage:* see my chance.

P. 142 L. 30　*Lancaster:* Henry VI, descended from John of Gaunt, Duke of Lancaster; see Genealogical Table, p. 384.

P. 142 L. 33　*church-like humours:* pious inclinations.

P. 143 L. 6　*milk-white Rose:* The White Rose of the House of York.

P. 143 L. 11　*bookish rule:* i.e., the King is a mere scholar, not a man of action.

P. 143 L. 16　*Ceres:* goddess of corn.

P. 144 L. 9　*staff:* the white rod of office carried by the chief officers of State.

P. 145 L. 26　*Grace:* the courtesy form of address of a Duke and his wife.

P. 146 L. 11　*Sir John:* A Bachelor of Arts was termed *Dominus* (= Sir); in the class lists in the University of Cambridge B.A.'s are still designated Ds. As most priests were graduates, the courtesy title of Sir was given them.

P. 146 L. 16　*Yet ... coast:* i.e., I am being bribed by their enemies.

P. 146 LL. 23–4　*A crafty ... broker:* a rogue can do his own dirty work.

P. 147 L. 6　*in the quill:* altogether. The origin of the phrase is unknown.

P. 147 L. 24　*Commons:* common lands. The *enclosing* of the common lands by the rich was one of the greatest scandals and grievances of the sixteenth century in England.

P. 148 L. 20　*be a pupil still:* always (*still*) be under the control of a tutor.

P. 148 L. 25　*tilt:* a friendly combat in which knights in full armour charged each other on horseback – a form of contest which called for considerable physical courage.

P. 148 L. 30　*Ave-Maries:* the prayer begining 'Hail, Mary'.

P. 149 L. 20　*revenues:* accented on the second syllable – revénue.

Sennet: a trumpet call announcing the arrival of a P. 150 L. 8
procession of important persons. The stage direction
in *The Contention* reads:
*Enter King Henrie, and the Duke of Yorke and the Duke
of Somerset on both sides of the King, whispering with
him: Then entereth Duke Humphrey, Dame Eleanor,
the Duke of Buckingham, the Earle of Salisbury, the
Earle of Warwicke, and the Cardinall of Winchester.*

Dolphin: the normal Elizabethan pronunciation of P. 151 L. 4
Dauphin, the title of the Heir to the throne of France.

execution: a 5-syllable word. The termination - *ion* P. 151 L. 13
was usually pronounced as two syllables, especially
in Shakespeare's earlier plays.

ten Commandments: slang for ten fingers.   P. 151 L. 25

most . . . breeches: a proverb of which the modern P. 151 L. 29
equivalent is 'the wife wears the pants'.

fast . . . verge: unable to escape from our magic circle. P. 155 L. 3

at an inch: closely.   P. 155 L. 31

The Duke . . . posse: The prophecy has a double P. 156
meaning as it is not clear whether 'that' means   LL. 19–21
who or *whom*. The answer, says York, is like the
famous warning given by the oracle to King
Pyrrhus when about to make war on the Romans:
'I tell you, son of Aeacus, you the Romans can conquer.' Pyrrhus in his arrogance assumed that he was
being promised victory.

hardly . . . understood: difficult to obtain and difficult P. 156
to understand.   LL. 30–1

The stage direction in *The Contention* reads: P. 157 L. 13
*Enter the King and Queene with her Hawke on her fist,
and Duke Humfrey and Suffolk, and the Cardinall, as if
they came from Hawking.*

Falconers: keepers and trainers of hunting hawks. P. 157 L. 14

old . . . out: the old hawk (Joan) would not have P. 157 L. 18
flown away. Hawks were liable to fly away in a high
wind.

point: place of vantage aloft from which the hawk P. 157 L. 19
swoops down.

pitch: the top of the hawk's flight.   P. 157 L. 20

and it like: if it please.   P. 157 L. 23

Tantae . . . irae: is such anger fit for heavenly minds? P. 158 L. 9–10

P. 158 L. 29   *factious numbers:* rebellious partizans.

P. 159 L. 15   *Medice teipsum:* physician [heal] thyself.

P. 160 LL.2-3   *Great ... multiplied:* he is greatly blessed on earth, but now that he can see he may become a greater sinner because he will have more temptations.

P. 161 L. 8   *But ... all:* only once.

P. 162   *Then Saunder ... again:* printed as irregular lines of
LL. 4-11   verse in the Folio.

P. 162 L. 14   *Beadles:* officers of the parish, responsible for keeping order and for inflicting minor punishments, such as whipping.

P. 163 L. 21   *apprehended ... fact:* arrested in the act.

P. 163 L. 29   *keep your hour:* maintain your normal way of life.

P. 164 L. 27   *close walk:* enclosed garden path.

P. 165 L. 2   *Edward the Third:* see Genealogical Table, p. 384.

P. 165 L. 18   *his:* i.e., King Richard's.

P. 165 L. 30   *Philipp:* Philippa.

P. 166 L. 23   *slips:* cuttings from a tree for grafting or propagating new stock.

P. 167 L. 19   *State:* all his Court.

P. 167 L. 25   *God's .... death:* see Exodus 22: 18 – 'Thou shalt not suffer a witch to live.'

P. 168 L. 15   *staff:* see note on P. 144 L. 9.

P. 168 L. 21   *of years:* of age, no longer needing a guardian.

P. 169 L. 1   *shrewd a maim:* such bitter mutilation.

P. 169 L. 15   *lists:* barriers fencing off a place of combat.

P. 169 L. 33   *fig for:* 'to Hell with!'. The fig was a gesture made by thrusting the thumb between the second and third fingers, with lewd significance.

P. 170 L. 22   *have at thee:* i.e., defend yourself.

P. 171 L. 7   *mourning cloaks:* as for a funeral. Mourners at funerals wore long black hooded cloaks covering everything but the face.

P. 172 L. 11   *papers ... back:* An offender condemned to public humiliation bore a placard on the back setting out the offence.

P. 173 L. 32   *in ... pray:* because I, who am out of favour, ask

P. 175 L. 2   The stage direction in *The Contention* reads: Enter to the Parliament. *Enter two Heralds before, then the Duke of Buckingham, the Duke of Suffolke, and then the Duke of Yorke, and the Cardinall of Winchester, and*

then the King and the Queene, and then the Earle of
Salisbury, and the Earle of Warwicke.

know . . . since: there was a time when.   P. 175 L. 13

give . . . day: say goodmorning.   P. 175 L. 18

Unsounded yet: the depth of whose treachery is not P. 176 L. 29
yet measured.

at once: this is enough.   P. 177 L. 6

steal a shape: assume a disguise.   P. 177 L. 20

watch'd the night: lain awake all night.   P. 178 L. 23

Murther . . . else: I punished murder more severely P. 179
than felony or other offences.   LL. 11–12

clerkly couch'd: politely phrased.   P. 180 L. 27

mournful crocodile: It was believed that the crocodile P. 182 L. 13
first attracted the passer-by with its pitiful lamentations and then snapped him up.

idly posted: negligently passed over.   P. 183 L. 8

impugns . . . doom: calls our judgement into question. P. 184 L. 1

kernes: the wild Irish foot soldiers, greatly dreaded P. 184 L. 32
by Shakespeare's contemporaries.

nourish: a one-syllable word.   P. 186 L. 4

Golden Circuit: royal crown.   P. 186 L. 8

caper: a movement in dancing (still common in ballet) P. 186 L. 21
where the performer leaps upward and beats the feet
together while still in the air. *Morisco:* morris-dancer.

The stage direction in *The Contention* reads: *Then the* P. 187 L. 8
Curtaines being drawne, Duke Humfrey is discovered in his
bed and two men lying on his breast, and smothering him in
his bed. And then enter the Duke of Suffolke to them. At
the end of the interview between Suffolk, he says,
'Then draw the Curtaines againe, and get you gon.'
Thereupon the King and his party enter.

Oh . . . do: would it had not been done!   P. 187 L. 12

Nell: Shakespeare seems to have forgotten that the P. 188 L. 8
Queen's name was not Eleanor but Margaret. The
mistake is repeated in the Folio at P. 189 L. 32, P. 190
L. 19, P. 191 L. 5.

wring . . . nose: rub his nose to restore consciousness. P. 188 L. 19

aven's note: The raven's croak was regarded as ill- P. 188 L. 27
omened.

basilisk: a creature with a cock's head, an animal's P. 189 L. 5
body, and a snake's tail, hatched out by a toad from

a cock's egg. It was a very deadly beast, able to kill by mere look.

P. 189 L. 14   *blood-consuming sighs:* It was believed that sighing consumed the heart's blood and so shortened life.

P. 189 L. 29   *adder . . . deaf:* It was a popular belief, founded on Psalm 58 : 4 – 5, that the adder resisted the music of the snake charmer by putting her tail in one ear and clapping the other to the ground.

P. 189 L. 32   *Dame Margaret:* the Folio reads *Elianor* here, at P. 190 L. 19 and at P. 191 L. 5.

P. 189 L. 33   *statue:* a 3-syllable word, the final *e* being accented.

P. 190 L. 8   *he . . . loos'd:* Aeolus, god of the winds, who kept them imprisoned in a cave.

P. 190 L. 34   *agent . . . inconstancy:* since Suffolk was the King's agent, and proxy at the wedding (see P. 135 LL. 1–4) he was to that extent responsible for the King's loss of love.

P. 191 L. 1   *Ascanius:* son of Aeneas, the Trojan, whom Dido, Queen of Carthage, loved madly.

P. 191 L. 34   The stage direction in *The Contention* reads: *Warwicke drawes the Curtaines, and shewes Duke Humfrey in his bed.*

P. 192 L. 9   *dread King:* i.e., Christ.

P. 192 L. 16   *timely-parted:* who died naturally.

P. 192 L. 18   *Being all descended:* because the blood has descended.

P. 193 L. 25   *with . . . badge:* by saying that I wear Murder's badge.

            badge: coat of arms worn by a nobleman's servant.

P. 194 LL. 5–6   *noble . . . slip:* a cutting from a base tree was engrafted into a noble stock – a round-about way of saying 'You are a bastard!'

P. 195 L. 1   *in our presence:* It was a capital offence to draw a sword in anger in the presence of the King.

P. 195 L. 16   *Free . . . intent:* this demand is not made from mere stubborn opposition.

P. 196 L. 3   *'Tis like:* it's likely – said sarcastically.

P. 196 L. 18   *His:* God's.

P. 196 L. 20   *breathe infection:* breathe out poison.

P. 196 L. 28   *If . . . thou:* Here the King turns to Suffolk.

P. 197 L. 7   *Fie . . . wretch:* Spoken to Suffolk because he does not curse the King. From this point Margaret becomes increasingly fiendlike.

mandrake: a root shaped like the lower limbs of a P. 197 L. 11
man, about which there were many popular beliefs.
It flourished best under a gallows; it shrieked when
pulled out of the ground, and its screams were so
fatal that a dog was tied to the root and made to
draw it out. In medicine it was used as an anodyne
and soporific.

cypress: The dark evergreen cypress was regarded as P. 197 L. 24
a dismal tree, fit for churchyards.

woeful monuments: i.e., the tears which she has been P. 198 L. 9
shedding – a far-fetched image.

'Tis ... want: So long as you are with me, I can P. 198 L. 15
only imagine what grief will be, just as a man who is
overful (*that surfeits*) cannot imagine hunger.

if ... thee: if I am separated from thee. P. 198 L. 18

southern: The south was the region from which ill P. 199 L. 19
wind, storm, and misfortune were supposed to come.

by me: by my side. P. 199 L. 22

from: out of. P. 199 L. 29

fretful corrosive: ointment containing corrosive was P. 200 L. 4
applied to infected wounds.

Iris: the rainbow, one of the messengers of the gods. P. 200 L. 8

The stage direction in *The Contention* reads: *Enter* P. 200 L. 18
King and Salisbury, and then the Curtaines be drawne,
and the Cardinall is discouered in his bed, rauing and
staring as if he were mad.

he: i.e., Duke Humphrey. P. 200 L. 30

soldiers ... prize: captured in our prize. P. 202 L. 2

What ... gentlemen: do you two, who claim to be P. 202
gentlemen, think that your lives are not worth LL. 12–14
2,000 crowns? In *The Contention* the price is £100 a
piece. *port:* bearing.

laying ... aboard: in boarding the prize. P. 202 L. 21

George: my badge as Knight of the Garter. P. 202 L. 25

Walter: pronounced 'Water'. P. 202 L. 27

cunning ... birth: a soothsayer cast my horoscope – P. 202 L. 31
though the prophecy was actually given by one of
the spirits in I.4 (see P. 155 L. 18).

Gualtier: the French form of Walter. P. 202 L. 34

But Jove: in *The Contention*, the previous line reads P. 203 L. 11
'*Iove* sometime went disguisde, and why not I?'

P. 203 L. 16   *foot-cloth mule:* riding a mule draped with an orna-
mental cloth which hung down to the ground on
either side, used on ceremonial occasions.

P. 204 L. 14   *Sylla:* Sulla, dictator of Rome, notorious for the
wholesale slaughter of his political opponents.

P. 204 L. 15   *mother's:* i.e., England's.

P. 204 L. 25   *guiltless King:* Richard II.

P. 204 L. 28   *half-fac'd Sun:* the heraldic device of the sun shining
through clouds.

P. 204 L. 29   *Invitis nubibus:* even if the clouds are unwilling.

P. 205 L. 13   *Gelidus . . . artus:* cold fear seizes my limbs.

P. 205 L. 34   *Tully:* Marcus Tullius Cicero, murdered by order
of Marcus Antonius.

P. 206 L. 2   *Pompey the Great:* Pompey, being defeated by Julius
Caesar, fled to Egypt where he was murdered on
landing.

P. 207 L. 11   *dog's leather:* used for making gloves.

P. 207 L. 20   *supposed Father:* Cade claimed that he was actually
the son of Edmund Mortimer: see P. 210 LL. 20–30.

P. 208 L. 3   *under a hedge:* i.e., as a homeless beggar.

P. 208 L. 11   *coat . . . proof:* proof armour was of fine tested
quality, but Cade's coat has been tested by beating.

P. 208 L. 13   *burnt . . . hand:* sheep-stealers and other felons who
escaped hanging were branded.

P. 208 L. 16   *three-hoop'd pot:* The quart pot was made of wood
with three hoops: a ten-hooped pot would hold
more than three quarts.

P. 208 L. 23   *on my score:* at my expense: see note on P. 217 L. 15.

P. 208 L. 31   *bee's wax:* used at this time for sealing wax.

P. 209 L. 2   *cast accompt:* keep accounts.

P. 209 L. 4   *setting . . . copies:* teaching schoolboys to write.

P. 209
LL. 14–15   *Emmanuel . . . letters:* It was a pious Protestant custom to head letters with the word *Emmanuel* (God
with us).

P. 209 L. 18   *mark to thyself:* do you use a mark instead of a
signature?

P. 210
LL. 2–3   *I . . . Mortimer:* Cade, having made himself King,
now proceeds to dub himself knight.

P. 211 L. 8   *span-counter:* a game in which the first player threw
a coin or counter and the opponent threw another
which had to hit it or fall within a span (nine inches).

clouted shooen: patched shoes – the mark of a poor P. 212 L. 3
man.

Lent: To prevent the slaughter of store cattle in the P. 212 L. 18
late winter, the Privy Council each year issued an
order that no meat should be eaten in Lent. Exemp-
tions were made for invalids and privileged persons
and certain butchers were specially licensed to supply
them.

hundred . . . one: ninety-nine families.   P. 212 L. 19

sword: The State Sword still carried before the Lord P. 212 L. 24
Mayor on ceremonial occasions.

Rul'd . . . Planet: like the planet whose movement P. 213 L. 20
controls my fate.

Southwark: the parish at the south end of London P. 214 L. 1
Bridge.

No my Lord, . . . Rebels: This speech and Cade's first P. 215
speech in IV.6 are printed as irregular verse in the   LL. 8–11
Folio.

London Stone: a large stone of immemorial antiquity P. 215 L. 22
in the City of London.

pissing-conduit: a fountain of drinking water in the P. 215 L. 25
City.

Savoy: at this time a great house in London, near P. 216 L. 14
the Inns of Court, used as a guest house for those
having business in the Law.

fifteens: see note on P. 139 L. 10.   P. 217 L. 1

Subsidy: a tax raised by Parliament to supplement P. 217 L. 2
the King's regular income for some special cause

Say . . . Serge . . . Buckram: different kinds of P. 217 L. 5
material, *say* being of silk, *serge* of coarse wool, and
buckram of coarse linen.

score: the record of drinks not paid for, the amount P. 217 L. 15
being written up in chalk on the inside of the tavern
door.

tally: a primitive method of recording accounts. P. 217 L. 15
Notches indicating the amount due were cut across
a thin piece of wood which was then split down the
centre; creditor and debitor each kept one half.

printing: Actually printing was first used in England P. 217 L. 15
in 1474 – twenty-four years after Cade's rebellion.

they . . . read: i.e., their 'neck verse'. 'Clerks', or P. 217 L. 23

persons who could read, were regarded as so valuable to the State that if convicted for certain capital offences they were given a second chance. To claim this privilege, the accused was called upon to demonstrate his literacy by reading to the court a verse (usually from the 51st Psalm). Amongst others Ben Jonson escaped the gallows by thus pleading 'benefit of clergy'. The pardoned clerk was branded on the thumb to prevent a second claim.

P. 217 *hose ... doublets:* breeches and coats. Fashionable
LL. 29–30 gentlemen wore also a cloak.

P. 218 L. 1 *bona ... gens:* a good country but an evil people.

P. 219 L. 32 *in Capite:* a legal phrase – by direct grant.

P. 220 L. 2 *take ... bills:* lit., acquire goods on credit, but with a pun on *bills:* weapons: see note on P. 224 L. 30.

P. 220 L. 19 *parley:* a trumpet call indicating a truce for negotiations.

P. 221 L. 17 *shift for one:* shift for myself.

P. 223 L. 26 *gallow-glasses:* Irish soldiers who fought on horseback and wielded an axe. *kernes:* see note on P. 184 L. 32.

P. 224 L. 11 *rough in terms:* i.e., speak gently. *terms:* phrases.

P. 224 L. 27 *sallet:* salad, with a pun on *sallet:* helmet.

P. 224 L. 27 *another while:* somehow.

P. 224 L. 30 *brown bill:* the hedger's tool, mounted on a long staff and varnished brown to prevent it from rusting – the countryman's weapon.

P. 225 L. 10 *that:* that which.

P. 225 L. 31 *Took odds:* had the advantage on his side.

P. 226 L. 24 *Herald's coat:* i.e., richly embroidered with a coat of arms. *emblaze:* signify, lit., paint – a heraldic term.

P. 227 L. 14 *Sancta maiestas:* sacred majesty.

P. 227 L. 19 *have I:* so sure as I have.

P. 227 L. 20 *fleur-de-luce:* fleur-de-lis, the emblem of France, borne as part of the coat of arms of English Kings for five hundred years.

P. 228 L. 6 *Ajax Telamonius:* After the death of Achilles, his armour was claimed both by Ulysses and by Ajax. When the armour was awarded to Ulysses, Ajax went mad and slew a flock of sheep supposing them to be his enemies who had insulted him.

make ... weather: accommodate myself to circum-   P. 228 L. 10
stances.

S. George's Field: an open space on the south bank   P. 228 L. 27
of the Thames.

That Gold: the Crown.   P. 230 L. 15

Achilles' spear: made for him by Vulcan, the black-   P. 230 L. 16
smith god. It was able to kill or heal by touch.

Neapolitan: because her father was Reignier, King of   P. 230 L. 33
Naples see P. 130 L. 17.

The stage direction in *The Contention* reads: *Enter*   P. 231 L. 4
the Duke of Yorkes sonnes, Edward the Earle of March,
and crooke-backe Richard at the one doore, with Drum
and Soldiers: & at the other doore, enter Clifford and his
sonne, with Drumme and Soldiours, and Clifford kneeles
to Henry, and speakes.

factious pate: rebellious head.   P. 231 L. 19

Call ... cried: This elaborate image is from the sport   P. 231 L. 28–
of bear-baiting. The bear was chained to a stake and   P. 232 L. 6
mastiffs sent in to attack it.

foul ... lump: The physical deformity of York's son   P. 232 L. 9
Richard (afterwards Duke of Gloucester and finally
King Richard III) was much stressed in the latter
plays, *III Henry the Sixth* and *Richard the Third*.

household badge: family crest, described in the speech   P. 233 L. 21
following.

sup: i.e., in Heaven.   P. 234 L. 2

La ... œuvres: the end crowns the work.   P. 235 L. 11

nor he ... valour: the man who has any thought of   P. 235
himself is not truly brave but only so by accident.   LL. 25–7

wild Medea: Jason, the Greek hero, won the Golden   P. 236 L. 12
Fleece with the aid of the sorceress Medea, with
whom he fled away. To delay pursuit by her father,
Medea slew her brother Absyrtus and cut the body
into pieces.

Aeneas ... bear: When Troy was sacked and burnt   P. 236 L. 15
by the Greeks, Aeneas took his old father Anchises on
his back and carried him away to safety on his ship.

the Wizard famous: Margaret Jordan's spirit (see   P. 236 L. 25
P. 155 L. 20) had warned Somerset to 'shun castles'.
Somerset was killed in the streets of St Albans be-
neath the sign of the Castle tavern.

P. 236 L. 29   *Excursions:* soldiers running to and fro on the stage to symbolize the rush of battle.

P. 237 L. 16   *To see . . . give:* to see their unlucky day when they in turn have our bad luck.

P. 237 L. 26   *Repairs . . . occasion:* how he renews his youth.

P. 238 L. 12   *got . . . have:* i.e., our victory is not yet complete.

P. 238 L. 14   *opposites . . . nature:* opponents who can recover their strength.

PART THREE

P. 241 L. 1   The stage direction in *The True Tragedie* reads Enter *Richard* Duke of Yorke, The Earle of *Warwicke, The Duke of* Norffolke, *Marquis Montague, Edward Earle of March, Crookeback Richard,* and the yong *Earle of Rutland,* with Drumme and Souldiers, with white Roses in their hats.

P. 241 L. 1   *Alarum:* noise of battle.

P. 241 L. 1   *Plantagenet:* The Duke of York.

P. 242 L. 25   *shake . . . bells:* a hawking metaphor; bells were fastened to the hawk's legs.

P. 242 L. 28   *Enter King Henry. . . . : The True Tragedie* adds 'with Red Roses in their hats'.

P. 243 LL. 6–7   *mourn in steel:* wearing armour, and not the customary funeral cloak.

P. 243 L. 31   *Earldom:* York had inherited the Earldom of March from his mother, through whom he claimed the throne. See *II Henry VI* II. 2. 9–52 [P. 165 L. 2 – P. 166 L. 16].

P. 243 L. 32   *Traitor to the Crown:* York's father was Richard, Earl of Cambridge, executed by Henry V for conspiracy: see *Henry V*, II. 2.

P. 244 L. 32   *Dolphin:* the Elizabethan spelling and pronunciation of *Dauphin* – the title of the heir to the French throne.

P. 248 L. 8   *Sennet:* a trumpet call to denote the approach or departure of a procession.

P. 249 L. 10   *entail:* settle an estate on an individual and his descendants.

P. 249 L. 13   *Callice:* the Elizabethan spelling and pronunciation of Calais.

Narrow Seas: English Channel.   P. 249 L. 14

White Rose: the badge of the Yorkist party.   P. 251 L. 24

Gabriel: the name of the actor who originally took P. 252 L. 5
the part.

for a need: if necessary.   P. 252 L. 29

Di ... tuae: may the gods make this your most P. 254 L. 31
famous deed – i.e., may you be disgraced for ever by
the slaughter of an innocent.

sands: i.e., in the hour glass.   P. 255 L. 31

Phaeton: the son of the sun god who tried to drive P. 256 L. 10
his father's horses but was thrown out of the chariot
and killed.

Phoenix: a mythical bird. According to the legend P. 256 L. 12
only one phoenix lived at a time. It lasted for five
hundred years. Then it built a nest of spices which it
set alight by the rapid beating of its wings. From the
ashes a new phoenix arose.

bandy: exchange, lit., hit the ball to and fro in tennis. P. 256 L. 26

Prodigy: omen of disaster. The physical deformities P. 257 L. 21
of Richard of Gloucester now begin to become
dramatically and psychologically important.

made issue: caused to flow.   P. 257 L. 27

Amazonian: The Amazons were a legendary race of P. 258 L. 27
female warriors who lived in South Russia.

Adage ... verifi'd: the proverb is to be proved true. P. 259 L. 6

Oh tiger's heart. ...: see Introduction, P. 15.   P. 259 L. 17

Hyrcania: the Caspian Sea district; the traditional P. 260 L. 3
home of tigers.

Where ... become: what has happened to.   P. 261 L. 12

bear encompass'd: The image is from the sport of P. 261 L. 17
bear-baiting. The bear was chained to a stake.
Mastiffs were sent in to attack him; and the sport
continued until bear (and spectators) had had enough.

Trimm'd ... younker: like a young man dressed in P. 261 L. 26
his best.

Dazzle mine eyes: are my eyes seeing straight? These P. 261 L. 27
suns were actually represented on the stage, as the
stage direction in *The True Tragedie* shows: 'Three
sunnes appeare in the aire.'

figures some event: foretells something to follow. P. 262 L. 2

breeder: female. Edward's wantonness was notorious. P. 262 L. 14

P. 262 L. 24   *hope of Troy:* Hector.

P. 263 L. 13   *my soul's ... prison:* i.e., I no longer wish to live.

P. 263 L. 30   *Chair:* the throne which York had claimed.

P. 263 L. 32   *gazing ... sun:* It was believed that the eagle's eyes were so strong that it could gaze into the sun.

P. 265 L. 5   *flail:* an implement for extracting grain from the ear. It was made of two heavy sticks joined by a leather thong and attached to a handle with which the straw was threshed.

P. 265 L. 13   *haste, post haste:* with the greatest possible speed. When the official postboy was required to carry a letter at top speed it was inscribed 'Haste, post haste'.

P. 265 L. 14   *Marches:* the Welsh Border.

P. 265 L. 24   *'Twas odds belike:* the odds against him must have been heavy.

P. 265 L. 27   *scandal of reture:* that he was disgraced by having to retreat.

P. 266 L. 5   *Numb'ring ... beads:* saying our rosaries – behaving like religious folk. *Ave-Maries:* the prayer beginning 'Hail, Mary'.

P. 266 L. 7   *Tell our devotion:* say our prayers.

P. 268 L. 18   *raise his issue:* promote his children.

P. 268 L. 22   *Unreasonable creatures:* animals which have no reason.

P. 269 L. 32   *Duke of York:* Edward, who has now succeeded his father. See P. 267 L. 3.

P. 271 L. 29   *his tongue:* he is a man of words, not deeds.

P. 272 L. 3   *Whoever ... stands:* we don't know who your father may have been, but you are certainly like your mother.

P. 272 L. 9   *Iron:* i.e., a worthless metal.

P. 272 L. 14   *wisp of straw:* Scolds were made to wear a straw crown.

P. 272 L. 16   *Helen of Greece:* The beautiful wife of Menelaus of Sparta, whom she deserted when she ran away with Paris of Troy. Agamemnon, King of Mycenae, Menelaus's brother, was the leader of the army which went against Troy.

P. 273 L. 2   *usurping:* because Margaret, as Henry's Queen, is a usurper.

P. 273 L. 17   *Excursions:* rapid movements of soldiers across the stage indicating a battle.

spite of spite: whatever happens.   P. 273 L. 22

have at thee: i.e., defend yourself.   P. 275 L. 28

The stage direction in *The True Tragedie* reads: P. 275 L. 29
'Alarums. They fight, and then enters *Warwicke*
and rescues *Richard* & then *exeunt omnes*. Alarme
still, and then enter *Henry solus*.'

of: on – to warm them.   P. 276 L. 5

carve . . . quaintly: carve elaborate (*quaint*) sundials   P. 276 L. 26
in the turf.

Priam: Priam King of Troy had fifty sons, all killed   P. 279 L. 27
in the Trojan War.

Clifford wounded: The *True Tragdie* adds 'With an   P. 280 L. 19
arrow in his necke.'

Lancaster: Henry, who was descended from John of   P. 280 L. 22
Gaunt, Duke of Lancaster. See Genealogical Table,
P. 384.

fear: fear of me.   P. 280 L. 24

commixtures: union of fear and love.   P. 280 L. 25

Phoebus . . . earth: see note on P. 256 L. 10. *Phoebus*:   P. 280
the sun god.   LL. 29–31

Clifford groans: The True Tragedie adds 'and then   P. 281 L. 31
dies'.

leaves . . . forth: when he was just reaching manhood.   P. 282 L. 5

screech owl: regarded as an evil omen.   P. 282 L. 14

Gloucester's . . . ominous: The title of Duke of   P. 284 L. 1
Gloucester had been borne by Humphrey (see *II
Henry VI*), Thomas of Woodstock (see *Richard II*,
I. 1. 98–102) and Hugh Spenser, favourite of Edward
II, all of whom had died violently.

Sinklo and Humphrey: the names of the original   P. 284 L. 7
actors who took the parts of 1 KEEPER and 2 KEEPER.

redress of thee: to thee for redress.   P. 284 L. 30

Nero . . . remorse: even Nero (the pattern of cruelty)   P. 285 L. 18
will lose his nature (*be tainted*) for pity (*remorse*).

tells his title: justifies Edward's claim to the throne.   P. 285 L. 26

Indian stones: pearls.   P. 286 L. 8

but while: only so long as.   P. 286 L. 27

keeps the wind: hunts contrary to the wind so that the   P. 288
deer shall not perceive him.   LL. 2–3

leave . . . crutch: until you are too old for lechery.   P. 288 L. 29

God's Mother: the Blessed Virgin Mary.   P. 291 L. 17

P. 291 L. 18   *other-some:* children of my own.

P. 291 L. 21   *Ghostly ... shrift:* During their conversation Lady Grey has been kneeling before Edward like a penitent at confession (*shrift*). She now rises to her feet.

P. 291 L. 22   *shriver:* one able to give confession, a priest. *shift:* trickery.

P. 291 L. 30   *ten days' wonder:* i.e., even greater than the usual Nine Days' Wonder.

P. 292 L. 14   *golden time:* i.e., when I shall be a King.

P. 292 L. 16   *Title buried:* even if the King dies.

P. 292 L. 18   *unlook'd-for:* as yet unseen.

P. 292 L. 20   *cold premeditation:* hopeless reflection.

P. 292   *And ... impossibilities:* I'll pretend that I can destroy
LL. 29–30   those who stand in my way, deceiving myself with what is impossible.

P. 293 L. 7   *And for ... not:* lest I should.

P. 293 L. 14   *unlick'd bear-whelp:* It was believed that a bear cub was born shapeless but was licked into shape by its mother.

P. 293 L. 26   *home:* my destination.

P. 294 L. 4   *frame my face:* suit my looks.

P. 294 L. 5   *mermaid:* Mermaids, like the sirens, were supposed to lure amorous sailors to destruction by their sweet singing.

P. 294 L. 6   *basilisk:* a creature with a cock's head, an animal's body, and a snake's tail, hatched out by a toad from a cock's egg – a very deadly beast able to slay by mere look.

P. 294 L. 7   *Nestor:* the Grand Old Man of the Greeks besieging Troy.

P. 294 L. 8   *Ulysses:* the cunning Greek general by whose device of the Wooden Horse Troy was ultimately captured.

P. 294 L. 9   *Sinon:* a Greek who pretended to desert to the Trojans. He persuaded them to take into the city the Wooden Horse filled with armed Greeks. When night came, Sinon released his friends from the Horse.

P. 294 L. 11   *Proteus:* the Old Man of the Sea, who cared for the sea-god's seals. If seized, he changed himself into some other shape.

Machiavel: Pietro Machiavelli, a Florentine, composed his famous treatise *The Prince* (*Il Principe*) in 1513. Machiavelli's cynical and realistic advice on statecraft was regarded by contemporaries (especially by those who had not read it) as so immoral and devilish that the word 'Machiavellian' was used to denote a man who utterly despised all religious, moral, and human laws.   P. 294 L. 12

strike her sail: lower the sail in sign of submission.   P. 294 L. 27

of a King: from being a King.   P. 295 L. 19

But ... worth: but in conclusion (*for the rest*), you are making a claim (*tell a pedigree*) which is sixty-two years old – a senseless (*silly*) period for making a claim (*prescription*) to the riches of a kingdom. The episode shown in this scene occurred in 1461 – 62 years after Henry IV deposed Richard II.   P. 297 LL. 25–7

Exempt ... pain: if the Lady Bona does not repay (*quit*) his passions (*pain*) with love, he will bear no malice (*envy*), but he will certainly suffer contempt.   P. 298 LL. 30–1

Post: the bearer of official letters, who used a horn to announce his arrival.   P. 299 L. 34

abuse ... Niece: Edward had attempted to seduce her.   P. 300 L. 31

Maskers: revellers – said ironically, in contempt for Edward's wanton habits.   P. 302 L. 1

willow garland: the sign of a deserted lover.   P. 302 L. 5

malcontent: one discontented with the present state of affairs.   P. 304 L. 2

at our abuse: the wrong we have done them.   P. 304 L. 6

will: the word *will* has various shades of meaning from *determination* to *lust*.   P. 304 L. 10

gave in charge: instructed him to accomplish.   P. 304 L. 30

But ... brotherhood: in favouring your new wife you forget the claims of your brothers.   P. 305 L. 24

Go to: an exclamation – 'all right!'   P. 306 L. 27

very words: see P. 301 L. 34.   P. 306 L. 31

Amazon: see note on P. 258 L. 27.   P. 307 L. 13

Ulysses ... steeds: The story is told in the *Iliad*, Book X. The oracle declared that if the horses of Rhesus, King of Thrace, grazed on the plains of Troy, the city would never be taken. Ulysses and Diomedes were sent by the Greeks to intercept   P. 309 LL. 25–7

Rhesus. In a night foray they killed Rhesus and seized his horses.

P. 312 L. 6   *My mind ... wheel:* though I must submit to evil fortune, I can endure it. For Fluellen's learned discourse on Fortune's wheel, see *Henry V*, III. 6. 3–40.

P. 313 L. 3   *makes ... change:* causes you to be changed so suddenly.

P. 313 L. 25   *blood-sucking sighs:* It was believed that sighs consumed the heart's blood and so shortened life.

P. 314 L. 15   *chiefest thicket:* densest thicket.

P. 315 L. 26   *fees:* A prisoner was charged fees by his keeper for his diet and lodging which had to be paid before he was released.

P. 316 L. 12   *thwarting stars:* unlucky fate.

P. 316 L. 19   *temper ... stars:* accommodate themselves to their fate.

P. 317 L. 27   *young Henry:* Ultimately Henry of Richmond was the final victor in the Wars of the Roses. He slew Richard III at the Battle of Bosworth and became King as Henry VII. See the last Act of *Richard III*.

P. 319 L. 16   *stumble ... threshold:* regarded as an unlucky sign.

P. 320 L. 14   *So ... him:* so long as it was not his responsibility.

P. 321 L. 14   *stand ... points:* are you so over-particular?

P. 321 L. 22   *out of hand:* forthwith.

P. 323 LL. 30–1   *meed ... fame:* my merit (*meed*) has won me support.

P. 325 L. 6   *Daintry:* the original spelling and pronunciation of Daventry.

P. 326 L. 7   *Atlas:* In classical mythology Atlas bore up the world on his shoulders.

P. 326 L. 14   *single ten:* i.e., the highest of the plain cards in the pack (*deck*); the other cards are all royal.

P. 326 L. 24   *strike:* lower the sails in token of surrender.

P. 326 L. 31   *Enter Oxford:* The staging and simple symbolism are worth noting. On the Elizabethan stage, there enter in succession by one of the doors, Oxford with one man carrying a flag and a second with a drum. Having delivered his lines, he with the flag-bearer and drummer, leaves the stage by the other door, so symbolizing his adherence to Warwick. Montague, accompanied by the same flag-bearer and drummer, then appears from the first door and repeats the movement. Then Somerset follows, and also leaves the stage. Clarence enters as if to repeat the movement, but stays. The stark simplicity of Elizabethan staging is often obscured by the embellishments added in editorial stage directions.

Jove's . . . tree: the oak.   P.329 L. 18

rids way: takes the weariness out of a journey.   P. 331 L. 20

For . . . charge: be allowed to steer the ship once.   P. 332 L. 15

If case: in case.   P. 332 L. 29

pitch our battle: draw up our lines.   P. 333 L. 28

The stage direction in *The True Tragedie* reads, P. 334 L. 15
'Alarmes to the battell, *Yorke* flies, then the chambers be discharged. Then enter the king, *Cla. & Glo.* & the rest, & make a great shout, and crie, for *Yorke,* for *Yorke,* and then the *Queene* is taken, & the prince, & *Oxf.* & *Sum.* and then sound and enter all againe.'

Jerusalem: i.e., Heaven.   P. 334 L. 25

Aesop: a Greek of the 6th century B.C. who devised P. 335 L. 11
moral fables. He was said to have been monstrously ugly and deformed.

charm your tongue: make you silent.   P. 335 L. 17

Petitioners . . . back: you never refuse anyone who P. 337 L. 9
asks leave to commit a murder.

Roscius: i.e., this play-actor. Roscius was a famous P. 338 L. 4
Roman actor of tragic parts.

fool . . . life: Daedalus of Crete and his son Icarus, P. 338
hoping to escape from Minos their King, attempted   LL 15–20
to fly by fastening wings to their shoulders. Daedalus successfully returned to earth, but Icarus crashed and was killed when the sun melted the wax by which his wings were fastened.

mistrust . . . fear: do not suspect (*mistrust*) any part P. 338 L. 34
(*parcel*) of what I fear.

aboding . . . time: foolishly foretelling evil times to P. 339 L. 7
come.

sort . . . day: find out a black day.   P. 340 L. 17

footstool of security: made safety our footstool.   P. 341 L. 13

if . . . laid: if once you (i.e. Edward) were laid flat. P. 341 L. 20

so Judas kissed: see Matthew 26, 47–49.   P. 341 L. 33

GLOSSARY

a' : he
abide : endure
abject : insulting
abodement : unlucky signs
abrook : endure
abuse : misuse, shameful treatment
accidents : events
accomplices : comrades
adamant : the hardest kind of stone or metal
admiring : wondering
admonish : advise
adsum : I am here
advance : bring forward, set up
adventure : risk, dare
advertised : informed, given notice
advice : careful thought
advised : wise, cautious
affect : incline to
affiance : confidence
affy : betroth
against : in face of
air-braving : lofty
Albion : England
Alcides : Hercules
alder liefest : dearest of all
almsdeed : charitable motive
amain : with full force, speedily
amort : sick to death, dejected
and't, an't : if
annoy : hurt
anon : by and by
antic : grinning like a clown
Antipodes : opposite side of the World

appal'd : made pale
apparent : clear
apparent : heir
appellant : challenger
apprehension : notion
approv'd : prove
argosy : great merchant ship
argues : indicates
arms : coat of arms
Art : formal learning
articles : clauses in a document
Asmath : the name of a fiend
aspiring : soaring
assay : attempt
asunder : separate
attached : arrested
attainted : condemned
attainture : attainder, condemnation, disgrace
attend : listen to
attorney : pleader, agent
avoid : be gone
awe : obedience, subjection
aweful : causing fear
awkward : adverse

bags : purses
baleful : deathly
balm : sacred oil
ban : curse
ban-dogs : watch dogs
bands : bonds, captivity
bandying : contending
bane : destruction
bark : ship
barter'd : exchanged
Basimecu : kiss-my-tail
battle : army

batt'ry: battery, assault
beard: insult
bearing: behaviour
bear-ward: keeper of the bears
beaver: helmet, lit., the face piece of a helmet
beck: bidding, beckoning
bedew: wet with tears
Bedlam: (1) Bethlehem, the London hospital for lunatics; (2) a lunatic
beldam: hag
belike: perhaps
benefit: right
bent: inclined
beshrew: ill luck to
besom: broom made of twigs
bested: be-sted, in such a condition
bestrid: stood over to protect
betide: befall
bewray: betray
Bezonians: beggars
big-swoln: swollen to bursting
bide: await
bill: writing
bode: foretell
bodg'd: bungled
boding: ill-omened
book: book learning
boon: favour asked
boot: advantage, booty
bootless: vain, profitless
boots: is profitable, advantageous
bow: give away, yield
brainsick: lunatic
brake: thicket
brave: full of spirit
brave: taunt
breach: gap

break: open, reveal
breathe: rest
breech: breeches
bridle: rein in, control
brinish: salt
Bristow: Bristol
broach'd: made flow, let out (as wine from a cask)
broker: agent
brook: endure
bruited: noised abroad
brush: bruising
buckle: fight at close quarters
buckler: shield
bucks: dirty clothes
bug: goblin
burgonet: helmet
burly-boned: hulking
but: only
butt: target

cade: herring barrel
cage: parish lockup
callet: low woman
came up: rose in the world
canker: maggot
canvas: toss in a canvas sheet
eaptivate: capture
car: chariot
care: sorrow, worry
cask: casket
cast: driven away
cates: delicacies
caudle: 'night-cap', hot drink given to invalids
cavil: raise frivolous objections
censure: judge, judgement
chafed: angry
chair-days: old age
challenge: claim as due, demand
chance: misfortune

channel: ditch

chaos: shapeless mass

chaps: jaws

character'd: inscribed, written

charge: command, responsibility

charneco: a wine (probably from Portugal)

chase: game

check'd: rebuked

checker'd: patterned in squares

cheerly: cheerfully

chid: ordered roughly

chines: roasts

choler: anger, hot temper

cited: incited

cites: summons

clapp'd up: confined

clip: embrace

close: secret

closet: small private room

cloy'd: bored

coffer: treasure chest

cognizance: badge

collect: gather, perceive

collop: slice

colour: excuse

colours: flag

commission: formal instructions

compact: agreement

companion: fellow

complices: accomplices

complot: plot

compound: settle

compromise: agreement

conceit: imagination

concluded: agreed to

condign: well-deserved

condition: state of life, rank

conduct: escort

confederacy: conspiracy

consort: concert

constrain'd: forced

content: agreed

controller: critic

contumelious: contemptuous

contusions: bruises

conventicles: meetings

convers'd: had dealings

conveyance: fraud

cony: rabbit

cope with: encounter

cornets: troops of horse

corrupted: regarded as of base blood

corse: corpse

couch'd: set in position for a charge

counterfeited: imitated

counter-pois'd: counterbalanced

counties: Earldoms

coursers: war horses

court-hand: handwriting used on legal documents

coverture: covering

craven: coward

crazy: feeble

credit: fame

crest-fallen: humble – like a defeated fighting cock

cross: thwart

cross: grief, suffering

culling: selecting

cullions: rascals – a low word

curds: cheese made of curd

curious: elaborate

currish: doglike

curst: bitter

cursy: curtsey

dalliance: love-making

dam: mother

darnel: a weed that grows in corn

darraign: set in order

dash: attempt

dastard: sneaking coward

daw: jackdaw

deathsman: executioner

decipher'd: revealed

deck: pack of cards

deep-fet: deep fetched

defaut: default, failure

deface: disfigure

defam'd: disgraced, made infamous

degree: step

deign: are willing

delicate: delicacies

demean'd: behaved

denay'd: refused

departure: death

depose: take an oath

deriv'd: descended

despite: spite

detect: reveal

Dian: Diana, goddess of chastity

diffidence: distrust

digest: get rid of

disanimate: discourage

disannuls: cancels out

discomfit: discouragement

dispense: come to terms with

dispensation: permission from the Church

dispos'd: has the nature of

dissemble: pretend

distract: mad

distrain'd: seized

doit: small worthless coin

double: talk thick, drunkenly

double: strong

doubt: fear

drab: harlot

draw: draw up

drift: intention

dub: confer knighthood on

dusky: smoky, extinguished

duty: sign of respect

ean: give birth

earnest: payment on account of the main sum, deposit

eclipse: extinguish

effuse: effusion

effus'd: shed

Elysium: Heaven

embassade: embassy, mission

empty: hungry

emulation: jealousy

enchas'd: enriched with gems

enfranchisement: liberty

engenders: begets

engirt: encircle

enlargement: release

enow: enough

entertain'd: treated

enthrall'd: made captive

enticing: decoying

entreat: treat

envious: hateful

environ'd: surrounded

equity: justice

espials: spies

espous'd: betrothed

esquire: landowner, gentleman

estate: condition

esteem: high rank

event: result

exclaim on: lament

exclaim: cry shame

execution: lit., action resulting from

exequies: funeral rites

exhibit: present
exigent: conclusion
exorcisms: charms, conjurations
expect: await
expostulate: argue
expuls'd: expelled
extirp'd: rooted out
extraught: extracted, derived

faction: party
factious: rebellious
fain: be glad
fain to: forced to
faint: dispirited
falchion: curved sword
fall'n at jars: fallen out
familiar: familiar spirit
fancy: love
far-fet: elaborate
favour: lenience
fealty: loyalty
fear: frighten
fearful: timid
fee-simple: freehold estate
fee'd: paid, rewarded
fell: dreadful
fell-lurking: treacherous
fence: skill in fencing
fetlocks: the tuft of hair above the hoof of a horse
field: expeditionary force
figures: foretells
fine: conclusion
flagging: drooping
flaw: gust of wind
fleet: pass quickly
foil: repulse
fond: foolish
foot-cloth: horse or mule, draped with a long cloth for ceremonial occasions

forfend: forbid
forg'd: false, feigned
forgery: deceit
forgo: forfeit
forlorn: a man abandoned
forslow: delay
forspent: exhausted
forswear: (1) commit perjury (2) swear to have nothing to do with (3) desert, reject
forth: out of
forwardness: zeal
frame: make, design
friend: lover
front: confront, face
frosty: white
frozen: cold, cowardly
fugitive: runaway, traitor
fume: rage, lit., smoke
furniture: equipment
furred pack: skin bag
furtherance: aid

gainsay: deny
Gallia: France
gather: understand from hints
gear: matter, business
gentler: more noble
get: win
giglot: wanton
gin: snare
given out: given up
gleeks: scoffs
gloss: glittering outside
God's Mother: the Blessed Virgin Mary
government: self-control, good manners
gown: dressing gown
green: still fresh
grin: show the teeth

groat : fourpence
guerdon'd : rewarded
guise : fashion
gulf : whirlpool

halberd : spear with an axe head, used by guards
hale : haul, drag
hallow : treat as holy
hammering : brooding on
hangings : costly tapestry
hap : fortune
haply : perhaps
happy : lucky
haps : happens
hard by : near
hard-favour'd : grim faced
haught : haughty
head : (1) army, (2) superiority
heat : anger
Hecate : goddess of witchcraft
Hector : champion of the Trojans
hedge-born : born under a hedge, beggar's brat
high-minded : arrogant
hinds : boors, yokels
hire : reward
hoboys : oboes
hold : castle
hollow : false, pretended
hot : haughty
house-keeping : hospitality
hulk : large sailing vessel
humour : whim, mood, nature
husbandry : cultivation

ill-boding : foretelling evil
ill-nurtur'd : illbred, wicked
immanity : savagery
impaled : surrounded, invested

impeach : calling in question
impression : shape
infallible : indisputable
infer : produce
infus'd : shed
inhears'd : coffined
injurious : insulting
ink-horn : portable inkpot
inly : inwardly
instance : proof
insulting : triumphing
intermissive : periodical
invention : device
ireful : angry
issue : child

jaded : contemptible
jades : horses in poor condition
jar : strife
jointure : marriage settlement given to a wife
jot : little mark
joy'd : enjoyed

keep : dwell
ken : perceive
kennel : gutter
kite : the lowest of the birds of prey

lade : ladle, bale
latest : last
lath : slip of wood
latter : last
laund : lawn, open space in a forest
lay : wager, stake
lays : songs
leave : cease
legative : appertaining to a Legate

lenity: gentleness
level: aim
liefest: dearest
liege: sovereign
liegemen: subjects
like: liken
liking: desires
lime: cement
limed: caught in birdlime
limits: boundaries
linstock: the match used to discharge a cannon
lists: place of combat
lithe: supple
livery: uniform
loaden: laden
lodged: laid flat
long: be impatient
long of: because of
Lordings: my Lords
lowted: treated like a lout

mail'd up: enveloped
malapert: impudent
map: pattern, picture
mark: 13s. 4d.
Mary: by the Blessed Virgin Mary
'Mass: by the Mass
match: marry
mates: confounds
maz'd: amazed
mean: (1) means (2) moderation
mechanical: labouring man
meeds: deserts
meet: fit
member: limb
meseemeth: I think
mess: lit., party of four at a table
method: argument

mickle: great
middest: midst
minions: favourites, darlings
minister: servant
misdoubteth: suspects
misproud: wrongfully proud
misthink: misjudge
mistrust: suspicion
mitigate: lessen
moe: more
moment: importance, weight
Mort Dieu: by God's (Christ's) Death – an oath
mortal: deadly
motions: purposes
mought: might
muleters: mule drivers
muse: wonder

naughty: wicked
neat: cattle
neglection: neglect
Nemesis: avenging Justice
noble: 6s. 8d.
nominate: give names to
nourish: nurse

obdurate: hard-hearted
objected: argued
obligations: contracts, bonds
obloquy: disgrace
obsequies: funeral rites
occasion: opportunity, advantage
o'ercharged: filled to overflowing
o'ercharging: laying heavy burdens on
o'ermatch'd: fighting against great odds
o'er-ruled: prevailed

o'erweening: too proud
office: business
opinion: (1) judgement (2) honour, good reputation
order: manner
orisons: prayers
otherwhiles: at other times
out of hand: at once
overgone: overcome
overpeer'd: overlooked
over-matching: overcoming

packing: be gone
pain: difficulty, labour
pale: enclose
palfrey: gentleman's riding horse
palmer: pilgrim
paly: pale
parched: dried up
parle: summons to negotiate
part: party, side
parted: pushed aside
particularities: types
pass: case
passed: uttered
passengers: travellers on foot, poor men
passing: surpassing
passion: emotion
patronage: maintain
pattern: type, model
pawn'd: pledged
peal: discharge
peel'd: shaven
peevish: silly
pent-up: frustrated
peremptory: overbearing
periapts: amulets, charms
period: end, full stop
perish: destroy

pies: magpies
pikes: spears with a long shaft
pilgrimage: lifetime
pinch: nip
pitch: height, the flight of a hawk at its topmost
pitchy: black
pithless: marrowless, feeble
plainness: honest dealing
plaints: lamentations
platforms: plans
pledges: pawns, hostages
plies: urges
plot: ground, place
plotted: planned
point-blank: close range
pointing-stock: thing pointed at
poise: balance
policy: cunning
politic: crafty
poltroons: lazy cowards
poniards: daggers
post: (1) official messenger (2) haste
post, in: hastily
posted off: put off
power: army
practisants: fellow conspirators
practice: plot
preachment: sermon
prease: press, crowd
precinct: allotted place
prefer: propose, put forward
preferr'd: gained promotion
premised: foreordained
preposterous: unnatural
presaging: foretelling
present: immediate
presently: immediately
pretend: purpose
prevent: forestall

prick: mark on a dial which shows the hour

prick'd on: goaded

pride: proud strength

privily: secretly

privy to: secretly acquainted with

press'd: conscripted

procurator: agent

professors: those who profess

progenitors: ancestors

progeny: descent

proper: (1) handsome (2) own, private

proportion: bodily grace

puissance: might

puissant: powerful

purblind: half blind

pursuivant: officer of the court

pussel: slut

puttock: kite

pyramis: pyramid

quailing: shrinking

quaint: clever

qualm: feeling of faintness

quillets: legal subtleties

quittance: repay

quitting: ridding

quondam: former

rack'd: tortured on the rack, stretched, plundered

racking: drifting (of clouds)

ragged: rough

rampant: upreared

ramping: upreared, enraged

range: roam

rare: wonderful

rate: abuse

rate: assess

ratsbane: rat poison

ravish: overcome

raught: snatched away

raw-bon'd: fleshless skeleton

reaching: far-reaching, influential

rear: set up

reave: rob

reclaims: subdues

recreants: traitors

redemption: salvation

reflex: reflect

refuge: defence

reguerdon: ample reward

remorseful: full of pity

remorseless: pitiless

rend: tear

repair: approach

repeal: recall from banishment

replete with: full of

reprove: disprove

repugn: oppose, reject

reputing of: brooding on

requite: pay back, counterbalance

resolv'd: convinced

resolve me: give me my answer

respect: comparison

respecting: considering

revell'd: played the drunkard

rid: cut off

rigorously: cruelly

rigour: ferocity

rive: discharge, fire

rook'd: crouched

rout: rabble

rul'd: directed

ruthful: piteous

sack: dry wine from Spain

sadness: seriousness

salve : healing ointment
satisfaction : recompence
sawyer : one who saws timber
saws : sayings
scathe : harm
scouring : cleansing
scruple : religious objection
seal : confirm
seal'd : guaranteed as genuine, completed
second : support
secure : make safe
self-place : same place
septentrion : north
sequestration : separation, imprisonment
servant : lover
several : separate, distinct
sever'd : separated
shag-haired : rough-headed
shearman : one who shears wool
shelves : shoals
shift : device
shoot : nodded
shroud : cover, protect
shrouds : sails
Sibyls : ancient prophetesses
significants : signs
sinew : join
silly : simple
sirrah : term of address to a junior or inferior
sith : since
skills : matters
slough : skin (pronounced sluff)
small beer : weak beer
smart : painful
smooth'st : flatterest
so : so long as, if
sophister : clever debater
sort : (1) choose, (2) fit

sort : (1) gang, (2) manner
sort : suits
sped : fared
speed : try their luck
spleen : wrath
spleenful : angry-tempered
spoil : lose
spoils : destroys
spray : young branch
stale : victim of a cheater
start : flinch
state : kingship
stay : support
stay : wait, delay
stay'd : withheld
stigmatic : branded, marked as foul by deformity
still : always
still : quieten
stomach : proud, quarrelsome temper
strait : strict
strangled : hanged
submission : loyal behaviour
subornation : encouragement to commit a crime
suborned : bribed to
subscribe : acknowledge
subverts : overturns
successive : by right of succession
suddenly : quickly
sugar : candy-coated
suit : petition
sullied : soiled
sunders : separates
supplication : petition
supply : fill up
supply : reinforcements
surfeiting : enjoying to excess
survey : inspect

suspect : suspicion
swain : rustic
swart : swarthy, dark
sway : have power
sweeps : stalks haughtily
swoun : swoon

tackles : ropes
taint : tainted
tainture : fouling
taper : candle
target : shield
tarras : balcony
temper : mix
temper : (of metal) quality, hardness
tender : regard
tends : that tends
terms : phrases
testament : will
thrall : share
through : thorough
tickled : excited
tiltyard : tilting ground
timeless : untimely
tire : feed greedily
title : claim to the throne
toss : wave aloft
toss'd : speared
toward : bold
tower : fly high
toy : trifle
train : long tail, followers
train'd : lured
trencher : platter
troth : truth
trow : know
truant : idle student
trull : whore
truncheon : staff

turmoiled : anxious
type : badge

unapt : unused
unavoided : unavoidable
unconstant : wavering
uncover'd : hat in hand
unfallible : infallible
unhallow'd : unblessed
unkind : unnatural
unneath : hardly
unready : undressed
unstaunched : unquenchable

vail : lower
venom : venomous
verses : incantations
via : away !
Villiago : villain
virginal : of virgins
visard-like : like a mask
void : empty
voiding-lobby : waiting room

waft : transport
waned : reduced
want : lack, be deprived of
ward : prison
warrant, warrantise : guarantee
water-standing : full of tears
weeds : garments
weening : thinking
weeping-ripe : on the point of tears
whelps : puppies
whenas : when
where : whether
whereas : where
whet : sharpen, encourage
whether : whither
whiles : while

whiles: until
will'd: commanded
winding-sheet: shroud, **wrap-**
ping for the dead
winds: sounds
wink: shut the eye
witch: bewitch
wittingly: intentionally
wont: be accustomed
wood: mad
world of: enormous
worm: serpent
worn: forgotten

worship: dignity
wot: know
would: wishes, needs
wrack: wreck
wreakless: reckless
wrest: distort
writ: summons to attend a
court
writhled: shrivelled
wrought: worked on

yclad: clad – an archaic form
yet: still

EDWARD III (1327-77)

EDWARD, The Black Prince d. 1376

WILLIAM OF HATFIELD o.s.p.

LIONEL, Duke of Clarence d. 1368 = ELIZABETH DE BURGH d. 1362

JOHN OF GAUNT, Duke of Lancaster d. 1399 = (1) BLANCHE OF LANCASTER d. 1369 = (3) CATHARINE SWYNFORD d. 1403

EDMUND, Duke of York d. 1402

THOMAS, Duke of Gloucester murdered 1397, ancestor of the Dukes of Buckingham

RICHARD II (1377-99)

ROGER MORTIMER executed 1330 Great grandfather of

EDMUND MORTIMER = PHILIPPA Earl of March d. 1382 d. 1381

HENRY IV (1399-1413)

(3) THOMAS BEAUFORT Duke of Exeter d. 1427

HENRY BEAUFORT Cardinal, Bishop of Winchester, d. 1447

(1) JOHN BEAUFORT Marquis of Somerset, d. 1410

RICHARD Earl of Cambridge, ex. 1415

EDWARD Duke of York k. in battle, 1415

The Yorkist Line See to left

EDMUND BEAUFORT Duke of Somerset killed in battle 1455

OWEN TUDOR executed 1461 = KATHARINE OF FRANCE Widow of Henry V

EDMUND TUDOR Earl of Richmond d. 1456

HENRY V (1413-22) = KATHARINE OF FRANCE d. 1437

JOHN Duke of Bedford d. 1435

HUMPHREY Duke of Gloucester d. 1447

JOHN BEAUFORT Duke of Somerset d. 1444 = JANE BEAUFORT

JAMES I King of Scots (1406-37)

Royal line of Scotland

MARGARET BEAUFORT d. 1509

(1) HENRY, Duke of Somerset, executed 1464

(2) EDMUND, Duke of Somerset, executed 1471

(3) JOHN BEAUFORT, killed in battle, 1471

HENRY VI (1422-61) murdered 1471 = MARGARET OF ANJOU d. 1482

ROGER Earl of March k. in battle, 1398

EDMUND MORTIMER d. 1409

Daughter of OWEN Glendower

EDWARD Prince of Wales k. 1471 = ANNE NEVILLE

JAMES II King of Scots d. 1460

EDMUND Earl of March o.s.p. 1424

RICHARD Earl of Cambridge executed 1415 = ANNE MORTIMER d. before 1415

RICHARD Duke of York executed 1460

JAMES III d. 1488

CECILY NEVILLE

EDWARD IV (1461-83) = ELIZABETH WYDE-VILLE d. 1492

EDMUND Earl of Rutland killed in battle, 1460

GEORGE Duke of Clarence executed 1478 = ISABELLA NEVILLE d. 1476

RICHARD III (1483-5) = ANNE NEVILLE d. 1485

ELIZABETH = JOHN Duke of Suffolk d. 1491

JAMES IV of Scotland (1488-1513) = MARGARET d. 1541

CHARLES Brandon Duke of Suffolk d. 1545

(1) LOUIS XII of France (1498-1515) = (1) MARY d. 1533

Royal line of Scotland

EDWARD Earl of Warwick executed 1499

SIR RICHARD POLE d. 1505 = MARGARET Countess of Salisbury executed 1541

EDWARD Prince of Wales d. 1484

JOHN Earl of Lincoln killed in battle 1487

EDMUND Duke of Suffolk executed 1513

RICHARD DE LA POLE o.s.p. 1525

ELIZABETH OF YORK d. 1503 = HENRY VII (1485-1509)

EDWARD V (1483) Murdered

HENRY Lord Montague executed 1538

REGINALD POLE Cardinal, Archbishop of Canterbury, d. 1558

SIR GEOFFREY POLE d. 1558

RICHARD Duke of York Murdered 1483

ELIZABETH = HENRY VII d. 1503 See to right

ARTHUR Prince of Wales d. 1502

HENRY VIII (1509-47) = MARGARET (2) = CHARLES XII d. 1533

MARY d. 1533

EDWARD V (1483) Murdered

Six other daughters, from two of whom were descended the Marquis of Exeter (executed 1539), and the Earl of Surrey (executed 1547), beheaded by Henry VIII for dynastic reasons.

KEY {
d. = died   k. = killed   ex. = executed
o.s.p. = obiit sine prole (died without issue)
----- = illegitimate (John of Gaunt's three Beaufort sons were born before he married Catharine Swynford)
}